DE 1 9

W9-ATF-306

An Irish Country Family

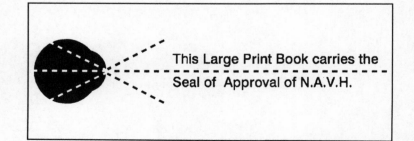

This Large Print Book carries the
Seal of Approval of N.A.V.H.

AN IRISH COUNTRY FAMILY

PATRICK TAYLOR

THORNDIKE PRESS

A part of Gale, a Cengage Company

Copyright © 2019 by Ballybucklebo Stories Corp.
An Irish Country Novel.
Maps by Elizabeth Danforth
Thorndike Press, a part of Gale, a Cengage Company.

ALL RIGHTS RESERVED
This is a work of fiction. All of the characters, organizations, and events portrayed in this novel are either products of the author's imagination or are used fictitiously.
Thorndike Press® Large Print Core
The text of this Large Print edition is unabridged.
Other aspects of the book may vary from the original edition.
Set in 16 pt. Plantin.

LIBRARY OF CONGRESS CIP DATA ON FILE.
CATALOGUING IN PUBLICATION FOR THIS BOOK
IS AVAILABLE FROM THE LIBRARY OF CONGRESS

ISBN-13: 978-1-4328-7185-7 (hardcover alk. paper)

Published in 2019 by arrangement with Macmillan Publishing Group, LLC/Tor/Forge

Printed in Mexico
1 2 3 4 5 6 7 23 22 21 20 19

To Dorothy

To Dorothy

ACKNOWLEDGMENTS

I would like to thank a large number of people, some of whom have worked with me from the beginning and without whose unstinting help and encouragement, I could not have written this series. They are:

In North America
Simon Hally, Carolyn Bateman, Tom Doherty, Paul Stevens, Kristin Sevick, Irene Gallo, Gregory Manchess, Patty Garcia, Alexis Saarela, Fleur Mathewson, Jamie Broadhurst, and Christina MacDonald, all of whom have contributed enormously to the literary and technical aspects of bringing this work from rough draft to bookshelf.

Natalia Aponte and Victoria Lea, my literary agents.

Don Kalancha and Joe Maier, who keep me right on contractual matters.

7

In the United Kingdom

Jessica and Rosie Buchman, my foreign rights agents.

To you all, Doctor Fingal Flahertie O'Reilly and I tender our most heartfelt gratitude and thanks.

AUTHOR'S NOTE

Once again it's time to welcome back old friends and bid new readers *céad míle fáilte,* a hundred thousand welcomes. Once again, because some aspects of this work require explanation, it is necessary for me to write another author's note.

In five of the preceding Irish Country Doctor novels I have told stories involving central characters in different time frames. Developments affecting a full cast of familiar players in the village of Ballybucklebo in the nineteen sixties have been presented in tandem with a story of one of the central characters at an earlier stage in life. Kinky Kincaid in the twenties, and Doctor O'Reilly in the early thirties, and during the start of the Second World War.

In this work in the hospital year of 1963–64, just-qualified-in-June '63 Doctor Barry Laverty and his friends are experiencing their houseman's (medical intern's) year, beginning in August '63 in the Royal Victoria Hospital Belfast before becoming fully licensed medical practitioners. A major teaching hospital is a very different place from a rural general practice and the young doctors must deal, under supervision, with a wide range of technically more difficult cases, and at a young age, on average about twenty-four, confront their own feelings about life and death, and with being, albeit in a junior capacity, at the cutting edge of medical progress.

I wish first to deal with that cutting edge, cardio-pulmonary resuscitation (CPR) and correction of ventricular fibrillation, and to thank everyone whose advice on these subjects has been invaluable.

Today we take for granted CPR and the availability of the ubiquitous Automated External Defibrillators (AEDs). While CPR had been devised in 1960–61, prior to 1963 there was no such thing as a portable cardiac defibrillator. In mid-1966 the first successful defibrillation of a patient at home was carried out by Doctor John Geddes and his Cardiac Ambulance team.

That triumph, which led to today's AEDs, was the brainchild of two remarkable men, Doctor Frank Pantridge and Doctor John S. Geddes, and their technical staff, Mister

Alfred Mawhinney and Mister John Anderson. They were all on the staff of Belfast's Royal Victoria Hospital. I have firsthand knowledge because I was Doctor Frank Pantridge's houseman on wards 5 and 6 from November '64 to February '65, and at that time Doctor John Geddes, a trainee cardiologist, was my immediate superior. I have always wanted to tell the story of the pioneers, but in a fictional setting. For dramatic purposes I have had to compress the time line, but I wanted the events as I describe them to be technically accurate. To that end my friend John Geddes, now retired, has read and corrected those chapters. John Geddes was a houseman on 5 and 6 in 1963–64 and the senior house officer there in '64–'65. I was privileged to work under his guidance in '64 and as a colleague at the University of Manitoba in 1989. He has graciously agreed to my condensing three years' progress into three months — but only on receipt of my solemn promise that in this note I will provide the entirely accurate history. Thank you, John.

Additional support came from my classmate and old friend Doctor Tom Baskett, who was also a houseman on 5 and 6, and who has provided me not only with his personal memories there but also critical information about the layout of other parts of the Royal, our duty hours, and pay scale. The excerpts from the Houseman's Concert of '65, heavily disguised as the Concert of '64, require my apologies to that class. Thanks again, Tom, for sending me the programme and some of the original script.

The other source is an excellent work, *The Evolution of Pre-Hospital Emergency Care,* by John S. Geddes, Ronald D. Stewart, and Thomas F. Baskett, Clinical Press, 2017, from which Doctor Geddes's words are provided verbatim below.

From those sources then, here are the accurate time lines.

The Lown defibrillator, which was portable but ran off the main electricity supply, was installed on the side ward of ward 6 in October '63.

The coronary care unit opened in December 1963 on ward 6.

The resuscitation by Doctor Geddes of the man on the pavement and subsequent defibrillation using a portable defibrillator by Doctor Pantridge was in late April 1964. In Doctor Geddes own words, "Brian Pitt and I were both housemen on ward 21. A hospital worker stuck his head in and told us a man was lying on the ground outside the building. Brian and I yelled for help and ran outside. A pulseless middle-aged man lay on the pavement. I started CPR. Dennis Coppel, an anaesthetist registrar, charged up pushing an anaesthetic trolley. He intubated the man and connected him to oxygen. Anand Garg, a neurosurgical registrar, helped us load the man onto a trolley and we got the patient to a side ward and took an ECG. Ventricular fibrillation." Copyright permission to use this has been granted by doctors Geddes and Baskett.

Doctor Pantridge and Doctor Peter Halmos brought the defibrillator from 5 and 6 and after two shocks had reversed the fibrillation.

In August 1964, Doctor Geddes began teaching CPR and defibrillation to the new housemen in batches of 1–3. The sessions took thirty minutes. I attended one, and in that month the in-hospital resuscitation programme was organised.

The specially equipped and committed to the programme ambulance and driver were ready by October 1965.

The first outing for the Cardiac Ambulance carrying the team led by Doctor Geddes was on January 6, 1966. A female patient who had suffered a myocardial infarction was successfully treated, brought to the hospital, and survived.

The rest is history, but I must make one other correction: Sister Crawford was the ward sister on 5 and 6. Sister Kearney, like Sister O'Byrne in Casualty, is a figment of my imagination.

In the other story set in 1969, Ballybucklebo general practitioners Doctor Fingal O'Reilly, a maturing Doctor Barry Laverty, and their associates tend to the ills of their patients and their community, both of whom the doctors regard as part of their family. Sixty-nine was a time of drastic political change in the wider community of Northern Ireland. This cannot be ignored and I will refer to it later.

My descriptions of places in North Down and the Royal Victoria are drawn largely from memory, mine and my wife Dorothy's. We grew up in north County Down and I was a medical student and houseman in the Royal from mid-1961 to August 1965. I am also indebted to *The Royal Victoria Hospital Belfast, A History 1797–1997*. Richard Clarke. Blackstaff Press, 1997.

As in my previous works, I next wish to acknowledge the actual people and real places that appear on these pages and make a comment on certain social habits.

When it comes to real people I have, where possible, named my contemporaries

14

both nonmedical and medical.

All of the political figures did hold the offices I describe, for example, Harold Wilson MP for Bromley was Prime Minister. I mention Joe Togneri with deep affection. His Italian family ran the Coronation Cafe in Bangor. As a child, he had developed kyphoscoliosis, a hunchback. His main delight in life was sailing his national fourteen dinghy. He taught a very young Pat Taylor to sail. RIP, old friend.

On the medical front, Professor John Henry Biggart was the head of pathology and dean of the faculty. Doctor Gerry Nelson was the chief of haematology and coincidentally shared a surname with my Doctor Connor Nelson. They were not related. Mister Willoughby Wilson was a surgical consultant on wards 9 and 10. Mister John A. W. Bingham was a thoracic surgeon. There were three senior neurosurgeons on ward 21, but Mister Charlie Greer was a contemporary of Fingal O'Reilly as undergraduates at Trinity College in Dublin in the thirties and is a figment of my imagination. Professor Graham MacGregor Bull was the senior physician (internist) on wards 3 and 4, and Muz Khan, an outstanding scholar, was a registrar at the time. Doctor Harold Millar was a senior neurologist. Professor Ivo John Carré taught us paediatrics and I still use his book *Aids to the Diseases of Children* as a trusted source. While much their junior, I knew them all.

Doctor Graham Harley was special. For those of us — myself, Tom Baskett, Brian Ireland, and Gerry MacCarthy — who went into obstetrics and gynaecology, he was our hero, the doctor we all aspired to be. I hope I have captured his skill and humanity in these pages. And Patrick Taylor. I decided it would be fun to give myself a supporting role, because in 1969 my chief, Mister Matt Neely, sent me to Oldham to learn laparoscopy from Mister Patrick Steptoe. I believe Doctor Eddie MacPhedran may have done the first one in Ireland, but I certainly was an active endoscopist then at the Ulster Hospital in Dundonald.

I did not know Rosalind Yarrow personally, but her discovery of radioimmunoassay in 1959 was integral to the research carried out on the hormone prolactin by my old friend Doctor Bernard Corenblum and me. Doctor Yarrow received the Nobel Prize for physiology in 1977, only the second woman to have done so.

I had mentioned social habits. One was smoking. The modern reader may have difficulty believing my references to smoke-filled pubs, restaurants, and even the hospital. Smoking during those years was the norm, despite clear evidence linking the addiction to lung cancer. That notwithstanding, my Christmas present from Doctor Frank Pantridge, senior cardiologist, was a packet of fifty Capstan Full Strength cigarettes, and I can still remember offering one to sister, our both lighting up in the clinical room, and no one thinking anything about it. I'm a slow learner, but I finally quit more than twenty years ago.

The other, which may also come as a surprise, is that a pregnant woman might drink alcohol. Some quit voluntarily because they found alcohol tended to nauseate them. Others thought it perfectly natural because the link with foetal alcohol syndrome was not established until 1973.

When it comes to the story line set in Ballybucklebo in 1969, I wish I could carry on as I had done with Ireland at peace, but alas, such was not the case. I began alluding to the increasing civil unrest in book 13, *An Irish Country Cottage*. I do not wish to belabour the matter in this work, but I have had to make mention of the critical political and sectarian events in April and May 1969. I have chosen to conclude the Ballybucklebo portion in July 1969, the month in which a man first walked on the moon on the 21st. Our story concludes prior to July 12, 1969. It was then, at the height of the "marching season," when Loyalist organizations held parades to celebrate the victories of the forces of Protestant Prince William of Orange over the forces of the deposed Catholic King James II of England in the late seventeenth century, that rioting erupted in Belfast, Londonderry, and Dungiven, leading to almost continuous civil strife until the Good Friday Agreement of 1998.

My picturing the tolerance of the two sides in Ballybucklebo one for the other is a reflection of how novelists often use their pages to set down how they would have liked the world to be.

One more thank-you and two apologies will conclude this note.

I had thought I was familiar with a host of Irish and Ulster expressions, but I must thank Brother Henry Gaither for one I had not heard before. "I have a thirst you could photograph." I'm not sure where he got it, but I think it's sticking out a mile. Thank you, Brother Henry. And as usual, a glossary defining these and other vagaries of the Queen's English as it is spoken in Ulster will be found in a glossary starting on page 607.

To my readers, I'm afraid the winner of the talent contest described in the last two chapters must remain a secret. Sorry. And my apology is to my nonmedical friends and classmates. There are a lot of characters in fourteen novels. In order to help me recall them, I have developed a habit of using real people's surnames although not their character traits. If you think you find yourself in here and are hurt — or worse, don't find yourself in here — I am truly sorry.

PATRICK TAYLOR
Saltspring Island
British Columbia
Canada
July 2018

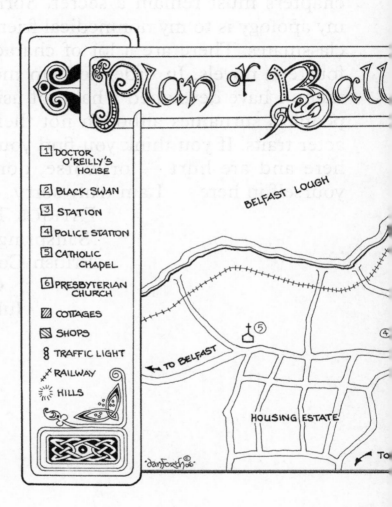

Plan of Ball

1 DOCTOR O'REILLY'S HOUSE
2 BLACK SWAN
3 STATION
4 POLICE STATION
5 CATHOLIC CHAPEL
6 PRESBYTERIAN CHURCH
▨ COTTAGES
▧ SHOPS
⎇ TRAFFIC LIGHT
✕✕ RAILWAY
☀ HILLS

BELFAST LOUGH

✝ ⑤

← TO BELFAST

④

HOUSING ESTATE

← TO

danforth©

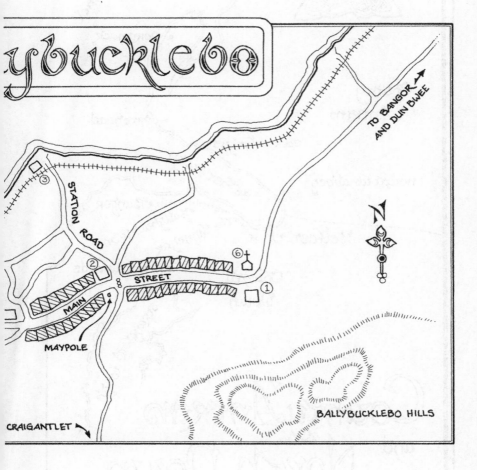

ybucklebo

TO BANGOR
AND DUN BWEE

N

STATION ROAD

③

②

MAIN

STREET

⑥

①

MAYPOLE

CRAIGANTLET

BALLYBUCKLEBO HILLS

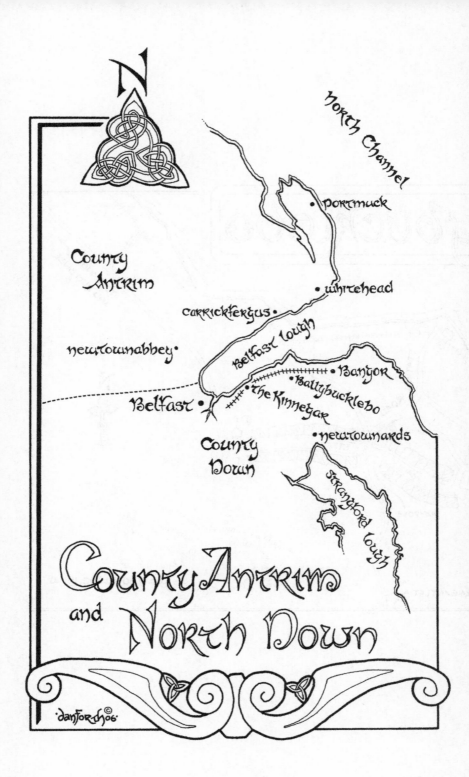

1
HOME AND BEAUTY

April 11, 1969

"Home is the sailor, home from the sea, and the hunter home from the hill." Fingal Flahertie O'Reilly, Doctor Fingal Flahertie O'Reilly, swept into the upstairs lounge of Number One Main Street, Ballybucklebo, yawned, and rubbed his gritty eyes.

"You look more like the wreck of the *Hesperus*," his wife, Kitty, said from where she sat in an armchair in front of a set but unlit fire. Their little white cat, Lady Macbeth, was curled up in Kitty's lap. She put a Dick Francis mystery on a wine table beside her. "Seriously, Fingal, I know you got your feet up for a while yesterday afternoon, but you were out again at midnight and you didn't come home until five this morning."

O'Reilly crossed the room and dropped a kiss on the top of her head, noting fondly that her raven hair was more than just tipped with silver. "Sorry if I disturbed you, my dear." He leant against the mantel. "Time, tide, and arriving newborns wait for no man. It took a while for me and Miss Hagerty, the midwife, to get everything squared away. You remember Aileen Mac-Cormack, the plumber's wife?"

"Cheerful redhead? Baby number two?"

"That's her. She and her child, all nine pounds of baby boy, are doing well." He yawned.

Kitty shook her head. "I know you enjoy midder, but you've a couple of youngsters in the call rota, one of them with extra training in obstetrics. Ever think of giving it up?"

O'Reilly shook his head.

"I'm not complaining," Kitty said, "but you know very well I hardly sleep when you're out on a call." She crossed her legs, trying not to disturb the sleeping cat. "Fortunately, you're not on call as much now. Even if you still want to deliver babies, one in four nights and weekends isn't bad. Not like when it was just Barry and you."

"Gives me more time with my lovely wife, and I'd get even more time with her if she'd think about slowing down too." He'd been encouraging her for more than a year about this, but she loved her job as senior neurosurgical operating theatre sister at the Royal Victoria Hospital.

24

Kitty shook her head. "We can talk about it, but not now. Not now. How was your refresher course for GP trainers today?" She looked at her watch. "Five fifteen. You made good time from Belfast."

"Traffic wasn't too bad." The two exchanged a glance. "We both enjoyed the course. Young Laverty's turning into a first-class teacher. I'm very lucky to have him as a partner." O'Reilly yawned again. "Had lunch with Professor George Irwin, Department of General Practice. He's impressed with Barry too. But George isn't sure he can find an assistantship here in Ulster for Emer McCarthy when she finishes her stint with us." O'Reilly pursed his lips. "It's worrying. It's April the eleventh today and she'll be leaving us on July thirty-first. She's a fine lass. I should be able to do something for her. I really should."

"And knowing you, you probably will, but that's three months away, Fingal, and getting your knickers in a twist now isn't going to help her find a job, is it?"

"No. It's not." He shook his shaggy head. "You're right."

Kitty nodded once. "I am right. You'll only get her worried too. So instead of fretting about your trainee, what you need now is a good brisk walk in the fresh air, so go on.

25

Give young Kenny a run too. The dog needs his exercise." She patted O'Reilly's tummy. "And he's not the only one."

O'Reilly grunted, stood up straight, and sucked in his gut. He offered his hand. "Coming?"

Kitty smiled. "No. Thanks, Fingal. Not this evening. We had an astrocytoma today. Brain tumour cases always take a while. I was scrub-sister for Mister Charlie Greer. On my feet six and a half hours. I think a visit to the Duck by yourself would be good for you, but be home for seven. Kinky was here today. Polished all the silver, hoovered every square inch of the place, and made a fresh batch of tomato soup, and beef and dumplings for me to heat up."

"Yum," said O'Reilly, unsure whether the prospect of a pint in the Duck and a bit of *craic* with the locals or one of Kinky Auchinleck's dinners with Kitty was the more appealing. His tummy rumbled.

"Go on with you, dear old bear," Kitty said, "and give me peace to read more of *Blood Sport*. The hero, Gene Hawkins, is on the trail of a kidnapped — if that's the right word — thoroughbred racehorse, and he's in all kinds of trouble. You'll enjoy it when I've finished." She picked up her book.

"I do love you, Mrs. O'Reilly. Seven sharp it is."

The Black Swan public house, known to the locals as the Mucky Duck, was a short walk from Number One Main Street, but O'Reilly and Kenny had taken the long way so they could make a stop at the shore. O'Reilly watched Kenny kicking up little sprays of sand as he raced after a series of sticks. Apart from a couple wandering along the tideline, O'Reilly and the chocolate Lab had the shore to themselves. The cries of a line of oyster catchers and the wavelets' insistent soft whispering just heightened the peace of the early Ulster evening. "Heel, Kenny," O'Reilly called, and when the big dog tucked in they retraced their steps under a mackerel sky.

Now O'Reilly and Kenny entered the pleasant fug of the low-ceilinged room to a chorus of cheerful greetings. "Good evening to this house," said O'Reilly, and beamed at Willie Dunleavy.

Willie nodded and put a pint of Guinness on the pour. As he let the first pull settle, the tubby publican decanted a pint of Smithwick's into a stainless steel bowl for Kenny.

O'Reilly smiled. This wasn't telepathy at

27

work. The man had been pouring Guinness for O'Reilly and beer for his gundogs since 1946. The feeling of continuity and changelessness was second nature, and very comforting.

A voice rose above the rest. O'Reilly recognised Lenny Brown. "Hey, I just seen pictures of them pair of buck eejits John Lennon and Yoko Ono having a 'bed in' at an Amsterdam hotel."

"I seen that on telly two weeks ago. You're behind the times, ould hand," Gerry Shanks said, and laughed. " 'Make love, not war.' Sounds good to me. Maybe they could do one at the Grand Central Hotel in Belfast."

There was a general muttering of agreement, O'Reilly thought. Things were still simmering in Ulster.

"Evening, Doctor." Bertie Bishop sat at a nearby table with Donal Donnelly's best mate, Dapper Frew, the estate agent. "Care to join us, sir?"

"Be my pleasure." O'Reilly lowered his big frame into a chair and ushered Kenny under the table.

The chocolate Lab lay down with a happy grunt.

"Evening, gentlemen," O'Reilly said. "How's the world abusing you both?"

"We're doing rightly," Bertie Bishop said,

but frowned. "We are, but poor ould Ulster's still got her worries. Your man Gerry's notion of 'make love, not war' sounds like what's needed."

"Excuse me, sir. Your drink." Willie Dunleavy set a pint in front of O'Reilly and put Kenny's bowl under the table. In moments, a feisty Chihuahua named Brian Boru had joined his young friend. Sounds of lapping drifted up to the table. Willie looked down and shook his head. "Sorry, sir. I keep telling Mary to keep yon animal on a leash but she's a soft heart, that daughter of mine."

O'Reilly laughed. "Daylight bloody robbery. I remember when a pint cost a shilling." He handed Willie five shillings.

"Just after the war, sir." Willie pocketed the coins.

O'Reilly glanced under the table. "Kenny likes to share his pint with his friend, just like Arthur did before him." Good old Arthur. O'Reilly shook his head and raised his glass to Willie, and then to the table. *Sláinte.* The pull he took on his drink left a white tidemark one-third the way down the glass.

Dapper looked down at the two dogs and rolled his eyes. "Anyroad, there's none of that there nonsense going on here in Ballybucklebo, praise be."

"Aye, you're right, Dapper, and I'm very glad you dropped in tonight, Doctor, so I am. We could use your advice."

O'Reilly looked from one man to the other as Bertie took a sip from the one pint a day he was allowed since his heart attack. As usual, the councillor was wearing a three-piece dark blue wool suit with the gold chain of a fob watch looped tightly across his still (despite his wife's best efforts) ample belly. A Masonic emblem in gold hung from the chain.

O'Reilly had never heard exactly why John Frew had been nicknamed "Dapper," but perhaps it reflected the neatness of his slim moustache, the set of his grey blazer, and the razor crease in his charcoal flannels.

O'Reilly looked around the pub. Usually when a scheme was underway, the prime mover was Donal Donnelly. But the buck-toothed, carroty-headed carpenter was not to be found. "All right, fire away."

Bertie leaned forward and spoke, so he could, with some difficulty, be heard over the rising din of the pub on a Friday night. "The rebuilding of the Donnellys' cottage, Dun Bwee, is coming on a treat. Can you believe it's been three and a half months since thon awful fire just after Christmas?" Bertie shook his head. "The outside walls is

30

all done. Donnacha Flynn and his son have finished the thatching and gone home til County Kerry. All the interior walls is finished, doors is being painted and hung, windows framed and glazed. Donal and his crew has done a great job. The whole thing'll be finished sometime in May."

"By God, I'm delighted to hear it," O'Reilly said, taking a second pull on his pint, leaving a fresh tidemark two-thirds down the glass, "but how can I help?"

"Me and Dapper here have a notion. Never mind all the other rubbish going on in Belfast, here in Ballybucklebo everybody's pitched in to see the Donnellys right. When they're ready til move I'd like," he glanced at Dapper, "that is Dapper and me'd like to give a housewarming hooley for Donal and his family and the whole community. It'd be fun for Donal and show the rest of the eejits in the wee North we can get along together if we try."

"Admirable," O'Reilly said. "You know, Bertie Bishop, for the worshipful master of the local Orange Lodge, you've a very open mind."

Bertie Bishop shrugged. "I'm not devout nor nothing, but me and Flo goes til church of a Sunday. I know in the past I've sometimes been a tough nut, but see thon heart attack?" He inhaled. "Since then I've no trouble with this 'love thy neighbour' thing, and I've another way I think we can make that work here."

O'Reilly was intrigued.

"The morrow's the last home game of the season for the Ballybucklebo Bonnaughts rugby team. They're playing the Portaferry Pirates. You'll be there, Doctor?"

"Mrs. O'Reilly and I wouldn't miss it," O'Reilly said.

Bertie waved an all-encompassing arm around the room. "This here's the social centre of our wee village. No orange-and-green rubbish here, but do youse notice anything strange?"

O'Reilly frowned and saw Dapper do likewise. As far as O'Reilly was concerned it was a typical Friday night, except perhaps for the notable absence of one Donal Donnelly.

"Donal's not here," said O'Reilly.

"He's taken his family to Rasharkin to see Julie's folks. I borrowed him my van," Bertie said.

Dapper frowned. "Must be the only pub in Ulster with a couple of piss-artist dogs under a table."

"Och," Bertie said, "run away on, Dapper. Sure, it's plain as the nose on your face.

No women, and that's the same in every public bar in Ulster."

"Because," Dapper said, "that's the law in public bars. You need a lounge bar or a snug for ladies and their escorts. The Duck's too wee for either." He grunted. "You can't even have any singing or dancing."

"I know that," Bertie said, "and the ladies go out in the daytime with their friends to that wee tearoom The Singing Kettle when we're at our work. But we need a place we can all get together of an evening."

O'Reilly nodded. Bertie had a point.

"I think we might be able til put the clubhouse til better use."

A voice O'Reilly recognised as belonging to Alan Hewitt rose above the hubbub. "Away off and chase yourself, Malcolm Mulligan. That there Concorde 002 aeroplane never went faster than sound, so it never. It was only up in the air for twenty-two bleedin' minutes. I don't think it'll ever go supersonic."

Ballybucklebo's long arm of the law, Constable Mulligan, laughed and said, "Only thing goes that fast is Cissie Sloan's mouth." A reference to Ballybucklebo's resident chatterbox.

Not until the universal burst of good-natured laughter had died down did Bertie say, "It's only a half-baked notion I have now. I need til get some advice and think on it some more, but I'll have my ducks in a row by the morrow."

"Fair enough," O'Reilly said. He was quite willing to wait. "Now, about this hooley, Bertie, I'm thinking we'll want it kept secret from the Donnellys until the last minute."

"That was my notion as well, Doctor."

O'Reilly finished his pint. "Dapper?" As the physician who had restricted Bertie Bishop to a pint a day, he could hardly offer the man a drink.

"You're a gentleman, Doctor. Please."

O'Reilly held up two fingers so Willie could see, and was rewarded with a short nod and Willie's attention to the pumps.

"Aye," said Bertie. "And we'd like for everyone who helped til be there, and all youse doctors —"

"Someone will have to be on call," O'Reilly said.

Bertie shook his head. "There'll be a phone in Dun Bwee by then."

O'Reilly frowned. "Usually takes months for the General Post Office to connect a new line."

Bertie assumed his Councillor Bishop expression. "Not if you know the right people." He grinned. "I'll say no more, but there'll be a phone at Dun Bwee all right."

"Fair enough," O'Reilly said, thinking that who you knew, not what you knew, was very much a fact of life in rural Ulster. He approved.

"And we'd like til have Father O'Toole and the Reverend Robinson, the Presbyterian minister, both say a few words," Dapper said. "And, well, Mister Bishop and me knows it's a bit impertinent, like, but do you think . . ."

"Excuse me." Willie set two fresh pints on the table and removed the empty glasses.

"Thanks, Willie," O'Reilly said, and paid. "Cheers."

"Thanks, Doc. Cheers." Dapper raised his glass. He wiped his upper lip with the back of his hand. "Do you think Lord MacNeill and his sister would come? They've been so decent in all of this, so they have."

"His lordship," Bertie said, "has a heart of corn. You'd think all of us was his family."

And to an extent we are, O'Reilly thought, and I for one count myself lucky to have John MacNeill a friend. "You can leave that one with me. I'll approach his lordship once we have planning matters farther along."

"Dead on," said Dapper.

"Some of it will be easy," Bertie said. "My Flo and Cissie Sloan and, I'm sure, Kinky'll

35

want to look after the catering." He puffed out his chest.

Oh-oh, O'Reilly thought, Bertie's going to address the meeting, but to his surprise Bertie shook his head, chuckled, perhaps at himself, and deflated. "I'll take care of the drinks and ask Willie or Mary to serve behind the bar."

"You'll pay, Bertie?" O'Reilly remembered a man who not so long ago would have squeezed a penny until it squeaked.

"Not exactly," Bertie said. "My building company will — as a legitimate tax-deductible, once-only bonus to my workers and a goodwill gesture to the others."

"That's dead decent, Mister B.," Dapper said.

Bertie Bishop shrugged. "There's no pockets in a shroud. Mind, Doctor, when your brother Lars put a word in with the National Trust to get permission to rebuild Dun Bwee and gave me a hand too with some business? I'd like him to come."

"Fair enough." Lars had helped Bertie Bishop draw up a will with many provisions for the Donnelly family. O'Reilly wondered if Bertie had told Donal about it yet. "It sounds like it's going to be quite the operation." Without being asked or having volunteered, O'Reilly seemed to have been co-

36

opted onto the planning committee. Oh well, hadn't he been up to his neck, and happy to be, in village affairs for more than two decades. He glanced at his watch, finished his pint, and rose. "You'll keep me posted?" he said.

"Indeed, we will," Bertie said, "but we know you're busy, so we'll have a couple of planning sessions first before we come after you for advice."

"Grand," said O'Reilly. "Now, I promised Kitty I'd be home by seven for Kinky's beef stew."

Dapper Frew looked at the packet of potato crisps he'd been eating and sighed as O'Reilly raised his voice. "Goodnight to all." Making a small bow in acknowledgement of the farewell from the room, he summoned Kenny and made for the exit. The bat-wing doors closed behind him and he started on the short walk home. Overhead the sinking sun shared the sky with a just-risen crescent moon, and O'Reilly turned the collar of his jacket to the evening chill. There's one for the books, he thought. A plot was brewing in Ballybucklebo of which Donal Donnelly was to be the recipient rather than the originator. The biter bit, but in a most pleasant way.

O'Reilly was still smiling as he put Kenny

into his doghouse and headed for the back door of Number One Main Street and the fragrant aroma of beef and dumplings.

2
ON WITH THE DANCE

April 12, 1969

"Standing in for Donal Donnelly this evening, Alan?" O'Reilly asked Alan Hewitt, who was behind the bar at the Ballybucklebo Bonnaughts Sporting Club.

"Aye, sir. What'll it be?"

"Two pints, and a gin and tonic, please."

"Right, Doctor. I'll see to it."

O'Reilly looked around the packed room. Drinks were kept in a separate room, behind a serving hatch. To the left of the hatch, a small dance floor stretched up to a low stage where a band might play for holiday functions. Along one side of the dance floor, and expanding to the full width of the room, were tables surrounded by simple wooden chairs. All seemed to be occupied. "Good crowd," O'Reilly said. About sixty people, smoking, drinking, arguing about the game, were slowly filling the room with laughter and the smells of beer and tobacco smoke.

"Brave clatter." Alan had the two pints on the pour and was seeing to the gin and tonic. "It's always a grand night when we play the Portaferry Pirates. Their team and supporters always come in for one or two after the game." He put the glass of gin and an opened small bottle of tonic water on a tray on the counter.

"Away off and chase yourself, Gerry." The ringing tones came from a table nearby. "Your man Monaghan couldn't beat the skin off a rice pudding. You telling me he won the flyweight match last night? Go home and feel your head."

The sally was greeted by an outburst of laughter.

O'Reilly smiled. There had been a boxing card in Belfast last night at the King's Hall. Boxing supporters were no less partisan than the rugby ones in here, who were either celebrating or drowning their sorrows over the Ballybucklebo Bonnaughts' sixteen-to-nine win over the Portaferry Pirates in the last game of the season played earlier today.

Alan set one pint on the tray. "Mind you," he said, "it might be busy tonight, but if there's no home game, mebbe only nine or ten members'll pop in of a Saturday. Have a jar. Play a few frames of snooker. Have a game of darts."

Like the snooker game he'd recently enjoyed with Father Hugh O'Toole while discussing his church's stance on contraception. Hugh had won the game.

Alan placed the second pint beside the first. "That'll be seven shillings, please, sir."

O'Reilly paid, grateful that drinks cost less in private clubs. O'Reilly helped his company to their drinks, a pint for John Mac-Neill, the club's president, the gin and tonic for Kitty, and set his own down on the table for six. "Just be a tick." He set off to return the tray.

"Thanks, Alan," he said, handing it over. "How's Helen doing?"

"My Helen?" said Alan, drying a pint glass with a Castles of Ireland linen tea towel. "I hardly see her since she started working at the hospital three-odd years ago." He shrugged. "Och well. I suppose they all have to leave the nest one day. She's her big exams in June, so she has." He took a deep breath. "And when she passes, me, a working man, I'll be the daddy of a doctor, so I will." He set down the dry glass and picked up another wet one. "I'm so proud of her I could burst."

"Good for her," O'Reilly said, "and good for you, Alan. You've every right to be

41

proud. She's a credit to you."

"Aye," said Alan. "I only wish —" He inhaled. "I wish my Brigit could have seen it."

O'Reilly well remembered Brigit Hewitt's death some ten years ago. "Och, Alan," he said, "we all do."

"Thanks, Doc." Alan managed a weak smile.

O'Reilly set off to return to his table. On the way he noticed the retired Doctor Ronald Fitzpatrick and Alice Moloney, Ballybucklebo's dressmaker, sitting cosily at a table for two. Kitty and the marquis would be happy enough chatting with each other until O'Reilly came back. "Evening, folks," he said.

"Fingal," Fitzpatrick said, "good to see you. I trust you and Kitty are well?"

"We are that."

Fitzpatrick's Adam's apple bobbed. "Excellent. And what did you think of the game? I thought it was terrific. Our forwards were magnificent. Don't you agree, Alice?"

Alice Moloney smiled fondly at her companion. "Of course, I agree with you, Ronald dear. I do believe I made the very same observation myself." She looked up at O'Reilly. "Ronald has learned a great deal about the game since I started teaching him at the Ulster Schools' Cup match back in March." She giggled. "Next season we're going to go down to Dublin in the spring to watch Ireland play Wales."

Interesting, O'Reilly thought. Things must be progressing with those two. And both had been such lonely people. O'Reilly was delighted for them.

Alice reached for and took Ronald's hand. "Will you be going to Lansdowne Road, Doctor O'Reilly?"

"I hope so," he said, suddenly transported to his parents' dignified, three-storey Victorian redbrick house, where he and Lars had grown up in the '30s. The house was not two hundred yards from the rugby pitch, and a world away, it seemed, from Ballybucklebo. "Might even see you there. Kitty and I usually have a jug in Davy Byrne's pub before kickoff."

"Remember when we were Trinity students, Fingal?" Fitzpatrick said. "You and Cromie, Charlie Greer, and Bob Beresford used to do that too."

"Aye, we did, while you, Doctor Fitzpatrick, were, as usual, cramming for exams." O'Reilly smiled. "A long time ago now." He glanced over at his table and saw Kitty smiling across at him. "Now, if you'll excuse me?" he said. "I mustn't keep Kitty

43

and his lordship waiting too long."

"Of course, Fingal," Fitzpatrick said. "Please give our regards to them both."

O'Reilly inclined his head and headed off. Before he reached his seat, he greeted Father Hugh O'Toole, as usual wearing his black cassock and biretta, and sharing a table with Mister Robinson, the Presbyterian minister, in a tweed sports jacket and white dog collar. "Hello, gentlemen. And Mrs. Robinson. Grand evening."

"Indeed," said Father O'Toole, "for the time of year it's in, so." The man had not lost his Cork accent. Nor had the two men of the cloth let the present upsets in Ulster interfere with their long-standing friendship.

O'Reilly sat down beside Kitty. "Had you given me up for lost?"

Kitty shook her head. "Not at all. How could you get lost here, when you know so many people and they all know you? It's a miracle you're back with John and me so soon."

"I agree." Lord John MacNeill, Marquis of Ballybucklebo, sat opposite. "I probably should be mingling a bit, but I'm much happier sitting here with your lovely wife." The iron-grey-haired peer was casually but immaculately dressed, from the mirror shine

44

of his black shoes to the neat half-Windsor knot in his Irish Guards tie. "Good game today," he said. "Myrna'll be sorry to have missed it, but she had some Queen's University chemistry department retreat."

"Poor thing," Kitty said. "Sometimes that happens to us nurses too. There was a time I didn't mind, but Fingal and I are getting used to having a bit more leisure."

O'Reilly nodded. "And I'm all in favour of it." He smiled at Kitty and lifted his pint. "Cheers." He savoured the bittersweet Guinness.

The marquis and Kitty returned the toast. O'Reilly took another pull on his pint and, as was customary in company, asked, "Anyone mind if I smoke?"

"Carry on, Fingal. I thought your brother might be here this evening, but Myrna informed me that Lars didn't care for rugby." The marquis chuckled. "Race cars were more his sport, as I recall."

The two men exchanged a glance as O'Reilly fished out his loaded briar and lit up. "I tried to tempt him, John, but Myrna's right. He's no rugby fan." As he exhaled a small cloud, he became aware of someone standing nearby. He turned to see Bertie Bishop and his wife, Flo.

"We don't mean to intrude, like, but I

45

wonder if, my lord, I could have a wee word?"

"It would be my pleasure, Councillor," said the marquis, standing in the presence of Flo and offering the Bishops chairs. "Lovely to see you both. You're looking very well, Mrs. Bishop. I've always admired that particular shade of green of your blouse."

Flo blushed, curtsied, and took a seat beside Kitty. "Thank you, my lord." Leaving an empty chair between himself and the marquis, Bertie parked himself beside Fingal.

O'Reilly let go a puff.

"Now, Mister Bishop, what can I do for you?"

"I've a request I'd like til put til the club, my lord. Seeing you're the president, I'd welcome your advice." Bertie inhaled. "We all know that since October last, things have been getting worser here in Ulster. We had them shenanigans at Burntollet Bridge in January, then riots. Thon bomb in Castlereagh at the electricity station in Belfast on March 30 done five hundred thousand pounds' damage." He shook his head. "People wonder what ordinary folks like us can do about it." He looked down, and back up. "I think the Ballybucklebo Sporting Club could help bring folks together, and set an example by doing it." He waved his arm to encompass the room. "Look around youse. Catholics and Protestants getting on like a house on fire. Just like the two teams. No animosity off the pitch."

"I see what you mean." The marquis looked round the table. "We're all old enough to have lived through the upheavals since 1916. I for one had hoped that when the IRA's Operation Harvest petered out in '62 that would be the end to it, but —" He leant forward. "I'd be in favour of anything that can be done."

"I think our wee village and townland, my lord, could show folks a thing or two right here, so I do."

"But how, Bertie? We're just one small village," Kitty said.

"Now look. We may be small but there's something special 'bout the place. Youse all know the two faiths here in Ballybucklebo" — he cleared his throat — "all get along rightly, so we do. We started coming together as friends after Belfast and Bangor was bombed in 1941 and folks from both sides helped each other."

The marquis said, "And we've had our combined Christmas pageant ever since, twenty-eight years ago. Started that year to celebrate our looking after each other as Ulsterfolks, not Catholics nor Protestants. Father Moynihan and a Mister Holmes, the priest and Presbyterian minister at the time, cooked up the notion."

O'Reilly released a fragrant cloud of smoke. "And apart from when Colin Brown caused chaos on the stage in '64" — he paused and saw the grins on every face — "the event has gone off as smoothly as a well-poured pint ever since '41."

"Aye, it has," Bertie said. "But apart from things like the annual sporting club Halloween and Christmas parties and after home matches, when we can all get together for a bit of *craic* and a jar or two, I'd like til suggest this building is underused on many weekend evenings."

"That is true," the marquis said.

"We've a licence to sell beer, wine, and spirits. There's nowhere near here where a fellah can take his missus for a pint and a bit of *craic,* except maybe the Crawfordsburn or the Culloden, and how many workingmen can afford them prices?"

Good point, O'Reilly thought. He saw John MacNeill nodding before he said, "So what are you suggesting, Bertie?"

"I think we should run events in here on Saturday nights."

"Now there's a thought," the marquis

said. "What kind of events had you in mind?"

O'Reilly heard the high-pitched notes of a pennywhistle embellished with occasional slide notes, the staccato rattling of spoons, and the rhythmic sound of a beaten drumskin.

"By Jove. Speak of the devil," said the marquis. "Looks like we might have an event going on right now."

Although no music was allowed in Ulster pubs, people here were no less fond of spontaneous performances than their cousins in the Republic of Ireland. The sporting club, a private venue, had no such restrictions.

Off in a corner, three men sat close to one another. One held a pair of kitchen spoons. Fergus Finnegan, the marquis's former jockey, now retired from that position and from his captaincy of the Bonnaughts, held a pennywhistle. The third man held a bodhran, the circular Irish handheld drum.

O'Reilly recognised the opening bars of "The Nightingale" and a voice called out, "Give us the words, Alan Hewitt."

"Come on, Alan. Let her rip."

Whistles. Applause.

Alan held up his hands, bowed his head, set his tea towel on the bar top, and van-

49

ished. He soon reappeared through a door, and as he moved to join the trio, all but one conversation hushed.

Alan faced the crowd, his blue eyes sweeping the room. He dashed a fair cow's lick from his forehead. "Youse all know the chorus, so join in when it comes."

The last chatty group stopped talking.

Alan looked at the whistle player, gave a three count, threw back his head, and began,

As I went a walking one morning in May
I met a young couple so far did we stray
And one was a young maid so sweet and
    so fair
And the other was a soldier and a brave
    grenadier

Fingal O'Reilly wasn't the only one to join in the chorus. He glanced round and saw just about everyone's mouth opening. Those who couldn't sing or didn't know the words nodded along in time. Tapped their feet.

And they kissed so sweet and comforting
As they clung to each other

Someone had two fingers in his mouth and let go a piercing whistle. Someone else whooped.

They went arm in arm along the road
Like sister and brother . . .

A pure contralto voice soared above the others.

They went arm in arm down the road
Til they came to a stream . . .

O'Reilly realised that the perfect sound was coming from Flo Bishop.

The applause was deafening when the song finished.

"You've a marvellous voice, Flo," Kitty said. "Quite lovely."

Bertie adopted his pouter pigeon pose, but out of pride for his wife. "My Flo's 'Blow the Wind Southerly' would give your woman Kathleen Ferrier's version a run for its money, so it would."

Flo bobbed her head, blushed, and said, "Bertie Bishop, behave yourself."

O'Reilly smiled and shook his head. "By God, Flo Bishop, I've been your doctor for twenty-three years. I never knew you could sing like that."

"My lord, ladies, and gentlemen." Fergus stood holding his whistle. "Now wasn't that grand altogether?"

More applause.

51

"But, I know there's some out there with their tongues hanging out and no one at the bar to pour for them, so thank you, Alan —"

A voice yelled, "Tongue hanging out? I have a thirst you could photograph."

The laughter was deafening.

Alan Hewitt bowed to Fergus and the crowd and headed back to his duty.

Already some of the groups that had quietened out of courtesy to Alan had restarted their conversations.

Fergus continued, "And the lads and I will give youse a few numbers. If anyone wants to sing a solo, join in." Fergus swept an arm around the room. "You want til give us a recitation, like 'The Charge of the Light Brigade,' or 'The Boy Stood on the Burning Deck,' just come on up."

A voice O'Reilly recognised yelled, "Will you give us a sea shanty, Doctor? You was in the navy."

"Not tonight, if you don't mind," O'Reilly said. He was proud of his baritone, but this was not the time or the place.

Fergus looked at O'Reilly. "But mebbe some other night, Doctor, sir? You just bide tonight." He turned back to the crowd. "We'll start with a jig, 'The Irish Washerwoman,' and instead of the usual three-jig set we'll just slip into a couple of hornpipes, 'The Plains of Boyle' and 'The Last Pint.' "

A slurred voice said, "Be jizziz, it bloody well better not be. I'm dying of feckin' thirst."

A woman yelled, "Shut up, Paddy. You're flying already."

There was general laughter and another woman called, "Take him home, missus. He'll thank you in the morning."

"Shush, you lot," a man called. "Give Fergus the floor, for God's sake."

Fergus let it all pass, raised his voice a bit, and concluded, "Later we'll get Alan to give us another number."

Mister Coffin, the undertaker, called, "Will you do 'Rocky Road to Dublin,' Mister Hewitt?"

"I'm your man," Alan Hewitt said, from his hatch.

More applause. Conversations started up again, as did the little band, in six-eight time. While many people went silent to listen, other groups were less inhibited. After all, O'Reilly thought, it wasn't as if they'd paid to hear a concert. If the musicians wanted to play? More power to their wheel, but some folks had come for the *craic,* not the music.

Bertie Bishop was one of them. "I was talking there now about having events. I had one thing in mind, but this here's just give me another notion as well. After you went home last night, Doc — Doctor O'Reilly was having a pint with me and Dapper Frew in the Duck — anyroad, Dapper's in the Ballybucklebo Highlanders. Them fellahs don't just play pipes and drums. Dapper says they've a uilleann piper, a fiddler, two pennywhistle guys, a banjo player who also has a mandolin, a squeeze-box guy who doubles up on the spoons. That's him over there tonight." He glanced at Flo. "You just heard my Flo sing. I think we've enough talent for to hold talent contests."

"I think that would be great fun, Bertie," Kitty said. "Don't you agree, Fingal?"

"I do, just as long as no one asks me to be a judge."

"I'm sure we can spare you that, Doctor O'Reilly," Flo said.

"You started off, Bertie, talking about bringing folks together," said Kitty. "I'm sure that sort of thing would help."

"Aye," said Bertie, "and the other thing I had in mind —"

He was interrupted by a round of applause coming from the dance floor. The band, as promised, had gone from a jig to

54

the even rhythms of a hornpipe, and two young women were facing each other on the floor, backs braced stiffly, arms and hands rigidly by their sides, step-dancing. O'Reilly recognised one, Jeannie Kennedy, who had had appendicitis in '64. Neither had on hard shoes, so the usual tap-dancing sound was absent, but O'Reilly enjoyed their light-footed grace.

Bertie Bishop laughed. "Funny that. Dancing. I was going til say, back in the '50s and early '60s, the Sea Scouts in Bangor ran a Saturday dance called the Fo'c's'le in their clubhouse. I don't know if it's still going on, but up in Belfast the Queen's University Hop is, and so's the one at Inst. Very popular with young people."

"So, you're suggesting we do dances here too?" the marquis said.

Bertie nodded. "For starters. See how it goes."

The marquis steepled his fingers. "I think this is a splendid idea. Bring the community together —"

A short burst of applause marked the end of the second hornpipe, and the girls returned to their table with Dermot Kennedy and his wife.

"For the love of God, sit down, Paddy."

The fellow, a heavyset redhead who had

shouted out earlier, was on his feet, swaying. Must be from Portaferry, O'Reilly thought, because he had never seen the man before.

The stranger threw back his head and roared to the tune of "Galway Bay,"

Maybe someday I'll go home again to
  Ireland
If my dear old wife would only pass away
She nearly has me heart broke with her
  naggin' . . .

Cries of "Shush," and "Houl your wheest, y'eejit."

Another member of his party dragged the man into a chair, and in moments two big fellahs were oxtercogging him, followed by his tearful wife, to the exit. Paddy's parting shot was "Shut up and get ready to drive, Mick. You're too feckin' drunk to sing. I know you're stocious, because your face is getting blurred." The door closed behind them.

The air was filled with tutting noises before the hums of conversation filled the room.

O'Reilly shook his head, but he was smiling. "Ah, the drink," he said, "it gets you drunk, makes you shoot at your landlord —

and it makes you miss."

"Steady on, there, Fingal. If there's a landlord to be shot at, it's probably me." But the marquis was laughing and so was everyone else at the table, although Bertie was the first to stop.

"All that carrying on would make a cat laugh, I'm sure. Dead funny, it is. But here's me trying til talk a bit of sense."

"Sorry, Bertie," O'Reilly and the marquis said together.

"We all know what you're saying is important," said O'Reilly. "Please go on."

"Thank you, Doctor. There's one other thing I was wanting to say. When the dances are going well, we'd need to have some special guests. We can do what we like among ourselves, but if nobody takes any notice, so what? I think we could put on a function, have our church leaders here showing that they are friends, a few primed spokesmen like your lordship, and you, Doctor. Maybe Alan Hewitt and Gerry Shanks? Everyone knows Alan's a Catholic and would like peaceful reunion of Ireland, and no one minds. He doesn't fight with Gerry Shanks, who wants Ulster to stay part of the United Kingdom." Bertie took a deep breath. "And that's the way it should be and that's what we want til show off. We'd invite

BBC Ulster, Ulster ITV and Radio Telefis Eireann along to see, and show other people how us folks in Ballybucklebo can get along."

O'Reilly nodded. "You never can tell what that might lead to. Good for you, Bertie."

"It is an impressive idea," the marquis said. "You've thought this through, haven't you, Bertie?"

"I have, my lord, and —" Bertie paused for effect. "I also think we could charge a small admission to every event and use that money, after expenses, til set up a fund."

"A fund? Oh, I like the sound of that," said Kitty. "And what would it be used for?"

Bertie sighed. "I don't want til sound like a pessimist, but I don't think things are going til get better in Ulster for a brave while. I think we could put away a bit of do-re-mi for seed money, and if we see a real need, like kiddies affected by what's going on, use our dosh til get a proper non-denominational charity, like, started. Maybe a summer camp where Catholic and Protestant kids could get til know each other. Something like that."

A spontaneous round of applause burst out from the crowd, as if all had heard and were in agreement. O'Reilly started clapping himself.

"Good gracious," John MacNeill said, "what a splendid idea. My sister Myrna and I would certainly contribute." He frowned. His voice was very serious when he said, "We'll need a majority vote of all members present in favour at an extraordinary general meeting to charge for admission. I think we should set up a steering committee so our proposal is watertight."

"I'll help," Bertie Bishop said, "and, Flo?"

"I'm on the Ladies' Committee. I'll ask if they'd like me to represent them."

"Excellent," the marquis said. "I wonder if the Reverend Robinson and Father O'Toole might serve? I'll ask them. I think you should chair the group, Mister Bishop."

"Thank you, sir," Bertie said. "And I'd ask that the chairman has no vote so there'll never be a tie."

"Fair enough," O'Reilly said. "And I'd suggest that's a big enough number."

Bertie Bishop grimaced. "There may be a wee snag. It only just came til me there now."

The marquis took a sip of his pint and leaned forward. "Oh? Please go on."

"These here grounds is out in the country, of course, 'cause land was cheaper to buy here," Bertie said. "But there is that one house fornenst the pitch and there's a thran

59

bugger, I'm sorry, your lordship, ladies" — O'Reilly was sure John MacNeill had heard much worse — "lives in it. Just moved in a couple of months ago. Lieutenant-Colonel Mullan, late of the Royal Ulster Rifles, has been complaining after every home game because of the noise. He was here half an hour ago, giving off. Chuntering on about sound bylaws. He'll likely object til dances too."

The marquis nodded. "Indeed, he might." John MacNeill frowned. "Rifles, eh? Fine old unit. Two regiments of foot, the Eighty-third (County of Dublin) and Eighty-sixth (Royal County Down), were amalgamated in 1881 as the Royal Irish Rifles. Did yeoman service at the Somme. Changed their name to the Royal Ulster Rifles in 1921."

"After the partition of Ireland," O'Reilly said. "The new Irish Free State didn't want them."

"They have a proud tradition," the marquis said. "I wonder if my sister Myrna and I had him round for dinner. Appealed to his regimental spirit? I wonder if he might withdraw his complaint."

Before anyone else could comment, there was a rattling of spoons and their player said, "My lord, ladies, and gentlemen.

Earlier we had a request for 'Rocky Road to Dublin.' Alan Hewitt, if you please."

As Alan made his way to join the musicians, there were whistles, cheers, applause. A cry of, "Go on, Alan, you-boy-yuh."

O'Reilly looked over to where the trio had re-formed.

The instruments played the intro and Alan began,

While in the merry month of May, now
    from me home I started
Left the girls of Tuam were nearly
    broken-hearted
Saluted father dear, kissed me darling
    mother
Drank a pint of beer, me grief and tears
    to smother . . .

Gerry Shanks's wife, Mairead, came and stood beside Alan, taking the alto part when the verse moved on:

Then off to reap the corn and leave
    where I was born
Cut a stout blackthorn to banish ghosts
    and goblins
A brand-new pair of brogues to rattle over
    the bogs . . .

O'Reilly sat back. He glanced round. Just

look how every face was smiling tonight. O'Reilly took a pull on his pint. Bertie Bishop's idea of using the clubhouse to bring the community together was going to take some planning, but who better to do it than the Bishops and the two men of God. And that was a stroke of genius Bertie had about getting the media in. None of this might solve Ulster's problems, but it couldn't hurt to try.

The alto and tenor notes filled the hall, soaring in harmony above every other voice in the place belting out the chorus in unison:

One two three four five hunt the hare
And turn her down the rocky road
And all the way to Dublin
Whack fal-al-dee-rah

3
Roaring He Shall Rise

April 12, 1969
Doctor Barry Laverty looked up at the white sails, both filled, taut, and drawing to perfection. He and his longtime friend Jack Mills had borrowed *Shearwater,* a GP 14 dinghy, from a friend, Andy Jackson. Jack was on the tiller and Barry was perched on the starboard side amidships as the little boat heeled to the wind. He loved the peace of being out on the waters of Belfast Lough.

They'd passed Luke's Point with its concrete outdoor roller-skating rink, and Barry could see the afternoon sun flashing from windows in the little town of Whitehead directly across the lough on the County Antrim shore. "Good to be back on the water, Jack," he said.

"Aye," said Jack. "I reckon both of us can use a break from Ulster politics, if only for the afternoon."

"You said it." Barry nodded. "And it's

good to get away from patients' problems too." He frowned. "Sue's visiting her parents in Broughshane today. She wants to have a chat with her mum, but she'll be home at six thirty."

Jack was the only other one privy to the Lavertys' apparent difficulty conceiving. "Still no luck?"

Barry shook his head. " 'Fraid not."

"I'm sorry, mate."

"Thanks." Barry managed a small smile. "She's being very brave about it." He stared out over the gentle chop for fifty yards to where a fisherman in a thirty-foot open motor launch was hauling in a net lobster pot empty of catch. Barry looked back at his friend. "Anyway. Let's try not to worry now. Enjoy the sailing."

"Fair enough."

The big farmer's son from Cullybackey sat to starboard on the stern cross bench, the dinghy's tiller in his left hand. He had a satisfied grin on his ruddy-cheeked face as he exerted just enough pressure so the angle of the rudder held the boat on course.

Barry sat controlling the jib, his feet under a central toe strap in case he might need to lie back outside the boat and use his weight to counteract the heeling effect of the easterly breeze blowing from the mouth of

Belfast Lough. Puffy clouds were gliding away from the distant Persian blue hills of Antrim and toward the smoky city of Belfast.

Now, in early April, although cellular long johns worn under jeans, thick oiled-wool Aran sweaters, yellow oilskins, and woolly hats were still in order, spring had come to Ulster and chased away Boreas, the bitter north wind.

The only sounds were the swish of the bows cutting through the water, the slap of wavelets on the boat's side, and the harsh overhead mewing of a couple of brown-speckled, immature herring gulls. A stronger gust made the dinghy heel, and Barry lay back out over the side, his leverage bringing the little vessel back on a more even keel. A burst of spray blew in his face and he felt its icy fingers, tasted the salt.

Barry could see his friend was having to put more pressure on the tiller to stop the boat being pushed off course. The gust passed, the boat righted, and Barry came inboard. "I'm sorry Helen couldn't join us today, Jack. She always enjoys a day out."

"It's her finals in June. Nothing, and I mean nothing's going to keep her from her studies. You remember what it was like when we were medical students? Pure bloody purgatory." He made a small helm adjustment and Barry trimmed his sail by tightening his sheet.

"I remember." Barry cast back to June 1963 at Queen's University Belfast and even now, six years later, shuddered at the thought. It had been a three-week test of endurance and knuckle-gnawing stress the like of which he'd never want to go through again. "At least I was finished with exams after that. You still had a fair share to face."

Jack grinned. "Behind me now. One early basic sciences exam called the Primary, four years training under supervision after our houseman's year, then the big one in London, written papers, practical cases at Saint Bart's, then orals at the Royal College itself."

"And you passed. You can put FRCS, Fellow of the Royal College of Surgeons, after your name, drop 'Doctor' and adopt the honorific 'Mister.' "

Jack laughed. "All because of some mediaeval academic dispute between physicians who demanded to be called 'Doctor' and barber surgeons who had to make do with 'Mister.' "

"I didn't think you cared much about titles, Jack."

"I don't, but I do care about getting a

senior position. I have to wait until a senior man retires before I can get a consultant job." Jack sighed. "Some of my lot have already emigrated. Much easier to get a senior post in Canada."

"You and Helen still thinking of going?" Barry hoped not, but the last time he and Jack had talked about this his best friend had seemed pretty set.

Jack answered quietly, "Helen has to get her finals first."

"She's not missed any of her exams up to now. I'm sure she'll be fine, mate."

"Huh," said Jack, "I agree, but try telling her that. She says she absolutely must pass, and not just for herself. She feels an obligation to a couple of people. Her dad, for one. And the marquis of Ballybucklebo for giving her that scholarship."

"You've got Fingal to thank for that," Barry said.

"From what I've seen of your senior," Jack said, "he keeps a lot of people on the straight and narrow, and you, my friend, you've been keeping this boat upright for more than an hour. My turn." Jack laughed. "Here, you helm for a while. I'll look after the jib." Jack prepared to move. He made sure the main sheet was cleated in.

"Right." Barry let his sheet fly and the jib

flap. He'd move aft to take the tiller before Jack relinquished control. Snug in its jam cleat, the main sheet could be left unattended during the changeover. Barry crouched, covered the short distance, sat aft, took the tiller, feeling the degree of tension required to keep the boat on course, and picked up the end of the cleated-in main sheet.

Jack moved forward and took Barry's old spot on the starboard side. Hand over hand he hauled in the jib sheet until the noisy flapping of the smaller sail had been stilled and the Teflon triangle was properly trimmed. He put his feet under the toe strap. He grinned. "All set."

Barry looked up. The sun had passed the top of the mast and shone directly down on him. He scrunched up his eyes, then opened them to watch the wavelets dance toward the boat. The wind ruffled his hair.

Both sails were set well. He smiled. " 'And all I ask is a tall ship and a star to steer her by.' 'Sea Fever.' "

Jack stood, knees bent to keep his balance, and struck a poetic pose. " 'I must go down to the seas again, to the vagrant gypsy life/To the gull's way and the whale's way where the wind's like a whetted knife.' "

Barry laughed. "That goes back a long

way. To Mister Wilcockson's fifth-form English literature class at Campbell College. Sixteen years since we met there in '53. I think the next line is, 'And all I ask is a merry yarn from a laughing fellow rover.' You and I have been fellow rovers, and by God, I can't count the number of times you've made me laugh."

"Many moons cross sky, Kemo Sabe. Much water flow under bridge."

"Eejit." Barry laughed. "See? You've done it again."

"Good old Campbell. I enjoyed our time there. Made some great friends. Played on a winning rugby team."

Barry knew his best friend had for years harboured a wish to play rugby football for Ireland, but it had not come to pass. Yet it seemed Jack had accepted that and got on with his life. That ability was something Barry envied in Jack Mills. Barry himself was more of a worrier and — Damn it, he wasn't going to think about his concerns today.

Jack bent and looked under the jib. "We're getting a bit close to the buoyed shipping lane, Barry, and there's a tanker heading up to the Sydenham tank farm."

"I'll alter course," Barry said. "You handle the jib."

"Aaar. Aye-aye, skipper." Jack exactly caught Robert Newton's Long John Silver from the '50s movie *Treasure Island*. He grimaced, widened his eyes, and said with a leer, "Was you ever at sea, Jim, lad?"

Barry chuckled. They'd seen the film together at one of the winter Saturday-night film screenings at their boarding school. Those memories, the happy ones like an old film, the serious ones like the exams they'd faced together — as Helen must shortly — and the remembrances of their houseman's year as freshly minted doctors, unsure of themselves, anxious, facing the stresses and the ridiculous moments, were all part of the foundation of their deep friendship.

Barry smiled over at Jack and altered course so the wind was coming in from almost directly astern. The boat, now running down the waves, began to pitch to the swells, bow and stern taking it in turn to rise and fall. Barry's memories were interrupted when Jack said, "Dear God, what's that?" He pointed to where a dark triangle in the water approached to starboard from ahead.

Barry leaned over the little boat's side and stared. "Damned if I know." The wind ruffling Belfast Lough made it impossible to see beneath the surface, but judging by the way the water was disturbed round the object, it was attached to something big. Very big. And it was coming their way.

The triangle, moving at about two knots, now was level with *Shearwater*'s bow. Barry peered beneath him as the creature passed close alongside. He could make out a blunt rounded snout, which meant the triangle, by now opposite Jack, was at least seven feet from the tip of the brute's nose. Holy Moses. If the triangle were a dorsal fin, the fish must be at least as long as the dinghy.

"What do you think it is, Barry, bye?" Jack's voice was strained.

"I think —" Barry jerked back, nearly losing his balance. He held on to the tiller but, flailing his free arm, dropped the cleated-in sheet.

Jack yelled, "Dear God," and flinched away. His movement hauled in on the jib. Deprived of its drawing power, it collapsed, flapping.

The ocean boiled as a vast dark fish with a pale underbelly breached. As it rose in the air, Barry saw its long snout, tiny eye, huge mouth, and gill slits that nearly encircled its body in front of a short fin like a half-moon on its back. The leviathan had to be at least

71

twenty feet long. He recognised it for what it was.

It reached the limit of its leap and fell back with a thunderous splashing, turning the sea into a maelstrom. To Barry it seemed to be an eternity before the last of the displaced water had returned to the sea, and some of it had fallen inboard, soaking them both. Water beaded Barry's oilskin jacket and coursed down the fabric in torrents, almost as if the skies had opened and it was raining. Barry's head was soaked. He ripped off his sodden wool hat. Short waves slapped against the dinghy's side, making her roll. For a moment he forgot about holding his course.

"Look out, Barry."

Barry swiftly corrected his helm. "Thanks, Jack. That could have been nasty."

"Bloody right," Jack said. "If we'd crossed the wind and the mainsail and boom had flown across the boat —"

"I know." Barry watched the dingy settle back on her course and Jack reset the jib. "We could have been dismasted. Silly of me to get distracted."

"You weren't the only one. Boys-a-boys," Jack said, eyes wide, "what in the name of the wee man was that?"

Barry watched the fin and its pursuing

wake moving sedately away in the opposite direction.

"There's no creatures like that near Cullybackey, hey. The biggest would be my dad's bull. Thon bye's as big as two of him."

Barry, his shock gone now he knew what they were dealing with, said, "I'm sure it's a basking shark."

"A shark?" Jack's voice rose in pitch. "Shark? Bloody hell. Sharks eat people. Let's get the hell out of here."

"Stop getting up to high doh, my friend. For one thing, the fish and us are going in opposite directions, and for another," Barry said, "that kind of shark's harmless, Jack. Basking sharks feed on plankton."

Jack frowned. "That twenty-foot monster feeds on plankton? You sure? Certain sure? Even if he doesn't bite, the bejeezusly thing had a mouth that could have swallowed Jonah."

"I know, I know, but trust me, Jack. The thing's harmless. I read all about them when we were at school. Dad had a book, *Harpoon at a Venture,* by the Scottish naturalist Gavin Maxwell. After the war, some ex-service chaps tried to start a commercial basking shark fishery on some island in the Hebrides."

Jack frowned. "What would be valuable in

a big ugly bugger like that?"

"Its liver. It takes up twenty-five percent of the animal's body and it's rich in something called squalene. And the shark's skin, properly tanned, makes a kind of tough leather."

"I'll be damned," Jack said. He shook his head.

"All the poor old basking shark does is swim around the oceans and eat plankton. Quite harmless to humans."

"Not entirely," Jack said. "When thon bye jumped I thought I was going to have a heart attack. I'm all right now you've explained." He grinned. "It'll be something to tell Helen about."

Barry said, "If I'm going to have time to let you buy me a pint in the club, we'd better be heading back."

"Fine with me," Jack said.

"Ready about," Barry said, starting to trim the mainsail while Jack readied himself to control the jib. "Lee ho." Barry called the executive order to put the boat's head through the wind, so it would be blowing on the dinghy's port side as she made her way to Ballyholme Yacht Club. "I'll sail her full and by," Barry said, an old square-rigger term meaning as close to the direction of the wind as possible with sails sheeted hard home.

Joe Togneri had taught a young Barry to sail. The son of Italian immigrants who ran the Coronation Café ice-cream and sweetie shop on Bangor's Quay Street, Joe had been full of old square-rigger terms. Barry grinned, remembering with deepest affection the little man with hunched back and twinkling eyes.

They settled down on course. "We should be in in about an hour."

"Lots of time for a jar," Jack said.

They passed the redbrick Royal Ulster Yacht Club and neared Luke's Point, where they'd turn into Ballyholme Bay on the last leg. "Thon shark, bye, it got me thinking." Jack shook his head. "Here we were sailing happily along on a perfect day, pretty much at peace with the world, when there's a violent eruption from the deep. Bit like Ulster —"

Barry guessed what his friend was thinking.

"Just when it seems all is sweetness and light, the old animosities have been festering under the surface, and suddenly burst through again."

"I still think things could settle," Barry said.

"They'd better," Jack said. "When, not if, Helen qualifies in June, she still has a houseman's year to do starting in August. We're still thinking about mebbe going to Canada, but," Jack grimaced, "Helen's having second thoughts."

"Oh?" Barry pricked up his ears. The last time he and Jack had discussed this subject, Barry had assumed it was a fait accompli, which had saddened Barry to think of losing his best friend. Now was there some hope that Jack Mills and his wife-to-be might stay in Ulster after all? "What's up?"

"It's not just that she feels an obligation to the marquis, she's worried sick about leaving her ould dad. You know he's a widower. She's all he's got by way of a family here since Helen's mum died ten years ago of kidney failure."

"Jack, it's your and Helen's call, I shouldn't try to influence you, but," he looked Jack in the eye, "I'd be delighted if you two stayed." Barry felt a glimmer of hope he recognised as selfishness. But it didn't stop him smiling.

Jack shrugged. "I thought I'd my mind made up. Certainly, my prospects would be better in Canada, but Helen's been thinking out loud to me about giving things here a chance to settle. One more year while she does her houseman's stint and gets full registration."

"Would you still get married?"

Jack nodded. "My folks won't like it. We'll have to hope Alan will."

"I don't know Alan Hewitt all that well, but by reputation he's a fair-minded man. And he loves his daughter."

Jack said, "We'll just have to see," and he brightened. "Who knows what will happen by next August?" Jack leaned aft and touched Barry's arm. "You and I had a lot of fun as housemen in the Royal Victoria. I'd like Helen to do hers there too."

Barry chuckled. "We did. I was thinking about it too, just before Moby Dick showed up." Barry shook his head. "Do you know what Cervantes said?"

"The *Don Quixote* bloke?"

"That's him. He said, 'A man must eat a peck of salt with his friend before he knows him.' We didn't just have fun together. There were some pretty hairy moments too."

Jack nodded slowly, and Barry was sure the allusion had not been lost. "A peck of salt."

"Dear Lord, Jack, is it really six years ago since we started?"

"It is," said Jack. "Indeed, it is."

"Remember our first day?"

"I'll never forget it," Jack said.

They sat together in companionable silence.

Barry Laverty kept an eye on the sail, the wind, and the sea, hoping Jack and Helen would stay, letting his mind drift. How Jack had felt on that day had been unclear to the young Barry Laverty, but he himself had greeted the challenges ahead with a mixture of pride and anxious anticipation about how he might cope.

Barry looked out over the sea. Back in '63 he'd been as churned up inside as that patch of ocean after the shark had breached.

4

IN THE FORCE AND ROAD OF CASUALTY

August 1, 1963

August 1, 1963. For the new batch of housemen at Belfast's Royal Victoria Hospital, this was the first day on duty, following qualification in June and graduation in July. Once the next twelve months were over, the newly qualified doctors would be fully licensed physicians and could pursue whatever career path they chose. But for now, they were at the beck and call of the service to which they were attached.

Doctors Barry Laverty and Jack Mills strode along the hospital's main corridor, the tails of their long white coats flapping behind them. They had been summoned from their breakfast in the housemen's dining room in the East Wing.

"God alone knows what's going on in casualty," said Barry. Four of them, including Barry and Jack, had been assigned there for three months in staggered shifts. "You're

79

supposed to be on the noon-to-six shift, Jack, and I've got the short night, six to midnight. Curly Maguire and Norma Fitch are there this morning. Shouldn't they be able to manage?" For a moment Barry wondered about Norma. He knew from their student experience how rough some of the casualty patients could be, and a few of the male housemen had wondered, would a woman, and a petite one at that, be able to cope?

"Should be, unless there's been some kind of multiple-victim accident. But we've been sent for, so we must be needed." Jack held open one of the double doors from the main corridor. "Holy Moses. Would you look at that?"

Both young men stopped in their tracks.

Ahead stretched row upon row of benches, filled by people waiting their turn to see a doctor. Some were standing or leaning against walls. Most of the men wore dunchers and many were smoking. The buzz of muted conversation was intermittently pierced by coughs, groans, and the lusty yelling of babies and children. Working-class women did not have the luxury of baby-sitters. Inured by three and a half years' exposure, Barry barely noticed the aroma of disinfectant that pervaded the whole hospital, but here there was a faint smell of unwashed socks and bodies. Even in 1963 not all the terrace houses in the slums of Belfast had running water.

"How the blazes are we going to get through all this? There's only four of us. There must be sixty people in here." Barry had never seen so many patients crowded into the waiting hall.

In the ten years Barry had known Jack Mills he had never seen him truly fazed, and his friend answered with his usual aplomb. "Remember what the very upper-class registrar said when we complained about the amount of routine work we'd to do?"

"Mike Patrick? Remind me."

Jack adopted plummy aristocratic tones. "In this life, young fellow, there will always be a certain amount of shite to be shovelled. Might one suggest you simply get yourself a long-handled spade?" Jack lengthened his stride and resumed his usual County Antrim accent. "Come on, hey bye. It won't be as bad as all that."

Despite his concerns, Barry managed to chuckle and followed his friend, now turning left onto a narrow aisle between the waiting crowds and the plaster room, where casts were applied or removed. Before turn-

81

ing right onto a corridor leading to the ambulance room, he saw a student nurse taking a patient into room B, directly ahead, where minor cases were seen.

They walked along the passageway to the casualty senior sister's office.

"Better report in with Sister," Jack said. "See what's up." He knocked on the door.

"Come in."

Sister Branna "Bernie" O'Byrne, originally from County Wicklow, sat hunched over her desk.

"Morning, Bernie," Jack said.

Smart in her red uniform dress, white apron, and starched white fall — the triangular headdress worn by all Royal nurses above the rank of student — the senior sister glared at Jack and Barry. "I know I've to call you youngsters 'Doctor' now, but by all that's holy, you're going to earn that title today. It's like Paddy's bleeding market out there."

The usually unflappable Bernie was giving Barry reason to worry. "But you and your nurses will help, Sister O'Byrne," he said, trying to keep his voice calm.

She sniffed. "We'll have to. I've never seen the waiting room so jam-packed." He had learned long ago that a student and now a houseman's best friends were the senior nurses. It was wise not to fall foul of them, and occasionally calling them by their full title was a sensible thing to do. Bernie pointed through the glass front wall of her office to the scene outside. The ambulance room had three curtained-off examining spaces on either side, separated by a central aisle. Past the last cubicle, double doors stood open. It was through them that stretcher cases arriving by ambulance were wheeled in.

"Your friends are already at work in there on two acutely ill recent admissions, and room B's chockablock. I want you two out there."

Barry smiled and felt relieved. He felt reasonably able to deal with minor cases.

"And if we need more help in here for something more serious, I'll send for one of you. Off you trot."

"Right, Sister," said Jack.

As they left her office, Barry heard retching coming from inside the nearest curtained-off cubicle. A voice he recognised as Norma Fitch's said, "Please try to lie still, Mister Duncan."

They retraced their steps to the waiting area and took a right turn to room B, with its six curtained-off spaces.

"Good luck, mate," Jack said, and pulled

back the curtains of the first cubicle.

Barry took the first examining space to his right, where a balding, middle-aged man, grey eyes with laugh lines at their corners, sat on a wooden chair holding a sock and shoe. His right foot and ankle were wrapped in a grubby pink tensor bandage. He grinned at Barry. "My God," he said, "is this what youse school kids do in your summer holidays?" He laughed.

Barry knew he looked younger than his twenty-three years. He was proud to have qualified as the youngest member of his class, but he'd never been one to stand on his dignity and he wanted to get a move on. "Only on Thursdays," he said, and inclined his head toward the bandaged ankle. "Bad ankle?"

"Aye. Gave her a right wrench, so I did. I should have known better than til be kicking a football around with a bunch of kids."

"Let me take a look at your card." Barry lifted a four-by-eight ruled card from a small rack attached to the wall. He read:

Alfred Stewart. 45. Labourer. Date first
    seen July 22. 17 Ravenhill Road. Protes-
    tant.
C/O Sprained right ankle.
O/E Tender swollen.

84

X-Ray NBI
R Strap D10

The hieroglyphics, when translated, meant: C/O, complaining of; O/E, on examination; NBI, no bony injury; R, treatment; and D10, follow up in ten days.

"So, how's it feeling today, Mister Stewart?"

"Dead on, Doc, and no offence meant when I said you look young. It's only oul' Alfie, taking a hand out of you, like."

"No offence taken," Barry said. "Let's have a look at your hoof." He bent, undid a safety pin, and unwound the bandage. No bruising. No swelling. Good. "Can you move it?"

"Aye." Alfie Stewart did, in all directions. "I can walk on it too."

"Go on then. Let's see."

He stood and paced along the floor. No sign of a limp. "I think I'm dead on," he said, "but you're the doctor, sir."

I am, Barry thought, and it feels very good. "I think," he said, "we can chuck out the bandage, and you can put on your sock and shoe." He opened a pedal bin and dropped the soiled bandage in. As Alf Stewart laced up his shoe, Barry wrote on the card, *Sprain healed. Discharge Aug 1,* and replaced it in the rack. "Off you trot, Alf. You're well mended."

"Thank you, sir." The moment he let himself out through the curtains a student nurse popped in to ready the place for its next occupant.

Barry, relieved he'd been able to deal with the patient so quickly, felt his confidence growing. Within the next fifteen minutes he'd discharged a man who'd had a foreign body removed from his eye three days ago, and sent home, cured, a nosebleed packed two days before. Then a sprained wrist treated a week ago. Barry was beginning to feel he was getting the hang of this.

Sister O'Byrne appeared, handed him a card, and said, "Nip over to the suture room, please, Barry. Nurse Clarke needs you there."

"Thanks, Bernie." Barry smiled. They were back to Christian names, which meant she was back in her usual, highly competent form. As he crossed the waiting hall, a patient, a woman at the extreme left of the front bench, stood and followed a student nurse into room B. In rapid succession, each patient moved up one seat, and one of the few now standing took the last vacated place at the back of the hall. It was this serpentine movement of the crowd that had led to some irreverent medical student of bygone years naming the unfortunates who came to casualty "the snakes."

Barry read his next patient's card.

Mrs. Dympna Kilpatrick, 32. Housewife. Date first seen July 27. 18b Falls Road, Catholic.
C/O Cut palm of left hand
O/E Two-inch incision sutured.
R Five black silk sutures. Tetanus vaccine D6

Sutures were usually removed on day seven. Oh well.

He went into the suture room where a woman sat wearing a knotted headscarf over red hair. Her left hand was stretched out palm up on a green sterile towel covering a stainless steel table on casters. The hand was painted brown with the antiseptic Betadine.

A student nurse wearing a mask and rubber gloves stood at the patient's far side, facing Barry. "Doctor Laverty," she said.

"Don't let me hold you up, Nurse Clarke." Barry had worked with the young woman before. He'd always admired Virginia Clarke's green eyes, auburn hair, and trim figure.

She bent over the patient. "Only one more to go, Mrs. Kilpatrick."

"Great." The patient looked at Barry. "Hello, Doctor. How's about ye?"

Barry smiled and said over his shoulder as he washed his hands, "I think I'm supposed to ask you that."

"I'm doing —" She sucked in her breath.

"Sorry," Nurse Clarke said.

"That's all right, dear, and I am doing rightly, Doctor. This wee nurse has a quare soft hand under a duck, so she has."

"All done," Nurse Clarke said, straightening up.

Barry dried his hands, crossed to be closer to the patient, and looked at the scar. It was red, as was to be expected, but there was no sign of infection and it was healing well. "Looks very good," he said. "Can you dress it please, Nurse?"

In moments, a fresh dressing had been applied.

"Leave that on for another five days," Barry said. "If it starts to feel sore or suppurate —"

"Excuse me, Doctor, but what's sup-supturate, like?"

Barry smiled. "If there's any sign of beeling" — Belfast for infection — "go and see your own doctor, please." He retrieved her card from where he had set it on a shelf. *Healed, Discharge. Aug 1.*

"I'll do that, sir." She turned to Virginia Clarke. "And thank you too, Nurse. I'll be running on." She left.

Nurse Clarke was stripping off her rubber gloves. Then her mask.

She really did have amazing depths to her eyes, but Barry told himself to get a grip. There were dozens more patients to see and he'd no time for dalliance. Pity. Physically she was a stunner and he knew she had a wicked sense of humour. "Thanks, Virginia," he said.

"Barry," she said, "I know its bloody bedlam out there, but may I ask you something?"

"As long as it's quick."

"I thought we took out stitches on the seventh day."

Barry frowned. He'd wondered about that too. Day six had seemed a bit early. "We do."

"I've seen two day-six removals today."

Barry frowned. "That is unusual. I'll ask Sister O'Byrne. I'll let you know. You're here all day, aren't you?"

She nodded. "Until four."

Damn it, there was something special about those eyes. Barry, always shy around

89

women, steeled himself. "I'll be off tomorrow night. I don't suppose you'd —"

"Sorry," she said, cutting him off and looking him right in the eye, "we have a class and I don't want to miss it. Getting qualified's important to me."

"Of course. I'm sorry." As always when he was flustered, Barry's right hand flew to his head to smooth a tuft of fair hair that never seemed to lie properly. "Well — yes — um — I'd best be off."

Barry Laverty, he scolded himself, why, why are you so ham-fisted when it comes to pretty girls? You tried to ask her out. She said no. He was embarrassed, yes, but he knew he embarrassed easily. Was his pride hurt? A bit, but it was hardly a catastrophe — nothing ventured, nothing gained. But, damn it, she was a very pretty girl.

He went back across the waiting hall.

The crowd was thinning. The last bench was nearly empty. He'd seen five patients, a couple a bit more quickly than he would have liked, and if Jack had done the same and Hilda or Curly had been able to pitch in, perhaps the task wasn't going to be as daunting as it had first seemed. Barry felt a certain relief. But already he was thinking about people as nosebleeds and sprained wrists. There was no getting to know your patients in this madhouse. Before he could turn into room B, a student nurse called, "Ambulance room, Doctor Laverty."

Barry swallowed. Here comes the real test, he thought, and lengthened his stride.

"In there, Barry," Bernie said, pointing to two ambulance attendants pushing a laden trolley into the area nearest the door.

He gave her Dympna Kilpatrick's card and closed the curtains behind him.

One blue-uniformed attendant was leaning over the patient, a man in his sixties, Barry guessed, who lay quietly under a grey blanket on a trolley. A chair at its head stood against a wall where an upright sphygmomanometer was affixed.

The attendant had a stethoscope in his ears and was wrapping the sphygmo cuff around the patient's left upper arm before taking his blood pressure. Barry noticed an Ambu bag, a face mask connected to a self-inflating rubber balloon, lying on top of the blanket.

The other ambulance man said, "Your man's doctor reckons he's had a heart attack. He has a two-year history of angina. About two hours ago he sent for his GP because he had bad chest pain going into his jaw and down his arm."

Certainly sounded like a coronary.

"When we got there, his blood pressure was one hundred over sixty and his pulse fast and very irregular. He was sweating. His doctor had given him a quarter of morphine for the pain and a tablet of digitalis for the irregular heartbeat and sent for the ambulance. Me and Bert there was sent out." He looked at his watch. "That would have been an hour ago."

"And his BP's ninety over fifty now," Bert said, pulling the stethoscope from his ears.

"He needs admission to ward 6, men's cardiology," Barry said.

"Bijizzis. He needs more than that," Bert said. "I've lost his pulse, sir."

Barry saw the patient's eyes staring, the pupils widely dilated. He grabbed a wrist. No pulse. Barry yelled, "Nurse. Cardiac arrest," then said as calmly as he was able, "Get the Ambu bag ready, Bert. I'll do the cardiac massage."

Barry clambered onto the trolley and straddled the patient's legs. He crouched and put one hand flat on the man's sternum, the other on top of the first, and began rhythmic chest compression of two inches, sixty times per minute. "Ventilate."

Bert placed the face mask over the patient's nose and mouth and started compressing the bag at a rate of one ventilation every thirty compressions.

"Yes, Doctor?" a student nurse asked.

"Ask Sister to phone 5 and 6. Tell them I'm bringing a cardiac arrest patient who I think needs defibrillation."

"Right."

"Ready, lads?"

The first attendant took hold of the rear of the trolley. Bert steered the front with one hand while continuing to compress the bag. Once they were out from behind the curtains, Sister O'Byrne assigned a staff nurse to bag duty while the two ambulance men steered the trolley.

Barry was tiring but could not stop his external cardiac massage. He was vaguely aware of passing into the main corridor and turning left, heading for ward 6. Those in the corridor — nurses, students, physiotherapists, relatives — cleared out of the way.

A voice said, "Hang on."

Barry felt the trolley stop. "What?"

"It's all right, Barry. The cardiac team's here."

Barry managed to gasp, "Thanks," before climbing off and letting Doctor John Geddes and his staff take over and immediately head for the cardiac unit, where the defibrillator would be standing by. Barry stood bent over, hands on knees, pulling in lungfuls of air before straightening up and saying to the staff nurse, "We'd best get back to casualty."

"I thought you did very well, Doctor Laverty," she said.

"Thank you," Barry said, and glowed. He'd been able to cope with minor cases and now he had not panicked in a critical situation. Maybe, after a few more weeks here, he'd begin to feel more like a doctor and less like a student. He hoped so. He looked back in time to see the team and trolley disappear through the ward's blue plastic doors. He hoped the anonymous patient would survive and recover.

Jack Mills was coming the other way. "Well done, mate," he said, and clapped Barry on the shoulder. "Bernie's a right good head. She said we're getting well ahead, Curly and Norma can cope for half an hour, it is their shift after all, and I've to take you to the cafeteria for a cuppa."

"I'd appreciate that," Barry said.

Jack lit a cigarette as they passed 5 and 6.

Barry hesitated, wanting to know how his patient was doing, but Jack said, "We'll look in later if you like. Give them peace now to do their job."

"Fair enough."

They went downstairs to the arched ceiling cafeteria known as "The Caves" beneath wards 6 and 7. Jack bought the coffee. They found a table.

"So," Jack said, "how are you enjoying your first day as a houseman?"

Barry put down his cup. "It's great to feel you're actually doing something useful."

Jack grinned. "Remember *Dr. Kildare* on the telly?" His accent changed to American. "Doctor Gillespie, the senior man, says, 'So how are you enjoying your internship, young man?' And Doctor Kildare, dripping sincerity, says, 'It's hell, sir — but I'm loving every gruelling minute.' "

Barry rolled his eyes and shook his head but couldn't stop laughing. He recognised it as a release from the anxious feelings of a few minutes ago. Then he managed, "You, Mills, are a buck eejit of the first magnitude, but I'll tell you one thing. I've wanted to be a doctor since I was nine. We've a year to decide what kind of doctors we'll be, and I intend to make the most of it." He took another mouthful of coffee. "Mind you, I hope every day in casualty isn't like this."

It was Jack's turn to laugh. "It won't be, I promise."

Barry frowned. "How do you know?"

"Did you notice how the return dates on the cards seemed a bit odd?"

95

"As a matter of fact, I did."

"Bernie told me that she's worked out that our immediate predecessors set it up for our, I hesitate to say, amusement. As long as it didn't jeopardise the individual patient's care, starting ten days before the last housemen were due to leave, they scheduled as many return visits as possible for today instead of spreading them out. We are in the middle of a deliberate deluge of return visits all timed for our first day. And that's on top of any new ones that come today."

"The crafty buggers," Barry said, but managed to smile. "Even so, we seem to be coping." He shook his head. With direct entry to medical school after high school, young doctors were exactly that. Young, and with a pretty immature sense of humour too. "And it's a relief to hear today is unusual. I need to tell" — Barry eyed Jack and decided not to mention Virginia's name — "one of the student nurses. She was wondering about the return dates on the cards."

"Aye. You wouldn't be meaning that wee nurse Virginia Clarke, would you?"

Barry's coffee cup stopped inches from his lips. "I would."

"She's a cracker."

"Would you come to the point, Mills?"

Barry's pulse had sped up.

"And not a bit shy."

"Oh?"

"I asked her to come with me tonight to see *Whatever Happened to Baby Jane?*"

Damn you, Mills, Barry thought. Damn you. Putting Jack Mills anywhere near a pretty girl was like setting iron filings close to a magnet. Instant attraction. Barry felt his pulse throbbing in his temple. He sighed. Faint heart never won fair lady, he supposed, but Jack was right, Virginia Clarke was a wee cracker.

Jack laughed and blew a perfect smoke ring. "She put one hand on her hip — and told me," Jack's voice became falsetto and indignant, " 'Take a hike, Jack Mills. If you were the only pebble on the beach I'd go for a swim first. Go out with a boy like you? Away off and feel your head.' " He took a drag and in his normal voice said, "She might be restful on the eye, but she's a feisty one." He chuckled. "Never mind. To mangle an old saying, and sticking with beaches, there is no deficiency of gill-bearing aquatic creatures in the seven seas."

Barry knew his tone was wistful. "I do think she's terrific."

Jack rolled his eyes. "Not again, Barry. When we were schoolboys in sixth form you fell head over heels for the mam'selle who was meant to be helping us with our French conversation."

"I know. It was silly, but she was a looker." Barry sipped his coffee. "You didn't know about the girl I took out in the summer holiday between leaving school and starting at Queen's."

"You never told me, you devil. I didn't know you had. And it wasn't love at first sight?"

Barry laughed. "I took her out twice. She'd a giggle that would have gutted a herring at six fathoms."

Jack grinned. "Love 'em and leave 'em. I tried to tell you that, mate, but did you pay attention? First week here you met a nurse, swooned, took her out for six months, and went into a year's decline when she decided to move on." Jack blew another smoke ring.

Barry pursed his lips and said, "I know, I know, but I don't seem to be able to help myself if I really like a girl."

"I understand," Jack said, and Barry heard the sympathy in his friend's voice. "That next one, that wee brown-eyed radiographer, hit you hard too. You were head over heels and she dumped you." Jack shook his head. "I think you're still licking your wounds."

Barry nodded. "A bit," he said. And he'd confess that to no one but Jack.

Jack leant forward. "Barry, we're both too young to get married. We have careers to make. Can you not see that right now girls are for fun, and lots of them feel that way too about us? One day for both of us the right one will come along, but for now?" Jack's voice adopted the tones of East Belfast, "Why would you buy a cow when you can get a bottle of milk at the grocers?"

Barry chuckled. "All right," he said, "point taken."

"And," said Jack, "if you do fancy Nurse Clarke, take another shot. I'll not stand in your way. The worst she can do is say no."

"Mebbe," Barry said, and laughed with his friend, but inwardly he was delighted. Maybe, just maybe it might be worth risking another rebuff if he asked Nurse Clarke again?

5
THINK ONLY WHAT CONCERNS THEE

April 12, 1969

Barry could still taste his yacht club pint when Jack parked outside the Lavertys' bungalow on its private peninsula on the south shore of Belfast Lough. "You coming in?" Barry asked. The Hillman Imp was here. Sue was home early from her folks' farm outside Broughshane. "Sue'd be pleased to see you."

"Sorry, but no thanks," Jack said, "I've a big list tomorrow, hey. A gastrectomy, varicose veins, a hernia, and two gall-bags." Surgeon talk for gall bladders, thought Barry. He'd never liked how surgeons referred to the conditions they were treating rather than the patients who had the conditions. "I'd like to put my feet up tonight."

"Fair enough. Keep in touch." Barry got out, and as he was closing the car door he heard Jack say, "Give Sue our love," before he drove off with a wave, bouncing over the rough ground.

Barry stood outside the low wall of his back garden absorbing the spring evening. A glossy blackbird, stiff tail jerking as it ran along the top of the wall, scolded him, and from the shore came the song of never-ending seduction of the rocks by the waves.

Barry had his hopes up now that perhaps Jack and Helen would stay in Ulster. Mind you, the glacial rate of promotion of junior surgeons could tip the scales. At least one-third of Barry's class had emigrated to America or Commonwealth countries, and even GP jobs were becoming tight.

The demented barking of Max, Sue's springer spaniel, came from behind the closed back door. "Shut up, Max," Barry called. You'd think the daft dog would recognise him by now.

Sue Laverty, née Nolan, her long copper plait undone and hanging free around her shoulders, stood in the open back doorway, smiling at Barry and holding on to the tail-thrashing Max's collar. "Jack not coming in?"

Barry shook his head and kissed Sue. "He's a big slate tomorrow." He patted a now-silent Max and followed Sue into the kitchen. "So, how were things in Brough-shane?"

"Pretty good. Mum's in fine form. We had our chat. Dad's keeping well, always a relief given his heart attack history. I rode Róisín, but poor old girl, she could only manage a trot. None of us are getting any younger."

"Come on then — old girl," and he patted her bottom, "let's go through to the lounge." She took his hand and her touch warmed him.

Barry, as always, let his gaze rise for a moment above the small front garden, out across Belfast Lough, where earlier he and Jack had been sailing. His thoughts of the shark vanished. "Good Lord, look at that." He crossed to the picture window.

Sue followed.

Heading up toward the Port of Belfast was a tall ship.

"Isn't she beautiful?" Barry admired the three towering masts, the long bowsprit standing proud above a creamy bow-wave.

"I've never seen one before except on the telly."

Barry was entranced. It wasn't every day he was privileged to watch a throwback to the romantic age of sail. C. S. Forester's books about Horatio Hornblower, a Royal Naval officer in Nelson's day, were still some of Barry's favourite reads.

He studied the rig. "All her square sails

are furled on the yards except the fore and main topsails. Those are the second from the bottom ones on the fore and main masts. And look." He pointed. Tiny figures were swarming aloft up the shrouds, then out along the main topsail yard. "They're going to furl that sail."

"Quite the sight," Sue said, "but I'm glad they invented the aeroplane. It would have taken us forever to get to Paris on one of those." She kissed him. "And I did so enjoy Paris, and on Saint Valentine's Day too. You were very romantic."

Barry had a moment of seriously erotic thoughts about that trip, but something more important had happened there. Sue, concerned about their apparent inability to conceive, had promised not to let her worries become an obsession and interfere with their life together, and bless her, she had kept that promise. "Come on," he said, "you'll be getting me all hot and bothered. Paris was a great adventure and Jack and I had one today too. Let's sit down and I'll tell you about it."

"In a sec," she said. "Let's watch this first."

"Of course." Barry and Sue watched as the flapping main topsail was hand-hauled up to the yard, then the topmen secured the sail to the spar and began making their way below.

"Bloody brave if you ask me," Sue said, leaving the window and plonking herself on the love seat, where Barry joined her. "Can you imagine climbing out along that thingy?"

"It's called a spar or yard," Barry said.

"All right. Spar. It must be fifty feet above the deck. And there's a bit of chop out there."

Max sprawled out in front of the fireplace and Tigger, a stray tabby they'd rescued from a December gale last year, climbed up on Sue's lap. She stroked the little cat.

"So. Tell."

"Well, we were pottering about, taking it easy, when a bloody great basking shark breached not ten feet from our beam. I could smell the fish, it was so close, and you should have seen the splash when it hit the water."

"Golly. A shark. Weren't you scared?"

"I'd read that the creatures are harmless, but poor Jack, to quote Cissie Sloan, he 'near took the rickets.' We'd a great afternoon, Jack and I, and he and Helen are having second thoughts about emigrating."

"Oh, Barry, that's good news." She snuggled closer to him. "I know how much you'd miss your old pal."

Barry nodded. "That square rigger got me distracted. I was asking you how things went in Broughshane."

Sue looked away. Stared out the window before looking him in the eye. Her voice was level. "I told you I had my chat with Mum . . ."

"And?" His doctor half well knew the mental torments women with apparent infertility went through, and he had been pleased Sue had been willing to open up to her mother. "What did she say?" He put his arms around her.

"She said I was a lucky woman to be loved by a man like you." And before Barry could say anything Sue kissed him and said, "I do love you, Barry."

He could feel his pulse speed up and the anticipation in the pit of his stomach.

"Mum said I should try to be patient. Carry on seeing Doctor Harley. That things often had a way of working out. It was all right to be unhappy sometimes. And if I needed to talk some more, she was always there." Sue smiled at Barry. "I'm glad I told her. It helps."

"That's all that matters."

Sue managed a tiny smile. "And that's all I'm going to say about Mum today, but it did help — a lot." The smile faded. Her words were matter-of-fact. "Today's the twelfth. My period's due in twelve days." She looked down, then back at Barry. "We might still get lucky, but if not, Doctor Harley wants to arrange my laparoscopy for about ten days after the twenty-fourth. That would be May the third, but that's a Saturday so he'll probably get it done on the Friday. That's not long to wait, is it?"

"No. No, it's not, my darling." Barry dropped a gentle kiss on her head and stroked her hair.

"So, we'll just have to bide, and I'll try not to say any more about it until after it's done."

The phone in the hall rang. He was tempted to leave it until the caller gave up. He wasn't on duty, after all, and he didn't want to interrupt this moment with Sue. But it went too much against the grain to not answer the thing. In their first junior clinical clerkship in 1960, students had been expected to take twenty-four-hour call, and nine years later he still couldn't ignore a ringing phone. "Just be a minute, pet," he said.

Sue moved aside.

"Hello? Laverty here."

"Doctor Laverty, I do be sorry to trouble

106

you, and you being off duty, so —"

Kinky Auchinleck. Was she on telephone-answering duty? Sometimes if all the doctors were out, O'Reilly would ask her and Archie to come over, watch telly, and field phone calls as she had done when she was O'Reilly's live-in housekeeper.

"— but Archie and I were watching telly at Number One and something's come up and I wonder if you could help?"

"I'll try, Kinky."

"Doctor Nonie's still away, Doctors Nelson and Emer are out on a maternity call, and Doctor O'Reilly and Kitty are at the Rugby Club. It's Guffer Galvin, sir, and he asked for you specifically."

"It's about Anne." It wasn't a question. Barry's old patient had had a lobar excision two years ago for an undifferentiated oat-cell lung cancer. The pathologist had not expected her to survive for much more than a year.

" 'Fraid so. She's short of breath and —"

"I'm on my way." He could take a detailed history when he got to their house on the council housing estate.

"Thank you, sir. I am sorry."

"It's all right, Kinky. Don't worry about it. Now, I'm off." Barry replaced the receiver. Damn. Damn. Damn. Sue needed him, but so did the Galvins. "I'm sorry, Sue," he said, "but I'm the only one —"

"And a patient needs you?" Sue smiled, shook her head. "If I'd known what I was getting into before we married. Go on with you. It's all right. I'll be all right. I'll get the tea started. Keep myself occupied."

Barry realised she was trying to make things easier for him. "Thanks, pet. I'll be back as quick as I can."

"Do what you have to, Barry. I do understand. Honestly." She pecked his cheek.

"I'll get my bag," he said, and left.

"Come on, on in." George "Guffer" Galvin was a short, bald man whose grey eyes were fanned with laugh lines at their corners. "Thanks for coming so quick, sir, and I'm sorry til bring youse out on a Saturday night, but my poor Annie's took a turn for the worser. She's in the parlour. We was waiting for Bruce Forsythe til come on the telly and she says til me, 'I'm awful short of breath, so I am.' Now we're not kiddies. We know what's been wrong with Anne. We know it can come back, so you'll not have til spare us the truth, Doctor, but I hate til see my Annie upset." The man's grey eyes blurred.

"Let's see what we can do." Barry put a

reassuring hand on Guffer's shoulder.

"You go on in, sir. I'll wait in the kitchen til you're done."

"Fair enough." As Barry watched Guffer Galvin walk slowly along the narrow hall, he took a brief moment to recap what he knew about his patient. Two years ago, both he and Fingal had thought they were dealing with a case of acute bronchitis in a heavy smoker of fifty-seven. They'd been wrong. She had been under the care of Mister John Bingham, consultant thoracic surgeon and his staff at the Royal since her bronchial carcinoma had been diagnosed and treated two years ago this month. And now she was short of breath. Get in there and see to her.

He opened the parlour door and went into the little room that was mostly occupied by a frayed maroon three-piece lounge suite.

Anne Galvin sat bent over on an armchair. Her grey-blond hair was untidy. She raised her head and Barry saw the fear in her eyes behind her wire-framed granny glasses. "How are you, Anne?"

"I've been better, sir," she gasped with a rasping sound ending in a dry, one-bark cough, "so I have." She screwed up her face and as she inhaled, her nostrils flared and the strap muscles in her neck stood out. Her lips had the slate-blue tint of oxygen shortage. She bared her teeth before making a grunting noise. "That's ferocious."

"Don't try to talk, Anne. Just nod or shake your head." He pulled a simple wooden chair over from beside the wall, sat, and put his bag on the floor. "You remember I popped in on you a month ago when I was up here seeing one of Eileen Lindsay's brood."

"I know, Doctor," gasp, "and I'd never asked for a call neither."

He put a hand on her shoulder. "Now, don't talk. We just like to keep an eye on folks, Anne, and the people at the Royal had written to say your recent checkup with them had been fine. Just wanted to be sure, that's all."

"Umgh." Anne inhaled.

Barry leant forward and laid the back of his hand on her forehead. It wasn't sweaty or hot, so she probably did not have a fever, but he noticed how her cheeks were sunken.

"Have you been all right since then — until tonight?"

She nodded, cocked her head to one side. Frowned. "But," gasp, "I think I've lost a fair bit of weight." She managed a weak smile. "I didn't mind that. Get my figure back."

Weight loss was ominous. Barry thought

110

he recognised denial when he heard it. Cancer patients were instructed to report any weight loss, but if she wanted to pretend it didn't matter? Fair enough. "Anything else?"

"Not until the night, about half an hour ago. I got this shortness of breath."

"And that's everything?"

She nodded.

"Have you boked? Had the skitters?"

She shook her head. No vomiting. No diarrhoea. No gastrointestinal tract involvement. Time to take a look. "Let me help you to the sofa."

She stood, leant on Barry, and he soon had her lying down. Already Barry was reasonably sure what he was dealing with. He'd forego the routine examination of pulse and blood pressure. If he was right, those matters could be dealt with once she'd been admitted to the Royal. "Can you pull your blouse up a bit? I need to examine your chest."

By the classic manoeuvres of inspection, palpation, percussion, and auscultation, Barry concluded that her right lower lobe had collapsed. The cause would almost certainly be blockage of a bronchus by a recurrence. "Just one more thing, and I promise it won't hurt. Can you sit up and loosen the neck of your blouse?"

She nodded.

Barry rapidly examined the triangular area to the right of her neck between the base of her skull, her collarbone, and her shoulder. It should have been smooth, but he could feel a craggy hard swelling about the size of a child's marble. Her cancer, as many lung cancers did, had spread to the lymph node there. "All done," he said. "I'm going to leave you for a minute and get Guffer so I can tell you both what's going on." He noticed a phone in the hall, new since he was last here. He'd get the ambulance equipped with portable oxygen on its way. Anne Galvin's condition was beyond the capability of a country GP.

After being assured a bed would be ready and an ambulance dispatched, Barry went to the kitchen.

Guffer sat at the table, toying with a cup of tea. He pushed it aside and leaped to his feet. "Well?"

"Come on through. I'll explain to you both."

Guffer followed Barry.

Back in the parlour, Guffer took an armchair and Barry remained standing.

"All right," he said. "There is no easy way to say this. I'm sorry, but I believe the disease has spread, Anne." He heard Guffer's whispered, "Shite," and saw Anne nodding. Her features were relaxed.

"I'm not an expert on what ails you, but I believe all is not lost. I —"

"But it's pretty serious, Doctor?" Guffer said.

"Wheest, dear," Anne said, and wheezed. "Let the doctor explain."

"I believe you will need oxygen and be admitted to the Royal. Mister Bingham's team will look after you, and I expect you'll be transferred to the Marie Curie Centre at Belvoir, but your specialists will be able to advise you better than me."

"That's not good, is it, Doctor?" Guffer asked. "Marie Curie's the place for X-ray treatments."

Barry shook his head. "To be honest, I don't think there will be a cure, but some radiotherapy at the centre may make you comfortable, Anne, for quite a while." Barry felt a lump in his throat.

Guffer put his hand on Anne's shoulder.

"Guffer, remember the last time you made up an overnight bag for Anne?"

"I'll see to it," said Guffer, his voice trembling. "And thanks, Doc."

"I think I've done very well." Anne Galvin gulped for air as she watched her husband

113

leave the room. "So I have, considering. All youse doctors have — have done your very best, and I know Mister Bingham's people won't give up without a fight."

Barry found himself biting his lower lip.

"I'll do whatever I'm bid." She dragged in more air and looked at Barry with pleading in her eyes, but her voice was strong when she said, "I'm not afraid. I've had a good two years to think on it, and if it's my time, then it's my time, so it is. The Reverend Robinson has me well prepared." A single tear trickled. "It's just I'm sorry for them as will be left behind."

So, her comment about weight loss hadn't been denial. It seemed this brave woman had come to terms with her probable fate. Doctor Barry Laverty found himself reaching for his own hanky so he'd appear to be composed when Guffer returned. He took one of Anne Galvin's hands. It was warm and solid in his hand. His patients were real people to him, not conditions, and that's the way he wanted it. But as he had learned not so many years ago, beginning with a lovely man with a gangrenous great toe, sometimes knowing a patient could be painful too.

6
EXAMINE WELL YOUR BLOOD

August 9, 1963

Barry put the last turn in the tensor bandage and anchored it with a safety pin. "Keep that ankle elevated when you get home, Sandy, and come back in ten days. Should be right as rain by then. It's only a sprain, but I'd rather you didn't try weight-bearing until someone's had a look at it then. And no hurling."

Barry handed the teen an elbow crutch a nurse had brought from the plaster room. "Don't forget to bring that back with you in one piece. It's not a hurling stick, Sandy."

The youth laughed and looked dubiously at the crutch. "Okay, Doc. I promise. See you in ten days."

A student nurse stuck her head into the room B cubicle. "Come quick, Doctor. A man's bleeding next door."

Barry dashed out and nearly collided with Norma Fitch, who was hurrying in the same

115

direction. "I'll see to it," he said.

"Thanks, Barry. Busy this morning."

Virginia Clarke appeared from the ambulance room, where she'd been working this morning. That was why Barry, still embarrassed after being rebuffed eight days ago, had been trying to avoid her, and had elected to work in room B today. She nodded at Barry, but said to Norma, "Sister'd like you to see a patient next door. The ambulance men said he'd had a fit. He's stopped now, he's still unconscious, but she suspects it might be epilepsy."

As Barry opened the curtains to his cubicle he heard Norma say, "Come on then, Nurse Clarke. Let's see if we can get this sorted, but it sounds like he'll need admission to the neurology ward."

A young man sat on a chair, a bloody towel held to his head. Brown dried blood had caked on his right cheek and coat collar, but no fresh blood was leaking past the towel. The compression was working.

Barry tugged the curtain closed. "Morning . . ." Barry scanned the eight-by-four card. "Mister Magee. What happened?" According to the card, James Magee was twenty-two, a labourer, and a Protestant, living at 19 Sandy Row.

"A brick fell out of my mate's hod. Hit

116

me on the nut, sir."

Barry could picture James Magee's mate climbing a ladder, holding the long-handled hod with one hand at waist level while its brick-carrying end rested on one shoulder.

Depending on the height from which the brick had fallen, it could have caused anything from a fractured skull with underlying brain damage to a simple scalp laceration. Given the rich blood supply of the scalp, they usually bled heavily. The patient would need a rapid head injury assessment before being trotted over to the suture room to have his wound cleaned and stitched. Barry got started. "Just keep holding the towel firmly to your head, Mister Magee. We'll get a look at it later. I want you to tell me your name, where you are, and what date it is."

"I'm Jimmy Magee, Doc. It's Friday, August the ninth, 1963, and I'm in the Royal, so I am. Nothing wrong with my marleys."

It didn't take long for Barry to satisfy himself that there was no brain injury or concussion, and that it was a simple case of laceration. He completed the card. "You'll need a couple of stitches, Jimmy. Come with me."

Once in the suture room, Barry sat Jimmy

on a chair, greeting a student nurse and an experienced senior medical student, an old friend. "Here's Jimmy Magee for you, Mike. Head laceration. I'd like to take a look when you have him cleaned up."

Barry waited until Jimmy was seated again before taking a careful look at a three-inch gash with red pouting lips and a slow trickle of blood draining from one end. "Carry on, Mike. Clip off some of the hair to give yourself a clear field, then three or four stitches should do the trick, Jimmy."

"Thanks a million, Doc," Jimmy said.

"You'll be fine. Mike's a great stitcher," Barry said, and left.

The benches in the waiting room were empty, but for a man giving his particulars to the receptionist. Barry noticed the fellow was swaying in his chair. Oh Lord, probably another not-quite-sober drunk coming in after a late-night binge looking for a hangover cure. As usual he'd be put on a stretcher in the ambulance room for fear he might fall off a chair in room B, injure himself, and sue. This one would need seeing to soon, but with a bit of luck he'd be one of the comical ones who just needed to sleep it off. At least there was going to be a short lull in the action, unless an ambulance case showed up.

Barry stepped aside as two ward orderlies hurried by pushing an unconscious man on a stretcher from the ambulance room toward the main corridor and admission to one of the wards. Probably Norma's epilepsy case.

He checked room B. Empty. He headed to the ambulance room, knocked, and let himself into Bernie's office, to find Norma Fitch already there.

"Bit of a lull now," said Bernie, who was reading the *Belfast News Letter.* "Praise be. Mother of God, would you look at that?" The senior sister handed the paper to Barry.

"Here?" He pointed to the top story, and Bernie nodded. "The General Post Office have confirmed that two-point-six million pounds were stolen in yesterday's train robbery at Cheddington in Buckinghamshire."

Norma let out an ear-piercing whistle. "That's a brave clatter of money." The five-foot-two brunette from Dungannon in County Tyrone had laughing eyes, full lips, a wicked sense of humour, and astounding stamina. It was a pity there were still some lingering concerns among the men about how she'd deal with belligerent patients. "I can't actually imagine such a sum."

"Actually," Barry said, "at a shilling a pint, it would buy you fifty-two million Guinness.

Or, at the three hundred pounds a year they pay us for working eighty-four-hour weeks, the Hospitals' Authority could hire about eighty-six thousand housemen."

"Golly. I never knew you were a mental arithmetic wizard, Barry," Norma said. "I still remember you asking for help with physics calculations in first year."

Barry laughed. "When it comes to sums, I'm a complete tube," he said. "Jack Mills worked it out on the back of a beer mat when we were having a pint last night in The Oak on the Grosvenor Road."

Virginia Clarke stuck her head round the door frame and Barry felt his breath catch in his throat. Despite Jack's suggestion that Barry try again, he hadn't. "Sister, we've a couple of folks in the waiting room and an ambulance has arrived." She smiled at Barry, who found he could not meet her gaze, but turned his eyes back to the newspaper in his hands. He would focus on his work and try to forget Virginia Clarke's green eyes for now.

The trouble was after only eight days on the job, he was getting bored with the routine work in room B and becoming less anxious about, even relishing, the challenges of the tougher ambulance room cases. Today he was on the eight-to-six "long day." His public school training had conditioned him always to defer to a woman. "Looks like our little break's over. Your pick, Norma."

She yawned. "I did the six-P.M.-to-eight-A.M. 'long night' last night, and it was a long one. And I'm still here until noon. Did a couple of major cases while you were in room B earlier. Unless there's more cases than you can handle, Barry, I'd like to do the easy stuff. Is that all right?"

"Fair enough. Off you go."

The double doors at the far end of the ambulance room, closed today because of a downpour, opened and an ambulance attendant pushed in a man in a wheelchair. His head, which he held between his hands, drooped.

"Cubicle one," Bernie called to the ambulance man.

"Right, Sister."

She handed Barry a blank eight-by-four card. "Here, Barry."

"Thanks." He left the office and went behind the curtains of cubicle one.

"Bout ye, Doc." The attendant helped the patient up onto the trolley, putting the man's head on a pillow and covering him with a blanket. "Dirty morning out there, so it is." The man shook water off his blue bus driver's peaked cap. "Even the ducks is

121

sheltering."

One of the few advantages of living in the hospital, Barry thought, was not having to brave the elements. "What can you tell me . . . ?" he began, but realized he'd never met this ambulance man before.

"It's Freddy, Doc. Not much. Your man, Mister Ivan Peters here, he's fifty-six, woke up this morning with a ferocious headache, dead tired, dizzy, and his left big toe had turned blue —"

The cyanosed toe was unusual.

"He lives at 2a Epworth Street. Docker by trade —"

His address, in the district of Ballymacarret, was in Belfast's dockland, so the man's occupation came as no surprise.

"His missus thought he'd taken a stroke so she dialled nine-nine-nine."

"Fair enough." Barry entered the pertinent details on the card. " 'Morning, Mister Peters. I'm Doctor Laverty. Not feeling so hot?"

The man, with obvious effort, turned his head to look at Barry. "I feel dead rotten, so I do, Doctor."

Barry heard a cough from behind them.

"Excuse me, sir," the attendant said. "Unless you need me, I'll be running along."

"Thank you, Freddy." Barry turned back

122

to his patient. Immediately he noticed that the man's face appeared to be very flushed — plethoric, in technical terms. Add it to the observation about the man's big toe, and a germ of a diagnostic idea was beginning to form. But routine must be followed. "How long have you been feeling like that?"

Ivan Peters sighed. "I've been tired for weeks. Couldn't tell you how long, but it's been getting worser. I started getting headaches about three weeks ago, and when one started I'd go dizzy."

"Have you seen your doctor?"

The man tried to shake his head, but grimaced, stopped, and said, "That stung, so it did."

Barry waited.

"Seen my doctor? See him? Not at all. He's one of them there 'Here's two aspirins' boys."

"You mean you've not been examined."

"Huh. My doctor's not an examining doctor," Mister Peters said. "That's why my missus sent for the ambulance when I took real bad, like."

It wasn't the first time Barry had heard the expression, and he knew some overworked physicians in the poorer parts of Belfast only had time to take a brief history, decide the complaint was medically simple, and prescribe accordingly, or simply refer the patient on for specialist care. "Don't worry, Mister Peters. I am." And always will be, Barry thought. "Tell me how and when you 'took real bad.' " A simple rule he'd learnt in the Royal. Don't talk down to patients, but always use language they can understand.

"I usually get up at six thirty, but this here headache woke me at quarter past. Tried til get up for a drink of water and a couple of Panadol — And damn it, didn't I take a dizzy turn and fall down? That woke Dora, the missus — and by the time she was full awake, so was I. And now here I am. Only other thing I noticed was that my toe was a funny blue-black colour. It's numb, but there's no pain."

"And that's it?"

"Aye."

"Give me a minute, please, to make some notes?"

"Aye, certainly."

Uncontrolled diabetes could cause a patient to faint and develop discolouration of the extremities, but once in coma they did not recover until treated. Disorders of the nervous system could cause headaches and fainting, but not discolouration. Athero-sclerosis, hardening of the arteries, could cause both, but rarely in a man of fifty-six. And so could . . . what? Damn it, Barry knew there was another condition, but like a naughty boy who had been called for tea and doesn't want to come, the answer refused to be coaxed out.

"I just need to ask a few more questions before I take a look," Barry said.

"Go ahead, sir."

As he took the man's pulse, which was normal, Barry led Ivan Peters through the standard questions to establish that he was orientated in person, place, and time.

"It's dead polite of you, young Doctor Laverty, to keep calling me Mister Peters, but I'm only a docker, so I am. Everybody calls me Rusky."

Barry was warming to this man. He smiled. "Why Rusky?"

"It's slang for 'Russian.' Ivan's a Russian name."

"I see. All right, Rusky. It's time to examine you, but before I do, is there anything else you'd like to tell me? Anything different happen to you in the last couple of months?" Barry had no idea what kind of answer he was hoping to hear, but sometimes, sometimes a fly cast over seemingly deserted water would produce a rise.

Rusky frowned. "Only thing I can think of

is I had a tooth pulled three weeks ago. I had til go back to have the socket packed twice, like. Thought it would never stop bleeding."

Uh-huh. The bad boy had come out from behind his bush, but not far enough to be recognisable. But Barry did have a nearly formulated idea. A single physical finding would clinch matters — and the disease Barry was now considering could be confirmed by some simple blood work after admission. "Thank you," he said, "now, let's have a look." He turned the blanket back.

Both pupils were equal and reacting to light, and Rusky had suffered no loss of motor or sensory function, because with veiled good humour he could move his limbs and respond to pinpricks on them. His elbow, knee, and ankle jerks were active and equal and his Babinski reflex, named for Doctor Joseph Babinski in 1869, was normal. When Barry stroked a blunt instrument along the sole of Rusky's foot from heel to big toe, it curled down. Had it curled up it would have been a sign of subtle but serious damage to the central nervous system. "Soon be finished," Barry said, "but you can stop worrying about having had a stroke."

"Dead on, sir. Thanks for telling me. It's great til get your mind set at rest, so it is.

And I don't think my headache's near so bad neither."

"Mind set at rest." A lesson well learned, Barry thought. There's always a very worried human being inside the symptoms and signs. "Can you slip off your left shoe and sock?"

Rusky's left great toe was blue-black, cold to the touch, and the man could feel nothing, nor move it. Gangrene. Not good, but dry gangrene due to poor blood supply of oxygen, not the more dangerous wet kind associated with infection. Barry was 99 percent certain now of what was wrong. "One last thing," he said. "I need to examine —"

As he spoke, Barry became aware of a raised, pleading, female voice he recognised as Virginia's coming from the next cubicle. "Look, Mister Shaw, sir, I only asked if you've been drinking. The doctor will want to know."

A slurred male voice yelled, "None of your bloody business, you stupid wee bitch. I've my rights, so I have. I'll not be asked questions like that. Not by nobody."

Barry well knew from his experiences here as a student how unpredictable drunks could be. How a seemingly simple question could in some trigger a violent outburst.

127

"Sir, I'm a student nurse trying to do my job."

"Well, feck off and do it somewhere else." The words were accompanied by something, probably a fist, banging on the plasterboard partition. "I just want something for my fecking head. Some bugger's hitting it with a hammer."

"Excuse me, Mr. Peters," Barry said.

The barrage of verbal abuse rose in volume, and Barry tried to tune out the words as he parted the curtains and went into the adjacent cubicle. Virginia Clarke was backed into the far corner, her eyes wide, her hands in front of her in what would be a futile endeavour to give herself some protection. A large, dishevelled man sat on the trolley, swinging his booted feet. His hair was uncombed, chin dark with stubble, puke stains on his darned jumper. Saliva trickled from one corner of his mouth. The place stank of stale drink. This was not a medical case.

The man slid off the trolley and began raising his fist to Virginia. Barry stepped forward and grabbed the patient's forearm with one hand and hauled, unbalancing and half-turning him so he now had his back to Virginia and was facing Barry. The brute was much stronger than Barry and ripped his arm free, throwing Barry against the wall, but at least the action had deflected the punch from Virginia. The drunk now stretched out a paw, making a grab for Barry, who retreated, but got stopped by the curtain. He steeled himself for a blow. He was vaguely aware of someone coming into the cubicle.

The torrent of insults dried up like a water intake when the Kingston valve is slammed shut, and Barry saw bravado being replaced by fear in the man's bloodshot eyes. Barry turned.

The cause of the sea change stood with her legs apart, feet firmly planted, arms tightly crossed in front. Norma Fitch's never-wavering gaze was fixed on her victim. Barry imagined the glare of Balor, the mythical one-eyed Fomorian, a gaze that could turn men to stone. Her voice was low, measured, and as cutting as aqua regia, a mixture of nitric and hydrochloric acids that can dissolve gold and silver. "No. You will not, I repeat, not threaten Nurse Clarke."

Frantic head-nodding. "No, miss. I will not. Honest to God."

"It's Doctor to you."

Head still nodding. "Yes, Doctor. Sorry, Doctor."

"You will apologise to Nurse Clarke."

"I'm dead sorry, so I am, Nurse. Cross my heart."

"You will give me your details, all of your details. Now."

The words poured forth. "Sammy Shaw, ma'am, I mean Doctor. Twenty-three. Occupation? Huh. Unemployed riveter. The bloody shipyard lost a contract and give a bunch of us our cards. Ten Balkan Street, ma'am. And miss, I mean Nurse, yes, I was on a bender." Virginia nodded to the man and Barry stepped to her side. "You all right?"

"Yes, thanks."

"Thank God for that, and thank you, Doctor Fitch."

Norma Fitch shrugged. "Doctor Laverty. I'd just come back from room B. Heard this horrible excuse for a man and thought I should do something. I didn't know you were in here."

"I'm very glad you came." For a moment Barry had been convinced he was a dead man. "I think Mister Shaw has discovered his manners now, thanks to you, and Nurse Clarke's safe too."

Norma looked back at the patient. "I can understand why you got drunk. I can understand you're angry, but it is no excuse for taking it out on Nurse." She smiled at

Nurse Clarke. "Mister Shaw understands that the RUC Police Station is a very short walk from here" — her volume increased as she fixed Shaw with her stare — "and he's promised to be a good boy."

Shaw flinched. "Yes, Doctor. That's right, Doctor."

"Abject" was the word that occurred to Barry.

Norma said, "I'll take care of this one, Doctor Laverty. I know you've a case next door."

He turned to go. It seemed any concerns about Norma Fitch were quite unfounded. Barry had the courtesy to feel embarrassed that he and his friends had doubted her abilities, and resolved to spread the word about what had just transpired. He glanced over at Virginia Clarke, who said, "Thank you, Doctor Laverty. My God, that was terrible. And thank you, Doctor Fitch." Then, to his surprise, as Norma began examining Sammy Shaw, Virginia Clarke moved closer to Barry and lowered her voice. "That was brave, Barry. Thank you."

And Barry was too pleased and too reticent to do anything but nod his thanks.

"You're back, Doc?" Rusky said when Barry arrived. "You got that bollix next door calmed down? My wee girl Jan? We're dead

131

proud of her. She's a staff nurse here at the Royal. She's told us about some of the shites that comes til casualty. No wee girl should be spoke til like that."

Barry shook his head. "I didn't sort him out. One of our lady doctors did."

Rusky whistled. "Tough lady."

"Actually," Barry said, "she's not, normally. But it is a mistake to rile her. Quite the woman." He pointed to Rusky's shirt. "Could you hoist that, so I can examine your tummy, and then we're done."

"Aye, certainly."

It took Barry moments to feel under Rusky's left ribs and no time to identify an abnormally enlarged spleen. He straightened. "Rusky," he said, "this is my second week on the job, so I'm still learning my trade, but the teachers here at the Royal trained us well. I can't give you a proper diagnosis here because you'll need some lab tests to confirm what I think ails you." Rusky Peters was staring into Barry's face. Hanging on every word. And why shouldn't he? Barry might still feel unsure of himself, but this fifty-six-year-old docker nicknamed Rusky, with a daughter Jan, a staff nurse in this hospital, was a human being with real concerns who needed answers. And Barry Laverty, Doctor Barry Laverty, had an answer. "I think," he said, "you have polycythaemia."

"Boys-a-boys. That's a quare mouthful."

"That's the short version. Its full name is polycythaemia rubra vera."

"I'll be damned." Rusky sat up.

"Your body is producing far too many red blood cells."

Rusky frowned.

"Did you ever try to wash boiled rice down a plug hole?"

"Aye. I always help Dora with washing up. If there's a lot of rice, the water can't get through and the grains stick. Everything gets clogged up."

"That's what happens with polycythaemia. And the body needs those cells to carry oxygen to nourish the tissues. If too many can't get through —" Barry shrugged and thought, Which is why you have gangrene in your toe, which will have to be amputated. But that was a bridge to cross later. No need to worry the man any more at this moment.

"Am I for admission?"

Barry nodded. " 'Fraid so."

"So, it's serious like?"

Barry took his time before answering. He'd learned as a student that questions like that could actually mean, "Am I going to die?" "Rusky, I told you I'm no specialist, but I was taught that you're stuck with polycythaemia once you get it, but that while it's not curable, it can be kept under control for years."

Rusky nodded. "You mean like sugar diabetes? I have a cousin with it."

"A little bit."

"He can't be cured, but as long as he takes his insulin he's okay."

"Very true." This was not the time to discuss the long-term risks of either condition.

"Thanks, Doc. You've taken a right load off my mind, so you have, so, admit away."

"I'll see to it, and if the senior staff there agree with me —"

"And why would they not?"

"You're very kind." Barry glowed. "They'll order blood work, and if it shows what I think it will, they'll either arrange treatment there and then or ask Doctor Gerry Nelson, who specialises in blood diseases, to consult. You'll be in good hands, I promise."

"Thank you, Doctor Laverty," Rusky Peters said. He hesitated, then asked, "Could I ask you for a wee favour?"

Barry smiled. "You can ask."

"You've been dead kind, so you have. I feel kinda safe here with you —"

Barry shrugged and felt the blush start.

"I don't know how long I'll be in for, but the missus and our daughter Jan'll visit me." His eyes misted. "I know all the staff here's dead good, and all, but when my da, God love him, passed eighteen months ago, I know he was properly taken care of, but nobody would answer my questions about him. Only young doctors like you might be around during visiting hours. The highheejins only came in in the mornings. Nurses were not allowed to go into details in case they disagreed with a doctor. One cleaning lady did her best til help with my questions, but — och. She tried, but . . ." He shrugged. "Doctor Laverty, would you consider popping in til see me once in a while?"

Barry didn't hesitate. "Of course," he said. "My pleasure."

"You're a real gent, sir," Rusky said. "Thank you."

And Barry Laverty felt humble. Sure, they'd all been warned ever since they'd set foot in the Royal three and a half years ago not to get too close to their patients, but this was the kind of medicine he was becoming even more sure he wanted to practise. And what harm could it possibly do?

"I'd better go and see if anyone else needs me." And without waiting for an answer he walked out, closing the curtains behind him.

To his surprise, Virginia Clarke stood in the cubicle opposite, one finger to her lips, beckoning with her other hand.

"You all right?"

"Perfectly, but I wanted to say thank you again."

"You already did. It's fine."

"Barry, you were trying to ask me out last Thursday. I said no. I usually do with young doctors because, well, I've a career to make, haven't I, just like you? I'm only twenty-one. I did have a steady boyfriend until about four months ago, but he — well, let's just say we don't see each other anymore —"

"I'm sorry," Barry said, but he wasn't really. His hopes were up.

"What I'm trying to say is," she smiled, "if we could find a time that we are both off duty —"

Barry felt as if Sammy Shaw had hit him. "We will," he said, and to his pure delight she kissed his cheek.

7
WITH A SAD SWELL'D FACE

April 16, 1969
O'Reilly leaned on Norman Devine's bedroom door frame as Emer finished their last morning consultation. The little lad by her side wore red-and-white-striped pyjamas. His face was flushed, sweaty. O'Reilly had seen him for a skinned and swollen knee and once with croup since the family had moved here four years ago.

He glanced at his watch, a Christmas present from Kitty. It told him the date, which he thought an extravagance. But sometimes it came in handy. April 16, the anniversary of the Battle of Culloden. Eleven fifteen. Still time to see how work was progressing at Dun Bwee and be home for lunch. Kinky had been in her element this morning getting the meal ready. Today lunch would be more than soup and a sandwich.

From where O'Reilly stood, he saw the right side of the boy's face was swollen behind the angle of the jaw. O'Reilly had made his diagnosis, but Emer had asked all the right questions, looked for all the right signs.

"All done," Emer said. "Button up your jammy jacket."

"Thank you, Doctor Emer." Barbara Devine pushed back her auburn hair and ruffled nine-year-old Norman's mop. It was the same colour as his mother's.

"You, Norman, you poor wee lad, have mumps."

"Aye. There's a wheen of it about this year, and my Normie's had his measles jag and polio sugar lumps, so I knew it wasn't one of them fevers."

Emer, still talking directly to Norman, said, "A nasty germ has got into your salivary gland."

O'Reilly saw Norman frown, but Emer explained. "Saliva is what doctors call spit. It's made in special places called glands. The one where you're swollen is called the parotid."

"Parroted? You mean I'm turning into a parrot, like?"

O'Reilly chuckled.

"No, I don't, son," Emer said. "It's doctor talk. You're going to feel peely-wally for a while. And have to stay in bed."

"I'm glad mumps is all it is, Doctor. Lots of kiddies get it and they get better," Barbara said.

"You're right, Mrs. Devine. They do."

Not entirely true, O'Reilly thought, but Emer now had the confidence not to mention potential but rare complications, sparing mother and child additional worry.

"I'm sorry we don't have any vaccine for it. It's probably better if they get it young —"

Particularly boys who, if they caught it after puberty, risked painful testicular infection that could lead to sterility.

"We'll have to let the disease run its course. Some of the other salivary glands may swell, but it usually goes down in ten days. Please give Norman lots to drink, keep his mouth clean. A semi-fluid diet will make it easier for him to swallow. Jellies, juice, clear soups, rice puddings." She turned back to Norman. "You look like a lad who likes rice pudding. You'll be fine, and if it gets sore, Mammy will give you an aspirin."

"I will."

"I'll drop in in a day or two. See how you're doing. All right?"

"Yes, Doctor Emer. Thank you. I'll show youse out," Barbara said. "I'll come back and see you in a wee minute, Normie."

O'Reilly let Emer and Barbara precede him into the low-ceilinged kitchen/living room of what had once been Maggie MacCorkle's cottage. Her old paraffin lamps had been replaced by electric ones and a TV set sat in one corner. Ah, progress, he thought. Any time now the Americans or the Russians will land a man on the moon, but we still don't have a cure for the common cold.

"I'm sure he'll be fine," Emer said, "but if you're concerned about anything, anything at all, don't hesitate to call."

"I'll do that."

"We'll be off," O'Reilly said.

"Except," Emer said, "could I use your sink? I'd like to wash my hands."

"Aye, certainly. Fresh towels in the top drawer."

O'Reilly said, "I'll wait outside."

The Devines' cottage sat on Shore Road between the railway line and the lough. Outside the air was soft, salty. A pair of common tern, fork-tailed and black-capped, their red bills and red legs vivid against the clear sky, alternated between hovering and plunging into the water in pursuit of small fish.

Emer appeared.

"Hop in." O'Reilly held open the door of his 1968 Rover 2000. Kitty had joined

140

forces with his brother and talked Fingal into getting rid of his ancient long-nosed model. He'd pretended enthusiasm when Kitty'd waxed lyrical about the 2000's de Dion suspension and four-gear fully synchromesh transmission. Enthusiasm about cars was something she shared with Lars. Fingal regarded the things as infernal machines for getting from A to B in relative comfort and — he chuckled at himself, fully aware of his own foibles — scaring the living daylights out of cyclists.

O'Reilly settled back into his seat, gazing intently at the single-storey, slate-roofed cottage. "Do you know this is one of the first places I brought Barry when he was my brand-new assistant. We'd popped in to check up on Maggie MacCorkle, as was, before she married Sonny Houston and moved into his house."

"I saw Maggie and Sonny with Barry yesterday," Emer said, "making sure Sonny's mild heart failure was under control yesterday. It was. Sonny asked me to do him a favour."

O'Reilly drove off. "Favour?"

Emer giggled. "Barry has warned me about Maggie's infamous plum cake."

O'Reilly guffawed.

"Sonny took me aside and asked if there

was any chance I could get Kinky to teach Maggie how to make it properly? I said I'd try."

O'Reilly turned onto Station Road. "Kinky can be the soul of tact. I'm sure she'll have Maggie making plum cake to rival Fanny Cradock's." He stopped at the traffic light and indicated left. "Maggie's baking is as tough as the armour of my old battleship, *Warspite.*" He made his left onto the Belfast to Bangor Road. "Incidentally," he said, "I thought you handled the Devines very well. You're learning fast."

She chuckled again. "I wasn't sure what you'd say when Mrs. Devine told us right at the door she thought it was mumps."

"I learned that lesson in Dublin in '36. A woman with a bellyache told me she had a tubal pregnancy. 'And what medical school did you go to?' I asked. 'None,' said she, 'but I had one in my other tube last year.' She was right, and I've never questioned a patient's self-diagnosis since."

"I'll remember that. Thanks, Fingal." Emer smiled.

The new Rover's suspension absorbed the ruts more gently than his old one had. Then the tyres were crunching on gravel. O'Reilly parked beside Bertie Bishop's van, his lorry, and a larger van from the General Post Office. Two of its employees strung wires between two new poles.

"Here we are," he said. "Let's see how they're getting on." He climbed out.

From above came the whine of engines. Jet service to Belfast's new Aldergrove Airport had started three years ago. O'Reilly looked up to see contrails disfiguring an otherwise perfect blue sky. His thoughts went back to the graffiti of intertwined white trails and black smoke on the late-summer English sky of 1940, and a badly burnt Hurricane pilot, Pilot Officer Flip Dennison. Nineteen years old and already decorated for gallantry. O'Reilly shook his head. The young lad would be forty-eight now. What had happened to him?

"Golly," said Emer. "It's really come on. That thatch's lovely now it's finished."

"And somebody's done a great job replacing those sandstone windowsills. Every one of them cracked, the fire was so hot."

Together they walked to the newly painted red front door, set in a narrow porch. O'Reilly had first approached this doorway when Donal was hoping to buy the place. They had thought the old plaque on the wall read *1795. Dán Buídhe,* or "yellow poem." The name had baffled everyone for

143

months. The sign had somehow withstood the flames, and whoever had cleaned it had made sure the first word was clear: *Dun Buídhe,* Dun Bwee, yellow fort.

The door opened and out came Bertie Bishop. "Good morning, Doctors. I only beat you here by a few minutes." He pointed to the GPO men. "The phone'll be connected soon."

During a conversation in the Duck, Bertie had said Donal would have no difficulty getting connected. Bertie knew the right people. Man of his word, was Bertie Bishop.

"I'm happy to tell you the roof, chimney breast, and walls are finished. The front frames and door are painted. Inside, all the structure's complete. Boggy Baxter's wiring the washing machine Donal plumbed in yesterday, and Buster Holland did the plastering. My lads is putting in the kitchen floor tiles, and the worthy Donal himself is painting round the back. It'll not be long until we move Donal and his family in. Mebbe three, four more weeks. Dapper and me's got the arrangements in hand" — Bertie hunched forward and put his hand to the side of his mouth — "for the house-warmin' hooley." He continued in a low voice. "My Flo and Cissie Sloan and Kinky have the catering planned, and Willie Dunleavy and Mary will work the bar and he'll give me the drink on 'sale or return' if unopened. We'll have no difficulty moving the Donnellys in. The trick's going til be getting them out again so we can get set up for the surprise. I'm damned if I can see how."

O'Reilly frowned. "Donal's the expert on tricks. But let me think on it."

They rounded the gable end. Unkempt grass studded with blooming primroses ran for fifty yards from the back of the house to a tall laurel hedge. From it came the constant twittering of a small flock of goldfinches. The lawn was bounded on each side by fifty-foot-tall leafless linden trees, known as limes in Ulster. Two small white butterflies danced to fairy music only they could hear.

"See that long mound on this side of the dog run, Emer?" O'Reilly pointed to a hillock clothed in long grass and a sunburst of dandelions. "That's a Neolithic grave. About four thousand years old. The National Trust look after it, and they insisted the cottage be restored to its original state."

"Like Newgrange in County Meath?"

"Not quite as old, and not as big, of course, but the same idea."

Donal turned to greet the newcomers.

"How's about youse all?" Wearing paint-spattered overalls and a paddy hat, he'd been standing back, head cocked, admiring his handiwork. The nearest window frame was wet, the red paint glistening.

Bertie said, "We're all grand, so we are."

"Great day for the painting," Donal said.

Emer said, "You're a man of many talents, Donal Donnelly. Carpenter, plumber, painter."

"Poacher, rare dog breeder, creator of ancient artifacts." O'Reilly reached into his pocket for his pipe.

"Och, now, Doctor. I'm done with them schemes. Now I'm just a jack-of-all-trades." Donal sang in a passable tenor,

I'm a roving jack-of-all-trades
Of every trade and all trades
And if you want to know my name
They call me jack of all trades.

He pulled off his paddy hat and bowed to Emer, who applauded.

Donal straightened and turned to Bertie Bishop. "You missed the man from the Trust, sir. He was here an hour ago."

"And?"

"He was pleased and said til carry on."

"That's good news," O'Reilly said. "You'll

146

soon be finished."

"Aye," he said. "Won't be too soon for me and mine."

"You and the crew keep at it, Donal," said Bertie Bishop. "Me and the doctors have til trot on."

"Right, sir." Donal clapped his hat on his head, picked up his pot of paint, and moved to the next window.

As they rounded the gable O'Reilly heard,

I'm a rovin' and a sportin' blade
They call me jack of all trades . . .

O'Reilly lit his briar and took a long puff. "What's up with the sporting club plans, Bertie?"

"Doctor McCarthy, we've been planning events at the sporting club on Saturday nights. Raise a bit of cash for a good cause. Bring the two sides together."

"The two sides, you mean the Catholics and the Protestants, Mister Bishop?" Emer said.

"Aye, I do. Me and Flo, the minister, and the priest, we've had a couple of meetings so we can bring the proposal to an extraordinary general meeting and members can vote."

147

"I applaud you, Mister Bishop," said Emer.

"Thank you, Doctor. Things was proceeding — until this morning. The county clerk phoned me. There's been a letter of complaint filed and the borough council will have til make a ruling before we can proceed."

"Bugger," said O'Reilly. "Let me guess. That Colonel Mullan?"

"Correct," said Bertie Bishop, "and he may have a point."

O'Reilly said, "He may. We need a plan. I'd suggest, Bertie, that your committee get its final report in quickly. If Mullan's request is rejected by council we can call an extraordinary general meeting at once and get the proposal ratified. The next council meeting is on May 19."

"I'll do my best to help."

"Good. But it would be even better if we could get him to withdraw his complaint. There may be a way to scotch his plans. Either way, we should be ready to get the events up and running." And, he thought, the best solution was to get the complaint withdrawn. But how?

O'Reilly held the back door open and ushered Emer into the warm kitchen.

Kinky was pouring milk into the bowl of a purring Lady Macbeth. "Right on time. Doctor Stevenson does be in the dining room, sir. She's got a secret, that one. And Doctor Laverty hasn't finished the surgery, but here." She straightened and picked up a plate. "Wheaten bread, chicken liver pâté, and smoked salmon pâté while you wait."

"Secret? Ahh, you, Kinky Auchinleck, are a wonder," O'Reilly said. "Thank you." He inhaled. "And those are wonderful smells. What's on the menu?"

"Sir, I'd like to have my own secret, so." Kinky chuckled and her chins wobbled. "I do not think you will be disappointed."

"I'm sure I won't," O'Reilly said. "Let's head on through."

"Fingal, I just want a word with Kinky. Sonny asked me to ask you for a favour, Kinky. He's too embarrassed to ask himself, but he wonders, could you teach Maggie how to make a proper plum cake?"

Kinky laughed. "Poor Sonny. Four years of eating Maggie's plum cake. Indigestible, it is. I'll get Maggie to join the catering for a certain housewarming hooley." She winked at O'Reilly.

"All of Ballybucklebo thanks you, Kinky," Emer said.

In the dining room, Nonie Stevenson, her

hair combed neatly, wearing no makeup, sat in a tartan dressing gown, reading the *Belfast Telegraph.* She looked up. "Fingal. Emer. Sorry about this, but I was out all night. Your patient, Fingal, Anne Enright? Mother and seven-pound-six baby boy they're going to call Lionel are doing well."

"*Céad míle fáilte,* a hundred thousand welcomes to young Master Enright." O'Reilly went to the head of the table and set down the plate of bread and pâté. "That grand news has given me an appetite." He took two pieces. The gods may have lived on nectar and ambrosia, but the poor divils never had the good luck to sample Kinky's pâtés.

Emer sat next to Nonie and pointed at the headline. "What do you think of this Bernadette Devlin. Can she win, do you think? The Mid-Ulster byelection to Westminster is on Thursday. She's up against the late incumbent's widow, Anne Forest. Devlin went to Queen's, you know. Took psychology."

"I do know. She's a firebrand, that one." Nonie shook her auburn bob. Her green eyes twinkled. "If she does, she'll be the youngest MP ever returned." She looked at the doorway.

"Hello, everyone. Sorry I'm a bit late from

the surgery. Kinky knows I'm here. She'll be in in a minute." Barry took a seat opposite the women.

Kinky entered, carrying a tray of steaming bowls, which she placed in front of the diners. "Pea and ham soup, and it does be hot," she said. "Eat up however little much is in it."

"Thank you, Kinky," O'Reilly said to her departing back. He took a spoonful. "This soup is one of Kinky's best."

"No argument there," Emer said. "Busy surgery this morning, Barry?"

O'Reilly tucked into his soup, happy to let his younger colleagues chat.

"It was a long one. The last customer was a real *Readers' Digest* patient."

Nonie rolled her eyes.

Fingal shook his head. He always explained things to patients, and he knew Barry did too. But many physicians kept patients in the dark with arcane language, believing it added to the mystique of their profession. More and more, patients armed with a little knowledge were now challenging that. Some politely, others belligerently. The latter were referred to as *Reader's Digest* types because the magazine carried medically related articles from which they quoted.

151

"I really don't mind folks asking questions, but my last one — he's going for a barium meal because I'm sure he has a peptic ulcer. He handed me an article from the aforementioned font of all wisdom entitled 'I Am Joe's Stomach.' I thought I was going to be there all day."

O'Reilly laughed. "I'm sure you handled it well."

Kinky came in and set a full tray on the table. "Has everyone finished their soup?"

Voices said, "Yes, delicious" or "Thank you, Kinky."

She smiled, then raised a large spoon to begin serving the next course. "Fish pie with champ topping and glazed carrots."

"Take a look at that before Kinky cuts into it," said O'Reilly. The pie sat steaming and fragrant, its peaked crust golden brown. O'Reilly breathed in the aroma. "The top of that pie is a work of art in potato and spring onions, Kinky."

"And inside is some of Hall Campbell's halibut. He gave me the pick of his early morning catch, so." She finished handing around plates to clapping and shouts of approval, then patted her silver chignon and acknowledged the applause with a little bow. "Enjoy it, and I will bring coffee and biscuits later, and, Doctor Laverty, I heard what you said. In Cork we say every patient is a doctor — after he's cured." She cleared the soup bowls and left to laughter.

For a while they ate in companionable silence, until Emer said, "When I was a houseman, some of the senior staff at the Mater Hospital were discussing being challenged. They reckon it began in 1958 when BBC started that documentary series *Your Life in Their Hands.* It went on until '64. Lots of folks are better educated about themselves today."

"In '58? That was the year after I started at Queen's," said Barry. "Each episode discussed a surgical condition from the point of view of patient and surgeon. We all watched it."

"I watched it too," O'Reilly said. "Learned quite a bit."

Kinky reappeared with a coffeepot and plates of her own ginger biscuits. As a sop to O'Reilly, she had included a plate of Jacob's fig rolls. "Two, sir," she said, and stared at his waistline. "Two."

"Yes, Kinky." She was the only person who could make O'Reilly feel meek.

"That was delicious, Kinky," Emer said. "Boy, am I going to miss your cooking."

Kinky was clearly pleased by the compliment. "And we'll miss you, Doctor McCar-

153

thy. May the saddest day of your future be no worse than the happiest day of your past."

A knock on the wall beside the open door turned heads.

"Connor. Come in," O'Reilly called. "You just missed Kinky's fish pie."

Doctor Connor Nelson, red-haired and sharp-nosed, limped in. "Afternoon, all. Last time I was here I forgot my walking stick. I've another at home, b-but I was passing and —"

"Coffee?"

"Love some." He sat beside Barry.

"Hi, Connor," Barry said, picking up the coffeepot. "Shall I be mother?" He started to pour.

Barry's attempt at an upper-class accent wasn't a patch on his friend Jack Mills's, O'Reilly noted, but everyone chuckled.

Connor, accepting a cup, crooked his little finger. "Thank you, young man, coffee would be delightful."

"How are things in the Kinnegar?" Nonie asked.

"G-going well," Connor said. "Having you folks to share call is terrific. And I've enjoyed having you with me on occasions, Emer," Connor said. "I'll miss you."

"It has been my privilege to work with you

154

all. I'll never forget my time here in Ballybucklebo."

"And we'd love to keep you," Barry said, "but —"

"So," O'Reilly said, hoping no one had noticed him snaffle a third fig roll, "Barry and I are pulling in favours from our contacts. Connor. Nonie. I'd ask you to do the same."

"Of course," Connor said.

Nonie nodded. "Please, Emer, don't put too much store in what I'm going to say. At the moment it's unclear, but, and it's a big but, I wanted you to know I may have something to offer. I'll not know for several weeks." She raised her coffee cup to her lips and smiled. "Don't ask me," she said as everyone at the table leaned forward. "My lips are sealed."

8
USELESS AND HOPELESS SORROW

August 13, 1963

A tired Barry wriggled on one of the hard wooden chairs in Bernie's office. Half an hour ago, Jack had beaten him to the only other comfy one. Bernie, as befitted her station, always had the best one. Barry's backside was beginning to ache, but not as badly as his feet. Apart from a half hour for lunch, he hadn't stopped. He'd lost track of the number of cases he'd seen: foreign bodies in eyes — a common complaint from workers at the nearby Mackie's foundry — cuts, bruises, two broken arms, one foreign body up nose, sore backs, and twisted ankles. Contrary to the way casualty departments were portrayed on TV in *Emergency — Ward 10* as all life-threatening drama, in real life it was a long procession of medically minor cases.

"Well, lads, it's five fifteen and it has been very quiet for the last half hour," Sister Bernie O'Byrne said. "Tomorrow you'll have been here a fortnight, and you know the ropes. I'm sure only one of you needs to stay until six when the others come on duty." Barry was finishing the eight-A.M.-to-six-P.M. "long day" shift. Norma had shared it with him from eight to noon, and Jack Mills had the noon-to-six "afternoon."

Bernie was in one of her generous moods, Barry thought.

Jack Mills grinned at Barry. "Toss you for it?"

Barry smiled back. He remembered how in their first years at Campbell College he and Jack had learned early on that one way to avoid falling out over trivia was a coin toss. "Heads," Barry said.

"Heads it is." Jack rummaged in his pocket for a penny and flipped it. "Tails it is, but off you trot anyway," Jack said with a grin. "You look knackered."

Typical Jack. "Thanks, mate," Barry said. "At least I have tonight off and only the short day tomorrow." And at four thirty he'd be picking Virginia up for their first date. Mind you, he'd been too busy working and sleeping to have had much time to dwell on it, hardly had time for anything but the occasionally exchanged fond glance when they were both on duty. He savoured the thought of her for a moment before saying to Bernie, "I want to pop in to ward 10, see how Mister Peters is, the man with polycythaemia."

"Good Lord," said Jack. "Do you think you're Saint Luke, the good physician? You're getting time off — and you want to see another patient? You'll make me regret giving you my toss win. Daft." He shook his head. "Barry, we've enough to do here without following admissions on the wards, don't you agree, Bernie?"

Bernie shook her head. "Doctor Mills, I'm a nursing sister, not a referee, but if Barry wants to see a patient, why not?"

Barry smiled. "Jack, this one's different." He turned to Bernie. "If you need me back in a hurry, Bernie, you know where to find me."

"I do, and you'll be on ward 6 too, but only for a shmall minute. I need a favour."

"Oh?" Perhaps her apparent generosity had a different motivation.

"Here." She handed him a ticket. "Wicklow are playing Down at the Gaelic football in Casement Park this Sunday. Sister Kearney of wards 5 and 6 supports Down, silly woman. My brother mailed me the tickets. He's a Mayo member and he gets them at a discount. That's hers. She can pay me at the game. She's going off this evening for a few days and I have paperwork to do here so I might miss her."

"I'll see to it," Barry said, slipped the ticket into his white coat pocket, and left.

"Keep me a seat for dinner," Jack called.

Barry took a short detour to the suture room, where Virginia was clearing up after the last case. "Just popping in," he said, "to say I'm looking forward to tomorrow."

"Me too." She flashed him a dazzling smile. "Don't be late."

"I'll not, and make sure you've got on walking shoes. Cave Hill is a bit of a hike." He backed out and headed for ward 10.

Barry pushed open the blue plastic doors and walked along a short corridor, passing the rooms connecting 10, the male Sinclair Ward, with its twin, 9, the female Honorary Medical Staff Ward. As usual, the faint niff that disinfectant could not stifle was coming from the sluice where bedpans were washed and housekeeping equipment stored. The ward kitchen came next. Many a frazzled student or houseman had been refreshed there in the small hours by a friendly nurse making "a wee cup of tea in your hand" and warm buttered toast. The side ward to his left was where Barry knew Rusky Peters was being nursed. Each of the

159

twenty paired wards had a similar floor plan. He reached the sister's desk with its full view of both fourteen-bed wards.

". . . and it's taken the police five days since the thieves struck to find more clues about the great train robbers."

"Is that what they're calling them now, Sister?" the student nurse asked. "The great train robbers?"

The senior nurse bent closer to the student nurse, who perched at the edge of her chair. "Aye. They've found their hideout at a place called Leatherslade Farm near Oxford. No sign of the villains yet, though." She turned from her companion and smiled. "Barry. How are you? Come to see your Mister Peters?"

Barry, who by now felt a proprietary interest in Ivan "Rusky" Peters, liked the "your." He nodded. "How's he getting on?"

"Well as can be expected. You know your diagnosis of polycythaemia was confirmed the day he was admitted. Doctor Nelson came to see him, decided not to use radioactive phosphorous, and went for immediate venesection. We took two pints of blood. That improved things at once. Mister Willoughby Wilson, ward 10's senior surgeon, amputated the left great and next toe to it on Saturday morning. I'm afraid the other

160

toe went black before we'd taken the blood. As a courtesy to his daughter, Jan, we put him in the side ward." She inclined her head back along the way Barry had just come. "She's with him now."

Barry knew he had no need to ask permission to visit Rusky Peters in the single-bedded ward that usually was kept for patients who needed isolation or intensive nursing, but sisters were important people to keep sweet. "May I?"

"Of course."

"Thanks, Sister." Barry turned, retraced his steps, and knocked on the door.

A woman called, "Come in."

He recognised Jan Peters's voice. He'd worked with her before and she'd been there when he'd kept his promise to pop in on Rusky on Friday evening. Barry let himself into the familiar windowless room with its light yellow walls and single iron bed. Rusky Peters sat propped up on pillows. A bunch of red grapes and a bottle of Lucozade stood on a bedside locker. Radio headphones hung from a hook on the wall and a temperature chart on a clipboard hung from the bed's foot. His blankets were humped up over a semi-cylindrical metal lattice cage over his left leg to prevent pressure on the surgical site. The white ceiling-mounted curtains surrounding the bed were drawn back.

Jan Peters sat on a simple wooden chair beside the bed. "Hello, Barry. Good to see you, and I know Daddy appreciates you coming very much." Her brown eyes sparkled under neatly plucked eyebrows. She must be off duty, because under a lime green woolly cardigan she wore a sleeveless yellow dress with a buttoned blouse, belted waist, and a knee-length flared skirt.

"Jan. You're looking well."

She lowered her head. "Thank you."

"How are you keeping, Rusky?"

"I can't complain, Doctor. All my headaches is gone. I don't get dizzy no more —"

And certainly his complexion no longer looked like a ripe tomato. The bloodletting had done him a lot of good.

"— and I know it's daft, but my toes — and I know they're gone — but they itch like bejazus. Thanks for warning me that might happen. You were right when you called it 'phantom toes.' The things is haunting me."

"Forewarned is forearmed," Barry said. "I'm happy to explain as long as I'm not muddling you. Too much advice can confuse anybody, and your specialists are the experts."

162

"Sure, I know that, but it's still nice having a doctor who isn't all cold and technical, like."

Barry smiled. It was his idea of good doctoring. That was all, at least he hoped it was, and not simply a way of polishing his own buttons so he'd feel good. A narrow table on wheels, covered in tools, glue, and black-and-white wood veneers, spanned the bed in front of Rusky. On a wooden square, hinged in the middle, Rusky was affixing squares of veneer to create a chessboard. Each square had in its centre a small fleur-de-lis of the colour opposite to that of its background.

"It's coming on a treat," Barry said.

"Aye," said Rusky. "I'm not much for the reading, and it gets boring in here, but this here is a great way til pass the time, so it is."

"Daddy's been doing marquetry for as long as I can remember," Jan said. "He's very good at it — and he knows lots about it."

"I must confess," Barry said, "I don't, and I'm a complete jackass when it comes to chess, but I do enjoy a game of draughts."

"Maybe if you've nothing better to do, Doc — oooh. Jasus. Sometimes that bloody itch is hard til thole." He took a deep breath.

163

"You all right, Daddy?"

Rusky nodded. "I think there's about a hundred fleas nipping at me, but it's passing."

"It will get better in time," Barry said. "I promise."

"Thanks, Doc." Rusky pointed at his handiwork. "Anyroad, as I was trying to say, maybe if I get this here finished before they let me out, you'd come and give me a game or two, sir?"

"It's so delicately built I'd be scared to scratch it. It's a piece of fine art." He was fascinated by people who were masters of their craft, and this man was a virtuoso, and presumably self-taught. What would Ivan Peters have achieved if he had come from a different background? "Would you ever think of doing this professionally, Rusky?"

"What? No harm til you, Doc" — Barry noted the Ulster softening of the inevitable contradiction to follow — "but not at all. It's only a hobby. The wee physio says I'll be able til get about rightly — in time, on a walking stick, but och, I'm not so sure. And you need til be agile working on them cargo ships." He looked at Jan and back to Barry. "I hope to God the physio's right, but I can see me doing nothing but this, playing draughts with my old mates, watching telly, and drawing the sick before I go on the bur-roo."

"The sick" was a sickness benefit paid for thirteen weeks from the time of onset of the illness, after which, if Rusky was still inca-pacitated, his money would come from the Unemployment Bureau — the burroo.

"Come on, Daddy," Jan said, "let's not worry about that now. Let's concentrate on getting you better and then home."

"That's very good advice," Barry said. "I'm delighted to see you coming on so well, Rusky, and I'm truly impressed with your skills. Now, I expect your missus will be here soon for visiting hours and I don't want to intrude, so I'll be trotting along. But I'll pop in again soon."

"Thanks, Doc," Rusky said. "You don't know how much it's meant to me. And if you do have time for a game?"

"I'll try," Barry said.

"Thanks, Barry," Jan said. "Thank you very much."

As he closed the door behind him, Doctor Barry Laverty felt the blush rise and the warmth suffuse him, inside and out. Patients were people, and if you got to know them, as a GP could, they could reveal all kinds of hidden depths. He'd never be like Rusky's GP. Not an examining doctor.

A cheerful Barry headed along the bustling main corridor with its terrazzo floors, narrow vaulted ceiling, and clerestory windows. The medical profession at the time of the Royal's completion in 1903 had put great faith in the curative powers of daylight.

Barry walked onto ward 6 along the corridor to Sister's desk. "Sister Kearney."

The senior sister turned from where she sat at her desk. She smiled. "Hello, Barry. What can I do for you?"

He fished out the ticket and proffered it. "Bernie O'Byrne asked me to deliver this. Says you can pay her for it at the game on Sunday."

"Thanks a million." She took the ticket.

"I'm off for my tea." Barry turned to go.

As he walked from the office he saw a familiar fair-haired man in the coronary care unit immediately adjacent to the end of the entrance corridor. Harry Sloan's ordinarily high complexion was flaming.

Harry glanced up. "Barry, give me a hand. Quick. Quick."

When Barry arrived at the bedside where Harry stood, he saw the patient he'd resuscitated thirteen days ago lying motionless and felt a moment of shame. He'd only dropped in once to visit the man and already he'd forgotten his name. He'd probably seen a hundred patients in the past two weeks.

The man lay bare-chested on the bed, sightless eyes fixed on the ceiling. The pillow had been removed and a board placed between his back and the mattress to provide a solid surface so that Harry's compression of the sternum would meet resistance and be effective. Barry looked at the screen of the electrocardiograph. All the lines were nothing but disorganised squiggles. Ventricular fibrillation. Cardiac arrest.

Barry stepped inside the curtains just before a nurse closed them to hide the drama from the rest of the ward.

"G-get the Ambu bag." Harry was already short of breath as he continued to give cardiac massage. Barry started to head for where it would be kept, but realized Harry had been asking the nurse, who produced it and gave it to Barry. He'd barely had time to give the patient a few puffs when the curtains briefly parted and the bespectacled Doctor John Geddes and a staff nurse rushed in pushing a trolley bearing the Lown defibrillator, which the nurse plugged into the mains. It was a bulky box with knobs at its front, a small upper screen for its built-in electrocardiogram, and a lower one indicating energy settings.

John Geddes nodded to the two men. "Please carry on, Doctors, until we get the defibrillator ready." Geddes busied himself in front of the trolley.

The staff nurse connected the defibrillator's arm, chest, and leg leads, and the ECG screen on the upper half of the defibrillator began to display the chaotic pattern of ventricular fibrillation.

In what seemed but moments Geddes said, "Right, we're nearly ready to go. Stop ventilating, but please stay, Barry. We may need you again."

Barry, still holding the Ambu bag, stepped aside.

The staff nurse inserted two cloth-wrapped tongue depressors between the man's teeth to stop him biting his tongue. The other nurse had applied KY jelly to two metal electrodes on wooden handles that Doctor John Geddes held. Their electrical cords came from the defibrillator. Harry Sloan stopped giving external cardiac massage.

"Clear," said Geddes. He waited until no one was touching the patient, placed the metal blades on the man's chest, repeated, "Clear," checked that it was, and stood on a foot pedal, sending an electric shock surging through the whole of the man's body.

His arms and legs convulsed. For a few seconds the monitor went blank, because it was automatically turned off when the shock was delivered, lest the current fry its inner workings. When a tracing reappeared, it was a flat line.

Barry and Harry resumed ventilation and massage until a second attempt to restart the heart had been prepared.

"Clear." Again, the man's limbs twitched. Again the monitor remained flat.

Three more attempts, three more failures, during which time the staff nurse had filled a syringe equipped with a long spinal needle with adrenaline, one millilitre of one-in-one-thousand solution.

"Needle," said Geddes. In moments he had swabbed the skin over the space between the fourth and fifth left ribs, thrust the needle through the chest and heart walls, and into the great left ventricle. When he pulled back on the plunger, smoky blood flowing back into the barrel confirmed he had hit his target. He injected slowly.

The last gasp of a dedicated team trying to bring a man back to life. The forlorn hope.

But the luminous green trace on the screen was as flat as the mood in the silent private space behind the curtains.

"Thanks everybody, but — I'm sorry. We tried." Geddes lifted the patient's chart. "If you need me, I'll be in Sister's office. I'll talk to the next of kin and fill in the death certificate for them. Thanks a lot, Barry. Good thing you were here. Harry already knows his stuff, but you'll be ahead of the class."

"Class?"

"I'll be starting soon to train all the house-men how to deal with cardiac arrest." He left.

Harry, still short of breath, jerked his head to the corpse. "I suppose you can't save them all."

Barry nodded, sad that everyone's best efforts had failed. He himself felt no sense of personal loss. He realised that was because he barely knew the patient. The unfortunate had been one of a crowd. Barry was honest enough with himself to know his earlier visit had been as much to confirm his having saved a life as it was out of concern for a stranger he hardly knew.

"Nyeh —" Harry often made that nasal sound as a preface to speaking. "God, I could use a smoke." He glanced at his watch. "I'm still on call, but I don't need to stay on the ward. Come on. The nurses'll take care of things here."

170

As soon as they were on the corridor, Harry lit up and strode off. He'd begun his year with this three-month stint on 5 and 6 — a position Barry would assume on December 1 when his time in casualty was over. He lengthened his stride and caught up.

"How are you, Harry?"

"Rotten." The man's lips turned down. His forehead was creased. He took a deep draw on his smoke. "I hate it when we lose them."

"Damn." Barry gritted his teeth. Poor man. He hadn't looked that old. And Harry was taking the loss hard. Barry immediately touched his friend's shoulder. "I'm sorry, Harry. I really am." He held open the door to the East Wing.

Harry stopped in front of a wall-mounted ashtray and stubbed out the half-smoked cigarette with a vicious twist of his hand. He shook his head. "Jesus, Barry. We were going to discharge him last week, but he had a bout of atrial fibrillation. Not as bad as ventricular. We put him on digitalis and quinidine and seemed to have it under control." Harry yawned. Inhaled. "I've been up since two this morning. We had two admissions and we lost one of them. Your man there, Robbie Martin" — Barry recog-

171

nised the patient's name now and yet still felt no real sense of loss — "was the second to go today. He was only sixty-one. It's bloody unfair." Harry stared into the middle distance.

Did Harry mean to the patients or to him? Probably the latter. They'd been working in the hospital long enough now to recognise that disease was inherently unfair to the victim, but the constant demand for perfection made of students and junior doctors, very often by themselves, could be upsetting if they failed to achieve it. Barry wondered how he'd be feeling now if he'd got to know this Robbie Martin as Harry must have.

Harry came back from wherever his reverie had taken him. "I thought," he inhaled, "mebbe, because I never saw anyone die when we were students, I thought being a doctor was about making people better. You always feel good when you get a winner, but losing them?" Harry shook his head. "It's getting to me."

Barry said, "At least we had to spend a year and a half dissecting a corpse early on and attending six postmortems last year. It's not as if we haven't seen dead bodies."

"That's true," Harry said, "but we hadn't known any of them when they were still alive. Your man there was a butcher and he ran greyhounds. His best one was a bitch called Molly."

Barry smiled. Here perhaps was an opportunity to try to get his friend out of his personal Slough of Despond. "Knowing a patient's occupation is part of the routine history, but, holy Moses, when did it become medically important to know about their hobbies?" Even though Barry had just learned of Rusky's marquetry, he thought his own interest, because he knew Rusky's daughter, Jan, was different from Harry finding out this kind of detail from a relative stranger.

Harry pulled out a packet of Gallaher's De Luxe Greens, tapped a cigarette on the packet to tamp the tobacco more firmly, and lit up. "Robbie's been in longer than any other patient on the ward. He didn't have many visitors. He's not married —"

Barry noticed that Harry was still using the present tense.

"I got into the habit of chatting with him before I went off the ward in the evenings. Nyeh, the poor man was terrified. He begged me not to let him die." Harry took another drag, then blew out smoke. "You know, Barry, I'm not sure I'm cut out for this."

"Come on, man. You're tired. Upset. Come on. We'll have our tea. You get an early night. You'll feel better after a good night's sleep."

Harry sighed.

"Come on, Harry."

But Harry Sloan shook his head. "I'm not hungry, Barry. And don't get all worried about me. I'm just dog-tired. I'm going for a bath and a lie-down."

"You sure?"

Harry managed a small smile. "I'll be fine." He turned to leave.

"All right, Harry. You've just had a rough session. Off to bed. You'll be fine." And as his friend walked slowly away, Barry hoped sleep would be all that was needed to get Harry back on his usual humorous even keel.

9
THE HEAVY BURDEN OF
RESPONSIBILITY

April 19, 1969

"Ba ba pom diddily pom." O'Reilly puffed his pipe and hummed along as Herbert von Karajan conducted Beethoven's Sixth Symphony in F Major. O'Reilly and Emer were on call for the weekend. So far, at ten fifteen, no one had needed them.

Emer had come down from Belfast last night and slept in Barry's old quarters. O'Reilly, always an early riser since his days in the navy, had let the lass have a bit of a lie-in. She was downstairs finishing the breakfast he had prepared for her. He was no cook, but years ago Kinky had taught him a few simple things, like grilling kippers. "Da da da da da diddly dada . . ." The last "dada" was punctuated with stabs with his pipe stem.

Kitty, with a sketch pad on her lap, sat in an armchair looking out the window. "There's a storm coming, Fingal," she said, "and I'm trying to get the feel of the leading edges of the clouds rolling in against the blue sky."

He stood and looked over her shoulder to see how, with charcoal, she had run an irregular line from one side of the paper, about a third of the way up, descending at a shallow angle across to the other side. She'd smudged the charcoal with her thumb to indicate the clouds' menacing darkness. The steeple of the Presbyterian church opposite was rendered in a few deft strokes.

She stared at the sketch and put down the piece of charcoal. "After we'd all talked about having events at the sporting club last Saturday I started thinking. You know I love to paint. I thought I might have a few new ones of local County Down scenes for sale hanging in the main hall of the clubhouse, and donate the proceeds to the fund."

"That's a splendid idea," he said, "and I think Bertie Bishop will —"

The telephone extension in the lounge of Number One rang.

He rose and switched off the new Bose stereo system he'd bought last year to replace his ancient Black Box. "Hello? Doctor O'Reilly."

"I'm sorry til bother you, Doctor" — he recognised Barbara Devine's voice — "but

Norman's taken a turn. He was still a bit sore, but pretty much all right yesterday when that nice Doctor Stevens popped in. But about half an hour ago, he took a headache and he's thrown off too."

"We'll be right out."

"Thank you, sir." The line went dead.

"Gotta go," he said.

"Take your coat, pet. It's going to pour." She bent to her sketch again and picked up the charcoal.

O'Reilly trotted downstairs and into the dining room, where Emer sat eating toast and Kinky's homemade marmalade. A plate with the wreckage of a brace of kippers sat on the table. "What's up?"

"I'm sorry to have to tell you that Norman Devine is having a setback."

"Oh-oh." She wiped her mouth on a napkin, stood, and said, "What are we waiting for?"

O'Reilly smiled. Good lass. "Only to get our hats and coats, because Kitty's been studying the clouds, and she says it's going to bucket down out there."

To underline his remark, the first wave of driven rain, sounding like the efforts of a drunken snare drummer, rattled off the windows.

Together they dashed across the back

garden, and Kenny didn't even bother to look out of his doghouse.

Sensible animal, O'Reilly thought as he dragged the car's door open and waited until Emer was settled beside him before driving off into the downpour.

Main Street was deserted. Rain drummed off the car's roof, the windscreen wipers danced a frenetic two-step, and water was thrown up by the tyres like spray hurled aside by a motor torpedo boat.

Emer's voice was matter-of-fact when she asked, "What are Norman's symptoms?"

"Headache and vomiting."

"All right. Could be a couple of things, but we'll not know until we've —"

"You. Until you've examined him. He's your patient."

"Right. Until I've examined him. Thank you." She settled in her seat.

O'Reilly knew from lab tests on the cerebrospinal fluid of studied patients that the mumps virus frequently invaded the central nervous system, but symptoms only appeared in 10 percent of victims. Depending on what part of the system was involved, most patients recovered, but in the remaining few in whom the brain itself was affected by encephalitis, the mortality was a terrifying 50 percent, with many of the survivors suffering serious residual damage. His hands grasped the wheel more firmly as his concern for Norman Devine increased.

He glanced over at Emer, who sat upright, her hands held stiffly in her lap, staring out at the rain. Was she concerned about not warning Barbara Devine of the possible complications? It had taken a couple of months for her to get over blaming herself when another child had developed a rare complication after scarlet fever.

The firmament was rent by a sizzling thunderbolt that lit up the inside of the car, and O'Reilly did what he'd been doing since childhood, counting the seconds before the celestial howitzers growled. "Eight miles away," he said as he parked outside the cottage and a single diesel-powered railway carriage, known to the locals as "the covered wagon," rattled past on its way to Bangor from Belfast. Although often full of commuters on weekdays, it was half empty today.

Even before they had climbed out of the car carrying their bags, Barbara had opened the front door. "Come on in out of that," she yelled over the gale. "It's coming down in stair rods." She closed the door. "Thanks for coming so quick. I'll take your coats. You're drenched, so you are, and after only a few seconds. Normie was getting along rightly, Doctors. He even had a visitor this morning. Colin Brown and his wee dog Murphy called in to talk to Normie about a puppy Colin knows about. Normie's been wanting a dog for months now and he's daft about that dog of Colin's. The boy's had the mumps so I let him in."

"Colin Brown's here now?" said O'Reilly.

"He is, sir. Colin was for going, seeing Normie's head had got so sore. He's boked twice, and the light hurts his eyes. But having Murphy beside him seemed to soothe Normie, and then the rain started coming down, so I asked Colin to stay. I have Normie teed up in there 'cause it's warm and I can keep an eye til him, and I have the curtains shut." She pointed to where Norman, today in blue pyjamas, lay in the dimly lit living room on a couch with what must be a cold wet towel on his forehead, a ceramic baking bowl on the floor beside him. "I done what you said, Doctor Emer, I give him an aspirin, but he boked it up, and then I called. I hope you don't mind on a Saturday, like."

Emer said, "You did exactly the right thing, Barbara."

Dear God, the consideration of rural patients for their physicians, O'Reilly

180

thought.

"Hiya, Doctors," Colin Brown said from where he sat on a chair near Norman. Murphy, Colin's mongrel, lay on the rug at Norman's side. "Mrs. Devine said that seeing it was so bad out, I could stay and she wouldn't mind if I watched you work, if that's all right with you, Doctor O'Reilly? If I pass my exams in June I'll be well on my way to being a vet, and sure don't doctors do more or less what vets do? I could learn something."

O'Reilly smiled. A couple of years ago, Colin had said when O'Reilly was examining a sick dog, "Sure isn't a doctor the next best thing to a vet?" Clearly his opinion hadn't changed.

"You sure, Barbara?" said O'Reilly. "You don't mind?"

Another thunderclap.

"Och aye. I think Normie's more comfy with Colin and Murphy here. He loves Murphy, so he does."

"Would you like Colin and Murphy to stay, Norman?" said O'Reilly. "You don't mind?"

Another thunderclap.

"I don't mind, Doctor. Murphy's all comfy here on the bed." The boy reached out to lay a hand on the dog's flank.

O'Reilly recalled with great clarity how two years ago, when Kenny had been a pup, how much his presence had cheered up Anne Galvin. Why not let them stay?

"We'll be good, Doctors. Honest to God," Colin said.

"All right. Just don't get in the way."

Norman's face and neck were still swollen. He looked flushed and he'd been crying.

Emer squatted in front of him. "Feeling poorly, Norman?"

"Yes, Doctor Emer. My neck's awful stiff, so it is."

The central nervous system is involved, all right, O'Reilly thought. Now let's see how badly. He crossed his fingers behind his back.

"I'm sorry to hear that. Do you know where you are?"

"At home."

"Good. What's your name?"

Norman frowned. "Sure you know it's Norman Devine."

She turned to Barbara. "Has Norman been hard to wake up?"

"Och, no, Doctor."

Making sure the child has not had any episodes of unconsciousness. Coma was frequent in encephalitis patients. "Have you anything here in your kitchen with a strong scent, Barbara?"

"I'll get something."

Emer turned back to the boy. "I have to ask you a few more questions and then examine you. Don't be scared."

"Here y'are, Doctor." Barbara handed Emer a bottle.

Emer held the open jar under Norman's nose. "What can you smell?"

"Cloves. I like clove rock, so I do."

"Me too," Colin said. "I wonder how you'd ask a dog what it could smell? They've terrific senses of smell. English springers and Labradors are likely the best sniffers."

"Wheest, Colin," Barbara said. "You promised to be good."

"Good lad, Norman." Emer returned the bottle of cloves to Barbara. "Now, Norman, what colours do you see me wearing?"

"You've a green sweater on, miss."

"Can you sit up for a wee minute?"

"I'll help," Barbara said, did, and took away the cold compress.

That's two of the twelve cranial nerves tested, the ones that carried their messages directly to and from the brain. If all were unaffected, the outlook would be getting better.

Another low rumbling, but less loud. The

183

storm was moving away.

"Norman, I want you to cover your left eye with your hand and look into my left eye with your right one. I'm going to wiggle my fingers, and I want you to point as soon as you see them appear, but keep staring into my eye all the time." She stretched out her left arm and began wiggling. Colin was covering his eye too, and the boy's serious expression made O'Reilly smile, despite his concern for Norman.

It took two minutes to complete the test of the boy's visual fields. He had no defects.

"Now before we get you lying down again, a couple more things." She held up three fingers. "How many?"

"Three."

"Now how many."

"One."

"I don't know what you're doing, Doctor Emer." Colin had been paying rapt attention. "But it wouldn't work with cats. They can't count, but I seen, I mean I saw, a dog at a circus once that could."

"Colin." Barbara held up an admonitory finger.

"It's all right," Emer said, and smiled, but she was perfectly serious when she added, "And Norman has no squint. Now, please, Norman, without moving your head, look straight up, down, far left, far right. Good. No loss of eye movements. Sorry I have to do this." She shone her pencil torch in his eyes.

He jerked his head away. "That hurts." He sniffed.

Murphy raised his handsome, square head from the sofa and licked Norman's hand. It seemed to comfort the lad.

"I am sorry," Emer said, but reported, "Pupils equal and reacting."

Nerves three, four, and six were intact, but photophobia was a sign of meningeal inflammation.

It took several more minutes for Emer to assess six more nerves. All were unaffected. "You've been a good boy, Norman. Now, I want you to stick your tongue out at me."

Norman looked to his mother for approval. A child sticking out his tongue at an adult was an unforgiveable act of rudeness. She nodded. "Mammy won't be mad." As Norman Devine stuck his tongue out at Emer, O'Reilly watched Colin struggling with what must be an urge to stick his out too. He succeeded. The boy was maturing. Emer was testing the twelfth, the hypoglossal nerve. If it were damaged, the tongue would deviate to one side.

O'Reilly uncrossed his fingers. His initial

anxiety on behalf of the boy was fading. And he was impressed with Emer's unruffled professionalism. He chuckled.

"That tongue is as straight as a die," Emer said. "Now, let's get Norman lying down again."

Barbara helped.

Emer assessed the boy's ability to move his limbs and feel pressure and touch, and tested his reflexes. None were abnormal. "Now, Norman, this is going to tickle." And Emer tested his Babinski reflex. The toe curled down.

"You could do most of that to a horse," Colin said. "Thank you, Doctor Emer. Boy, I knew I'd learn something."

Barbara smiled. "My mammy says you should learn something new every day."

Emer stood. "Now, let me explain what's going on."

Colin hunched forward, his frown indicating his attention.

"I believe the nasty bug has caused some —"

Norman moaned, hung his head over the bowl, and threw up.

O'Reilly's nostrils were assailed by the acrid smell, but he'd been exposed to it for thirty-eight years. He didn't even wrinkle his nose.

"Poor Normie," Colin said, "but there'd be worse smells in a byre or a pigsty, I reckon."

Norman Devine might be feeling rotten, but Emer's thoroughness had removed encephalitis as a diagnostic possibility. The examination was conclusive proof that the boy's brain itself was not infected, praise be.

Barbara cradled her son's head, wiped his lips with the towel that had been his cold compress. " 'Scuse me. I'll just go and empty this and get you a glass of water, Normie," she said, picking up the bowl.

"Don't worry, Norman," Emer said, "you're going to be fine." She pulled a hanky from her sleeve and dried the boy's tears.

O'Reilly heard a toilet flushing. Tap water running.

Barbara came back and replaced the bowl. "Sorry about that." She held a glass to her son's lips so he could drink.

"Hardly Norman's fault," O'Reilly said, inclining his head to Emer to indicate she should carry on. He was going to be interested in her explanation.

"Sometimes the mumps bug can inflame membranes in the head —"

Barbara's hand flew to her mouth. "Has

Norman got the meninjitees?"

O'Reilly knew what Barbara must be thinking. There had been an outbreak of meningococcal meningitis, cerebrospinal fever, here two winters ago. It was a virulent disease and one little boy had died. Emer couldn't know about that and how it was affecting Barbara.

"Yes," said O'Reilly quickly, "but it's a very different kind to the one you're thinking about, Barbara. No need to worry. None at all. I promise."

She took a deep breath, and put her hand on her heart. "Thank God for that." She was blinking back tears.

Colin mumbled to himself, "I read once how animals can get it too. I'll have to learn all about how to diagnose it."

"Please carry on," O'Reilly said to a frowning Emer. And rightly so. Norman was her patient, and she had not sought his opinion or his interference.

"Doctor O'Reilly's right. The meningitis caused by the mumps bug is much, much milder. When it does affect the membranes called meninges, the poor patient, that's you, Norman, usually has a not-too-nice two or three days, but I can give you some medicine that will help to bring your fever down and help the headaches." She turned

188

to Barbara. "Can you cope with the nursing? We'll get the district nurse, Colleen Brennan, to drop in every day. Norman should be over this stage in two or three days."

"He'll not have til go til the fever hospital?"

"No, no hospital for Norman."

Barbara folded her arms. "I will cope, so I will."

"I never doubted it," Emer said. "So, let's see. You got sick last Wednesday the sixteenth, today's Saturday the nineteenth; you'll be feeling much better by Thursday, and by the way, Mammy, Norman won't be contagious after next Thursday, and you should be better by Saturday, son."

"Did you hear that, Normie? This time next week you'll be fit as a flea and we can get your daddy to drive us to Crawfordsburn to look at that pup Colin has been telling you about." Barbara smiled. "My husband Jamsie's working this weekend but he's off the next. Thank you, Doctor Emer. Thank you very much."

Colin grinned and Murphy wagged his tail.

Emer lowered her voice. "One last thing," she said. "Do you know how to use a suppository?"

189

Barbara nodded.

"You stick them up your —"

"Colin," three voices yelled.

"Sorry."

O'Reilly shook his head and hid a grin. You may be maturing at sixteen, Colin Brown, but the lad who told Joseph to "feck off" in the 1964 Christmas pageant was still alive and well in there.

"I'm going to prescribe something containing Panadol. One every six hours."

"Excuse me, Doctor McCarthy," O'Reilly said. "It'll be hard for Barbara to get to the chemist's until her husband comes home tonight." He opened his bag and handed her a box of six. "That'll see to Norman until his dad gets home after his work tomorrow with your scrip filled. I know the chemist in Holywood's open tomorrow."

"Jamsie gets free travel 'cause he works for the railway. He'll nip up and back on the train, so he will," Barbara said.

"Good," said Emer, handing Barbara the prescription, "and now I just need to wash my hands and we'll be off. And if you've any worries at all, call."

"I will, Doctor, and thank you too, Doctor O'Reilly, for explaining. When I thought my wee dote had them other menijitees, I near took the rickets."

190

O'Reilly nodded his acknowledgement, but said nothing.

"Don't you worry, the pair of you. You'll be fine, Norman," Emer said as she dried her hands.

Colin said, "Thank you very much everybody for letting me watch. I did learn a lot. I think now it's going to be harder to be a vet than a doctor."

"Oh," said O'Reilly, "why?"

" 'Cause you can ask your patients questions. Can you see me asking a ram, 'What colour of shirt am I wearing?' He'd probably butt me."

O'Reilly tousled the youngster's hair. "You really do want to be one, don't you, Colin."

"I've never wanted anything as much." The boy nodded. "And not only will I have Mister Bishop's scholarship, if I get good enough marks in my exams, I could win a county or a state exhibition, that's money the government pays for your fees and stuff. It'll take me five years and then I'll come back as Ballybucklebo's first vet."

"You study hard, Colin," Emer said. "All of Ballybucklebo is cheering for you. Don't let them down." Barbara handed them their coats and opened the door to a calm, freshly washed world under a clear blue sky.

On the way home, with the sun splitting

the heavens and the road steaming as it dried, O'Reilly said, "Sorry to take over like that. We had an outbreak of meningococcal meningitis here in January of '67. One wee lad died from it."

"I've been working with you for nine months, Fingal, and I know you'd never let a little matter like a starchy old medical tradition come between you and good patient care. I thought Barbara was going to break down and now I understand why. No need to apologise. You did exactly the right thing."

"And so did you, Emer, when you first made the diagnosis of mumps. Not knowing the local history, if you'd whispered meningitis back then she'd have been worried for days and right up to high doh today. You accepted a risk that you could be blamed if a complication arose — which it did, and you did that for the patient's peace of mind. In my opinion, Emer McCarthy, another three months with us is a waste of time. You're ready for independent practice right now."

Her voice was low, but O'Reilly could hear a trace of pride. "Thank you, Fingal. Thank you very much. It's good to know you think that. It really is."

10
I To the Hills Will Lift
Mine Eyes

August 17, 1963
Barry drove Brunhilde, his Volkswagen
beetle, toward the car park at the foot of
Cave Hill, a 1,200-foot-high mound of
ancient basalt that overlooked the city of
Belfast. He'd shaved twice today and had
been nervous when he'd met Virginia at
precisely four thirty at Musson House. The
nurses' home had been named in 1951 for
Miss Anne Musson, one of the previous
matrons of the Royal Victoria. Virginia had
looked lovely standing on the steps of the
old six-storey redbrick building, and Barry
had told her so. He was rewarded with a
smile and a "Thank you, sir." And her laugh
had been like warm honey.

They'd chatted on the twenty-minute run
up to the park north of the city, mostly of
inconsequential things, because Barry, still
suffering from his closeted boyhood in a
boys-only boarding school and his fear of

193

being repulsed, found talking to girls difficult.

Then, out of nowhere, she had said, "You are a bit shy, aren't you, Barry Laverty?"

"Yes," he said. "Is it so obvious?"

"Not really, it's just that us girls, walled up in Musson like a bunch of nuns, did talk about you lads, you know, when you were students. We all thought you, the quiet one, were cute. We liked the way you cared for your patients too, and you didn't make passes at us. Try to pinch our bottoms like a farmer's son from Cullybackey I could mention."

Barry knew his friend Jack had quite the reputation among the nurses.

Her smile was radiant. "I find your being shy attractive. And I did think it took real guts to tackle that lout last Friday. Thank you again."

As he parked, he berated himself for not having had any better reply than "It's Norma Fitch you should be thanking."

She smiled. "I'm not going to argue with you, Barry, on our first date."

Was that a hint she was hoping this might lead to a second? "Here we are," he said, "and we couldn't have asked for better weather to climb the hill."

"I've lived in Ulster all my life. Born and

brought up in Magherafelt, County Derry, and I've lived in Musson for nearly three years, but I've never been up here."

"Excuse me." Barry leant across her, inhaling the suggestion of her light perfume as he unlatched her door. "Hop out," he said, leaning back. "We've four and a half miles to cover, half of it uphill. I'm going to give you the conducted tour. My dad used to bring me here, teach me about the place. There's a lot of interesting stuff."

He reached behind him for his walking stick, an ashplant with a crook for a handle, then joined her in the warm air, pointing to a four-storey granite-block building with a five-storey tower at its rear left corner. It was a complex design with curved corners surmounted by conical roofs, intricately twisting staircases, and apparently randomly sited bay windows. Small cannons mounted on wooden gun-carriages were arranged in the forecourt. "Belfast Castle," he said. "Took from 1811 to 1877 to build it, Dad told me. Apparently it's in the Scottish Baronial style."

"Looks like something the Brothers Grimm might have designed." She took his hand as if it were the most natural thing in the world and said, "Come on then, Mister Tour Guide."

"Would you like to use the stick?" he asked. "It gets pretty steep in places."

"I'll be fine."

"I'll bring it anyway and if you do want it, sing out." He pointed with it. "First left," he said and set off, "then right at the first junction."

As they trod together along the footpath toward a small wood of birch and fir, he admired her sensible outfit. A green head-scarf bound up her auburn hair. The collar of a silky green blouse was folded over the neck of an Arran sweater, which hung loosely over black pants. Heavy brogues would be ideal for scrambling up over the rougher ground where they were going. Despite the cerulean cloudless sky, cold winds could tear in across Belfast Lough, and once past the wood there was no shelter. The three caves were well above the path and difficult to climb up to.

They entered the wood, and the sharp, clean, resin smell of the fir trees filled him with a sudden sense of well-being. Out of sight of any other walkers he stopped, moved to her, took the plunge, and gently put his lips to hers. She did not, as he half expected, pull away. Their softness and the taste of her made him shiver, and that she responded made his pulse quicken. They parted. "Nice," he said. "Very nice."

"Mmmm," she said, and her green eyes sparkled. She cocked her head and smiled at him. "I think I could grow quite fond of you, Barry Laverty." And she kissed him back.

He was a little breathless when they parted. "And — and I of you, but Virginia, it's about a two- to three-hour hike, and —"

She chuckled. "Lead on."

They left the wood and Barry said, "The view is even better from higher up, but it's worth stopping here too."

"Golly," she said, "it's quite the panorama. Belfast, the River Lagan, the lough, the County Down shore in the distance, and Antrim directly below. And is that a hint of Scotland's Mull of Galloway in the far distance? It really is very beautiful."

"Just wait until we get to the top." He pointed ahead at a basalt outcrop. "That's what the locals back in the early nineteenth century called 'The Emperor's nose and cocked hat.'"

She peered at the black ridge. "It does look like them," she said, and clapped her hands. "It really does."

Barry smiled at the innocent way she took enormous pleasure from this new sight.

"The emperor was Napoleon. It's said that Jonathan Swift saw it, imagined it was the head of a giant keeping watch over the city, so he trotted off and wrote *Gulliver's Travels.*"

On they tramped, climbing, descending into little valleys, and climbing again. The earthen footpath wound among hillocks of springy grass highlighted by clumps of purple heather and yellow gorse that bathed them in its almond scent. When they crested one hill and went down into a small valley, Barry noticed they were alone again, but before he could act, Virginia said, "My mum always says that when gorse is out of bloom, kissing is out of fashion." And she kissed him long, deep, and hard, her tongue tip flickering on his.

"Golly," Barry said as they parted.

"I told you I thought I could become fond of you."

Barry, still savouring her kiss and her words, was tongue-tied, and before he could think of anything witty to say, a middle-aged couple had crested the hill behind them. "Um, I think, ah —" He gave up and sighed. "Next left." And holding her hand more tightly, he climbed with her to the new hilltop. "Look, that jumble of rocks and boulders to your left is the Devil's Punch-

198

bowl. Celtic farmers kept their cattle penned in there. The path goes down to it then passes beneath a large cave off to the right and begins climbing again."

They kept on, occasionally being overtaken by other hikers. As they passed beneath the first cave, he said, "That one is twenty-one feet long, eighteen feet wide, and varies from seven to ten feet in height, and —"

She snuggled up against him. "Oooooh. It looks dark and spooky in there." She laughed and snuggled closer. "Barry, please don't think me ungracious, but isn't there a bit of the 'seen one, seen them all' about caves if we can't go in? Bloody great holes in the side of the mountain?"

He laughed. "Point taken." She was right, and besides, he was much more interested in this lively young woman. She caught him off guard when she stopped and faced him. "What I'd really like is a short travelogue round Barry Laverty. Please tell me about yourself."

"There's not too much to tell." Particularly, he thought, when you've had it drummed into you since you were a nipper that gentlemen do not blow their own trumpets. "I'm twenty-three, born in Bangor, Bangor Grammar School, Campbell

199

College, got my colours for swimming. Queen's for six years, and now I'm a houseman trying to make up my mind what to do next year."

He heard the tinkling of a bell and pulled Virginia to one side of the path as a boy in a Belfast Royal Academy school cap, open-necked white shirt, and shorts, sweat running down his cheeks, puffed past, pedalling like crazy on a three-speed bicycle.

"It is warm," Virginia said. "Hang on." She crossed her arms in front of her and stripped off her sweater. As she tied the sleeves around her waist Barry was treated to a breathtaking view between the creamy roundness of two delightful breasts. He felt his pulse quicken and, realising he was pretty warm himself, took off his tweed sports jacket and carried it over his shoulder. He was so entranced with her he barely noticed the spectacular, ever-changing views. They climbed steps leading to a cattle grille in a fence.

"All right, that's your professional biography. I want to know a bit about who you are. What do you do in your spare time?"

Barry laughed. "You're a student nurse. When you turned me down you told me that getting qualified was important to you."

"It is. Very. But all work and no play —"

Barry smiled. "If you're working as hard as I had to to get through, and I'm sure you are, you should know the answer to that is 'What spare time?' " He only hoped she was going to be able to find more for him in the future. "I used to like to sail, build model boats, fly-fish, read —" They were alone, so he kissed her long and tender before saying, "And I love climbing up Cave Hill with beautiful green-eyed nurses."

She squeezed his hand as they crossed the metal strips of the grille to walk on a grass path. "Less of the nurses, plural, Doctor Laverty." Then she stopped in her tracks. "Oh dear Lord, look at that. I've never seen a view like it. This must be how a bird sees the world." She shook her head in wonder. "Tell me what I'm seeing, Barry, please."

They had come to the summit.

It had been on the tip of his tongue to say it was her turn to tell him something about Nurse Virginia Clarke, but her enthusiasm was infectious. "All right, you already know that all of the city of Belfast and Belfast Lough are in the foreground. You can see the gantries of the shipyard, the enormous yellow Goliath crane, the steeple of Saint Mark's at Dundela, Holywood, Ballybuck-lebo, and Bangor on the far shore, and on this side the semicircle sweep of the Antrim shore."

"And is that Strangford Lough in the middle distance and Scrabo Tower at its head?"

"It is, and beyond that you can make out Slieve Croob in the middle of County Down, and behind it the Mourne Mountains. Now, look left. Do you see the far horizon under that thin white bank of low clouds?"

She turned to stare.

"You were right, that is the Mull of Galloway in Scotland to your left, and way away to your right in Saint George's Channel is the Isle of Man."

She stood in awe, saying nothing, and Barry decided not to tell her about the legend of Finn MacCool, the Irish giant who had built the Giant's Causeway in order to fight the Scottish giant Benandonner. When the Irishman had run out of stones, he'd torn out a sod and hurled it. The crater became Lough Neagh and the sod the Isle of Man.

"Gosh, Barry," she said. "Thank you for bringing me here. It's wonderful. Makes me feel small and insignificant. I like the feeling. Puts things into perspective."

"I know what you mean," he said. "I was

seven or eight the first time Dad brought me up here. He had to haul me up some of the steeper places. He made me look out at that panorama and I'll never forget what he said. 'Take a good look, son, and always remember this any time you feel important. Man in comparison to nature is really not important at all.' "

She smiled. "I think I could like your dad, Barry, even if I've never met him."

Barry, who was not close to his father, said nothing.

Rising on a thermal, three glaucous gulls, wings stiffly arched to catch the air currents, rose higher above the escarpment.

"Look at that," she said. "How lovely. So graceful, and just after me saying this must be how a bird sees the world."

For moments neither spoke.

"And what's that?" She pointed to a crumbling earthwork wall running from one side to the other across the narrow escarpment where they stood.

"It's an old *ráth,* a hill fort. On this side, it's protected by that earthen wall and a deep ditch, and there's a steep cliff at the far side. It's called MacArt's Fort. The two leaders of the United Irishmen, Wolfe Tone and Henry Joy McCracken, both Protestants, met here in 1798. They wanted civil and religious freedom for everyone, regardless of creed, and took an oath of allegiance before the uprising."

She chuckled. "So not only are you a sailor, model boat builder, fly-fisherman, and reader, you're a wonderful tour guide—"

He glowed in her praise.

She leant closer and whispered so he felt her warm breath on his neck, "And you kiss very well too."

Barry would have savoured the moment, but the cycling schoolboy was back. "Excuse me, mister, can I get by, please?"

"Of course." Barry stepped aside and the lad mounted and pedalled away. "Come on," he said. "The path down the south side is much gentler. Won't take us long to get back to the car."

Virginia sighed and then breathed in a deep breath. "One more good look?" She stared all around her, turning slowly. "Beautiful," she said. "I'll always remember this."

I'll not forget it either, Barry thought, seeing the beauty of her. "Now," he said, "let's head for home."

They set off.

"And it's time, Virginia Clarke, for me to find out a bit about you, please."

"All right." She frowned and said with a

204

serious tone, "My CV reads: I'm twenty-one, in my third year of training. I told you I'm from Magherafelt. Went to Rainey Endowed School. It's an old co-ed grammar school. My best subjects were science and mathematics, and I played left wing on the first eleven hockey team." Then she grinned. "Now. Wasn't that exciting?"

Barry shook his head and laughed. "Exhilarating," he said.

"On a more personal note, Dad's a solicitor in Magherafelt and Mum writes children's stories for BBC Radio. I like ballet and short stories and history." She stopped and faced him. "And just so you know, I am very serious about wanting to be a nurse."

"Why did you pick nursing?"

Before she could answer, they passed the young cyclist, who, well away from his teachers and his school, nestled at the foot of Cave Hill, was having a smoke.

"Why? I like people, I suppose. And when I was fourteen, my dad gave me a book by Cecil Woodham-Smith —"

"She's a fantastic historian," Barry said. "I've read her *The Great Hunger* and *The Reason Why.*"

"So have I, but Dad bought me *Florence Nightingale*. That's when I decided on nursing." She lost her smile and her voice was serious when she said, "And I love it. And I'm going to finish my training and go on to be a midwife."

"I think that's terrific. I really do."

"Thank you, Barry." They started walking.

"I'm not in it like a lot of the girls who want to snag a young doctor. Marry up. I don't blame them for wanting to avoid working in a linen mill or a shop. Not at all. They're smart, they did well in school, and they want something that leads to a better life, and there aren't that many options for us girls. But I'm not like the ladies who used to go out to the Raj and try to land an army officer. They called them 'The Fishing Fleet,' you know."

Barry laughed. So, as well as being beautiful, it was clear that this Virginia Clarke was a self-possessed young lady. He liked that.

"I don't need to, and don't be hurt, in fact I've tried quite hard to not get involved in anything long term. I want to succeed in my career."

Barry shrugged. "I understand," he said, "and I'm not hurt, because so do I, even though I'm not quite sure yet what kind of doctor I want to be." And as Jack had guessed, Barry was still smarting a little from the loss of that brown-eyed radiographer nine months ago. From ahead came a scream and the sound of metal crashing against rock.

Barry instinctively let go of Virginia's hand, grabbed his jacket, and took off like a liltie. He rounded a corner to see first a school cap and then a fallen bicycle with its owner lying in a heap beside the path. Barry knelt beside the boy. "You all right?"

"I am not." His face was tear-stained. "Stupid bloody hare ran in front of me and I braked too hard. I think I've bust my leg." He lowered his head to indicate his right, dirt-stained shin. "I hit it a right dunt and heard it snap."

"Here." Barry laid his jacket over the boy for a blanket. Shock could accompany broken bones. "Where does it hurt?"

The lad put his hand down to about six inches above the ankle joint on the outside of his leg.

"I'm Doctor Laverty. I'm going to help you if you'll let me."

Virginia arrived and knelt beside Barry. She held a finger to her lips. "Don't let me intrude" seemed to be the unspoken message.

"This is Nurse Clarke. What's your name?"

207

"Ronnie Houston." He brushed away a tear.

"How old are you?

"Thirteen."

Small for his age. "I'll try not to hurt you." The skin wasn't broken over the place that hurt, so if there were a fracture, it was a simple one involving only bone, not a compound or open fracture with its attendant risk of serious infection. Neither was there a great distortion of the limb, so it was unlikely that the tibia, the larger bone in the lower leg, was broken. "Can you move your foot, Ronnie?"

"Don't want to. It hurts too much."

"All right." Sign one of a break. Loss of function.

Barry very gently laid his fingers where Ronnie said it hurt the most. Gentle pressure allowed Barry to feel a grating sensation, crepitus, and Ronnie yelled, "Holy Jesus, that hurts. Stop it."

"Sorry," Barry said.

"No. I'm sorry, Doctor. I shouldn't have sworn."

"It's all right." Two more signs. That was enough to satisfy Barry even in the absence of the other two, abnormal movement and displacement, that the fibula, the smaller of the two lower leg bones, was gone. This would need temporary splinting, transport to the children's hospital, and an X-ray. "Did you hit your head, Ronnie?"

"Nah."

That could wait for a fuller assessment because Barry could do nothing here anyway. "All right," he said. "Just be a jiff." He stood and examined the bike. The walking stick would act as one splint and, he thought as he wrestled the bicycle pump free from its clips on the bike's frame, this long rigid cylinder would suffice for the other.

"Nurse, could I borrow your scarf?"

She took it off, loosing her hair to fall to her shoulders to frame an oval face. It would serve in lieu of a bandage. But he needed three more. He unbuckled his belt. He said, "Please don't be offended, but I don't suppose you'd be wearing stockings?" Most young women since the advent of Mary Quant's miniskirt now favoured tights.

She laughed. "As a matter of fact, I am. They're more comfortable under trousers. You two look away." In moments she had handed Barry a pair of tan nylons.

With Virginia's help it took a very short time to apply a makeshift splint, with the walking stick fixed by Barry's tie and belt immobilising the knee joint above and the ankle below the break, and the pump held in place by Virginia's stockings stabilising the outside of the leg. "Right, young Houston," Barry said, "put your arms around my neck and hang on."

He did. "My leg's not so bad now, but please go easy, Doc."

"I will." Barry put his arms under the lad's good thigh, letting the foot dangle as he supported Ronnie's back with his other arm and stood. "Can you wheel the bike, Nurse? It's not too far."

Ten minutes later it was beginning to feel like it was, and when a big strapping lad, who introduced himself as Seamus O'Malley, caught up with them and offered to carry Ronnie Houston the rest of the way, Barry agreed with relief. The four of them trooped into the lobby of the castle, where Seamus made his good-byes after setting Ronnie on a sofa.

It took little time to phone the boy's parents and then Sick Kids, who agreed to arrange for an ambulance. When it arrived and the ambulance staff had re-splinted the leg, Barry collected his stick and their items of clothing and they said their good-byes.

Together they walked hand in hand back to the car park. "Barry, I want to thank you for a lovely afternoon. I know it's not the grand sweep of the summit, but just look at the view from here and how the lough glistens down there."

"It is beautiful, and so are you."

She laughed. "Coming from a shy boy like you, that is a real compliment."

Inside Barry felt warm.

Virginia was serious when she said, "And I want to tell you how impressed I am with the way you look after your patients. You're going to be a fine doctor, whatever path you choose."

He glowed.

"I'm committed to my career," she squeezed his hand, "and I know you are to yours, but I hope we can find time to see each other again. You are a lovely man."

And at that moment, true to form, the brown-eyed radiographer forgotten, Barry Laverty knew he was falling. He looked up to see birds, clearly pigeons now, flying to reach the top of the castle, and inside his heart flew with them.

11
YOUR LOCKS WERE LIKE THE RAVEN

April 21, 1969

Snip-snip-snip. Snip. Snip-snip. Silence.

"Thundering jasus, Doctor O'Reilly, for the last time would you bloody well sit still, you bollix. One more snip and you'd have lost the top of your flaming ear." Dougie George, Ballybucklebo's bellicose barber, was in good form this morning.

O'Reilly laughed.

"Mind you, them great cauliflower lugs of yours are like feckin' Dumbo's and they could use a pruning."

Dougie, who must be at least seventy, had the reputation for being the rudest man in Ballybucklebo. He'd have insulted royalty if given the chance. O'Reilly suspected it was all a carefully constructed façade that, far from driving people away, had the opposite effect of attracting customers. Those who braved Dougie's decent haircuts and brutal remarks got lots of attention in the Duck after a trim. They'd take a long pull from their pints, heave a great sigh as if they'd just had a close encounter with death, and retell Dougie's latest insult. "Honest til God, Dougie says til me, 'I was going til give you a nasty look, Constable Mulligan — but you already have one,' " or " 'You, Willy John, have a nose that would take a thorn out of a greyhound's arse.' "

Well inured to the man's antics, O'Reilly had been getting his hair cut here since 1946. Originally Kinky had had to make a fuss to remind him. Now Kitty kept him right, bless her, with remarks like this morning's: "Fingal, you look like a perambulating haystack and we're going to the MacNeills' tonight. Get your hair cut."

"How much longer are you going to be, Dougie?"

"I'm seventy years old, Doctor. I think I've finished growing, you great glipe."

Snip-snip-snip.

A bell tinkled as the door opened. A tall, middle-aged man with an erect bearing walked in and took one of four hard wooden seats.

The snipping stopped, and Dougie said, "In for the usual, Colonel Mullan?"

"Please."

"I'll be with you in a wee minute. I have

213

the razor stropped and ready."

"Thank you."

Interesting, O'Reilly thought. This must be the man Bertie Bishop had referred to as a "thran bugger." O'Reilly decided to let the newcomer make the running. He listened to the *snip-snip-snip* as what seemed like enough dark hair to stuff a mattress slipped down the sheet pinned with a clothes-peg round his neck to lie on the linoleum floor. The single swivel-chair faced a mirror with a fading 1940s advertisement for Brylcreem stuck on one side. The red-and-white-striped pole outside the shop halfway along Main Street, once the symbol of the Company of Barbers and Surgeons formed in 1540, was reflected on the other side. A glass shelf in front of the foot of the mirror carried bottles of patent hair restorer and disinfectant-filled glass cylinders, one holding combs, the other scissors. Three ivory-handled cut-throat razors lay side by side and the leather strop for honing them hung from the back of the chair. Although it was not openly advertised, Dougie was also the source of Durex condoms for those too embarrassed to ask at the local chemist's. They were not on display. Their presence was only mentioned in code. "And will sir be needing anything for the weekend?"

The only thing that had changed since 1946 was that Dougie and O'Reilly had both aged twenty-three years.

Snip-snip-snip.

O'Reilly peered in the mirror at the newcomer's reflection. This was the man who was interfering in the sporting club's efforts to start running functions. His dark brown hair, parted to the left, was clipped in a military style above deep-set blue eyes. He sported a thin, neatly trimmed moustache, but his cheeks were stubbled. The colonel's navy blazer was decorated with the crest of the Royal Ulster Rifles — a harp supporting a crown with the motto *Quis Separabit* below — his grey flannels had a razor crease, his black shoes a mirror polish.

Shuffling through ancient magazines on a low table, Colonel Mullan put aside *Practical Mechanics, Playboy,* and *The Ulster Tatler* before selecting an old *Shooting Times.*

Snip-snip-snip.

"Anyroad, Doctor O'Reilly, what do you reckon to this Bernadette Devlin, the civil rights Republican getting herself elected til Westminster last Thursday? I read she'll be making her maiden speech tomorrow, the twenty-second, in Parliament. Dead historic day. I'll bet it will be full of digs at thon Prime Minister Macmillan."

"Miss Devlin? It's a democracy, Dougie. I don't get involved with politics, don't believe in taking sides, but if the majority of her constituents want her, they can have her. That's how democracy works. Someone a bit younger in Parliament might be refreshing too."

"Aye, she'll be refreshing all right, in her miniskirts and them go-go boots the young ladies wear these days. I can just see her in question time. 'Will the right honourable member for Bromley take a long walk off a short pier?' "

Snip-snip-snip. "Will you stop bloody laughing, you eejit. This here's a delicate operation. Don't want to send you out of here with only one ear."

The colonel lowered his magazine. "Um, I say, that is, I don't mean to intrude, but are you by any chance the Doctor Fingal O'Reilly?"

His accent was clipped. Very British, and yet certain words had retained their Ulster inflections. This was typical of an Ulster youngster who'd been sent to a minor English public school and tried to acquire the tones of his upper-class fellows. The natives, ever sensitive to speech patterns, referred to it with some derision as being like buttermilk coming through the cream.

Snip-snip.

"I am."

"Oliver Mullan." He began to rise, but O'Reilly said, "I'm sorry, but under this sheet I can't shake your hand, Colonel."

"Perfectly all right." He sat, and his tone was self-deprecatory. "And actually, it's only lieutenant-colonel, but convention gives me the honorary full rank conversationally."

"I understand," O'Reilly said. He had seen his share of action in the war, had tucked it away at the very back of his mind, never mentioned it, and vaguely disapproved of ex-military men who clung to their old rank. But at least this Mullan was honest about his. "I've heard you were with the Stickies."

Snip-snip.

"Royal Ulster Rifles. That was our nickname because we stuck to things like glue. We don't exist anymore. Sad, really. Last year we were combined with other fine regiments like the Inniskilling Fusiliers to form the Royal Irish Rangers. Pity, but I didn't spend much time with the Rifles. I was on detached duty." He coughed. "It's not actually something I talk about much."

O'Reilly respected that.

Snip-snip.

Dougie said, "The Stickies? That's what the Irish Republican Army started calling

217

themselves two years ago, because at Easter they wear a lily held on by sticky tape."

"An Easter lily," O'Reilly said. "To commemorate the heroes, martyrs, who died or were executed in or after the Dublin Rising in April 1916."

Snip-snip.

"One doesn't wish to be contentious, Doctor, particularly on first acquaintance, but that's one perspective. As a loyal British subject and an ex-serviceman, I'm more inclined to regard them as rebels against duly constituted authority, and I'm very concerned that we may see that kind of nonsense starting again here in Ulster."

The snipping stopped.

Dougie said, and his tone was level, "Excuse me, Colonel, you've not been here in Ballybucklebo very long. We try very hard not til take sides. Get along with each other, like."

"Hah-hmm." Colonel Mullan held up a placatory hand. "If I've caused offence I apologise, but are you both not concerned? There was rioting in Londonderry's Bogside, NICRA against Loyalists on Saturday. Bombs exploded yesterday at the Silent Valley Reservoir. That's Belfast's main water supply, and it led to a water shortage for firemen when mobs with firebombs stormed nine post offices and the central bus station in Belfast last night."

"It is very worrisome," O'Reilly said, "but we keep hoping it'll settle down."

"That's right," Dougie said. "Nobody here in Ballybucklebo wants trouble." He held up a mirror behind O'Reilly's head. "That look all right, Doc?"

O'Reilly looked at his reflection. "Thing of beauty," he said. "Thanks, Dougie."

Dougie opened the clothes-peg and removed the sheet, showering the floor with clippings. He lifted a broom from the corner and started sweeping up.

O'Reilly swung round until he was facing the Colonel. He stood and offered his hand, which Colonel Mullan took. His grip was firm. "Welcome to Ballybucklebo, Colonel. Don't worry about having Loyalist sentiments — as long as you keep them to yourself."

"Thank you, old boy. Much appreciated. A wink's as good as a nod to a blind horse."

"Unless it's a horse Donal Donnelly has money on," Dougie said. "Anyroad. Hop up, Colonel, while I get the lather ready."

"I shall." He smiled. "Got into the habit of having my batman shave me — he'd been a barber on Civvy Street. My little extravagance. Having dinner with the marquis this evening, you see."

O'Reilly, remembering John MacNeill's remark nine days ago about appealing to the man's military spirit, said, "I'll look forward to seeing you there." He turned to Dougie and paid, adding ten percent for the tip. "Thanks, Dougie." He started to leave, but just as he opened the door, making the bell ring, Mullan spoke. "It has been a pleasure to meet you, Doctor. And thank you for the advice. I really will take it to heart."

And O'Reilly wondered why Bertie Bishop, usually a fine judge of character, had called Colonel Mullan a thran bugger. He hardly seemed bloody-minded, and despite his understandable Loyalist leanings, he had been a perfect gentleman.

Maggie MacCorkle, wilted primroses in the band of her red straw hat, was standing at the kitchen counter of Number One Main when O'Reilly returned home. She smiled her toothless smile. "Afternoon, Doctor dear."

Kinky was mixing something in an enormous yellow mixing bowl. "I'll be with you in a minute, sir, but Maggie and I do be at a very important part. We're making a very easy boiled fruitcake, and I did put the fruit,

220

sugar, and tea to soak in this large bowl last night, so, and the oven's heated to three twenty-five and the baking tins are ready."

O'Reilly noticed a tray of Kinky's freshly made hard fudge cubes and helped himself to a handful, making sure Kinky did not notice. He popped one in his mouth and the rest in his trousers pocket. He'd take a chance they'd not become crumbly until he got to his room and emptied them out to be enjoyed at his leisure.

"Now Maggie, I want you to stir the egg and marmalade into the fruit mixture. Give it a really good stir, now."

"Right, Kinky." Maggie, whistling the Rolling Stones's "Honky Tonk Women," attacked the batter so enthusiastically O'Reilly reckoned she should be on a building site mixing cement. The bowl rocked and shimmied.

Kinky said, "Carefully now, Maggie, or you'll be having it on the floor, so. Maggie knows all about the surprise party for the Donnellys next month, sir. She's going to help with the catering, and when I explained to her at the Women's Institute meeting last week that my kind of plum cake is best if it's made a little in advance, she asked if I would show her how it's done."

"Sometimes, Doctor dear," Maggie said,

"I get a half-notion that dear oul' Sonny would like a change from my cake, so I asked Kinky til show me how til make one of hers."

"An excellent idea," O'Reilly said, trying not to sound too enthusiastic. "I'm sure Sonny loves your plum cake, but we could all do with a change from time to time, Maggie."

Kinky gave O'Reilly a penetrating stare and made a gesture that suggested his help was no longer needed. "Now Maggie," Kinky said, "it's time to stir in the two kinds of flour and the baking powder." She pointed to the counter. "The baking tins are ready."

"I think," O'Reilly said, "you two are going to find yourselves running a TV cookery show soon, but speaking of running, Kitty doesn't like to be kept waiting, and you know we are going to Ballybucklebo House tonight for a formal dinner."

"I do, sir. Alice Moloney's let out the waist of your dinner suit — again — and it and your cummerbund are ironed and ready on your bed. Your patent leather shoes are as shiny as a calm sea in the setting summer sun."

"Ah, well, thank you, Kinky. I'd better be trotting along."

"You do that, sir." Kinky cocked her head to one side and said, "But next time say please before you pinch my fudge that I know is in your pocket, so."

A suitably chastened Fingal Flahertie O'Reilly slunk off, but enjoying the lumps of fudge was going to be worth it.

12
TAKING OUT HIS FALSE TEETH

August 29, 1963

Barry yawned. He had never felt so tired in his life, and his whole head was throbbing.

"It's not urgent," said Bernie to the student nurse who'd appeared at the doorway. "Pop him in a wheelchair and take him to room C." Being popped into a wheelchair and taken to room C sounded pretty good, Barry thought, if they'd let him sleep. He and Norma were having a rest and a cup of tea in Bernie's office during a late-afternoon lull in the production line of mostly minor cases. "Get him teed up, and I'll send a doctor over in a minute or two." She mouthed the words, "Finish your tea." Sister O'Byrne was protective of her young doctors.

Barry nodded at her and took a mouthful. It tasted like tepid dishwater.

"I don't think you heard the Reverend Martin Luther King Jr. on the telly last night, Barry."

Barry sighed. "I was here, Norma. Missed the news." It wasn't all he was missing. Decent meals, sleep, fresh air, Virginia Clarke.

"Pretty powerful stuff. He's a riveting speaker. He told two hundred and fifty thousand people in Washington D.C. 'I have a dream,' and that the struggle for one man, one vote would go on 'until justice rolls down like water, and righteousness like a mighty stream.' "

"Huh," said Barry, "we could use him here. Ulster people have been protesting about voting inequality like Doctor King's lot are doing." He finished his tea. "But I don't think two housemen like us are going to solve that problem this afternoon." He yawned, considered letting Norma see the case, but damn it, he only had a bit of a headache really. "Sit you there. I'll go." He nodded in Bernie's direction. "Bernie's giving me 'the look.' " The senior sister had a grin on her face she reserved for out-of-the-ordinary cases. And after four weeks of practically nothing but impersonal medical trivia, Barry thought something different might be interesting. Perhaps it would lift his feeling of malaise.

Norma chuckled. "Thanks," she said. "You are a real gent, Barry Laverty."

He stood up and felt the small world of Bernie's office whirl around him. What the hell was wrong with him? He knew being overly tired could cause dizziness, but this was only the fourth week of his houseman training. He had to be tougher than this. He'd be damned if he was going to give in to it. He sat again and took some slow breaths before rising.

Bernie was frowning. "You all right, Barry?"

"Bit tired is all."

"I see." She said something to him about the patient, but the words seemed to be coming from the end of a long tunnel. Had she said something about a tooth? "A what, Bernie?"

"Come on," she said. "I'll show you, because I want to see this myself."

He shrugged at Norma. It must be interesting if Sister O'Byrne, with all her years of experience, wanted to take a look-see. Barry followed Bernie.

"I don't suppose you'll mind, Barry, that Nurse Clarke will be coming from the suture room to help you?"

Nurse-doctor fraternisation was discouraged by senior nursing, but it was rumoured that Sister Barra O'Byrne, a spinster herself, was of an understanding nature and willing to turn a blind eye. She also seemed to know what her student nurses were thinking before they did themselves, and was as protective of medical students and junior doctors as a she-wolf of her cubs.

"No, Sister. I will not mind." Although Barry wasn't sure he felt strong enough to hide his feelings right now. He and Virginia had seen Gregory Peck in *To Kill a Mockingbird* last week at the Hippodrome, and in the darkness of the theatre, away from the hospital, it had hit him that he was in love. In love with Virginia Clarke. He had not dared to tell her then, and another opportunity had not presented itself. Today, with the headache and the exhaustion, he felt as weak as a newborn.

"You take care of my nurse, young man. Treat her well, or I'll —"

"Yes, Sister," he interrupted, blushing, yet there was no feeling of warmth in his cheeks, and he shivered.

They crossed the waiting hall where, praise the Lord, all the benches were empty. Only a solitary floor cleaner pushed his wet mop along, and the receptionist at her desk near the front door had her head buried in a dog-eared copy of *Woman's Own*.

"Sorry, Bernie," Barry said. He cleared his throat and coughed. It felt raw. "I missed what you said about the patient. Something to do with a tooth? Isn't that why we have a dental houseman? I don't know anything about teeth." He'd tried not to let his irritation show, but he knew it had.

Bernie stopped in her tracks. "Are you sure you're all right, Barry? It's not like you to be tetchy."

"Sorry, Bernie. Don't worry. I'm just not at myself today." And while he knew their complaints were of vital importance to the patients, the steady flow of anonymous medical trivia was starting to bore him. He was already looking forward to his next rotation on paired medical wards, handling more complicated cases and getting to know them as people. But that was still two months away. "Please tell me about this case."

"Are you sure you're not coming down with something?"

Barry shook his head. "Look, Bernie, I'm fine. Sometimes I get tired, that's all." From the way she pursed her lips Barry wasn't sure she believed him, but he wasn't going to let this tiredness get to him, and while Bernie might think the case unusual, he didn't think much could surprise him after almost a month on casualty. Most had been unremarkable. One or two had been different. Memorable. Like the unfortunate with tertiary syphilis, also known as general paralysis of the insane, who believed, to quote the patient, that he was "John the feckin' Baptist," and who was now "preparing the way of the Lord" in Purdysburn mental hospital. The most bizarre so far had been the man who had got his penis stuck in the nozzle of the hose of a cylindrical vacuum cleaner, and to get to the Royal had travelled by bus, cylinder under arm, hose disappearing inside his raincoat. As the surgical registrar later told Barry, even after a general anaesthetic, it had looked like the unlikely couple were going to be united " 'til death did them part."

"Are you sure?"

Barry nodded.

Bernie shook her head, glanced at him, but preceded him into the room where the student nurse and Virginia, who kept her green eyes above her surgical mask off Barry's, had got a tousled-haired, muddy-faced young man lying on an examining couch under a blanket.

The nurse handed Barry the eight-by-four: *John Stewart. 20. Student. Date first seen August 29. Queen's Elms* — so he was a student living in the men's halls of residence — *Protestant.* "Hello, John," Barry said, and forced a smile. "I'm Doctor Laverty. You have a toothache, I believe."

"Not exactly, Doctor." John Stewart sat up and threw his blanket back.

The patient's face wasn't the only part of him daubed with mud. His studded boots, white shorts, and royal blue jersey with white collar were well and truly splattered. "Playing rugby for Queen's?" Barry asked, recognising the uniform.

"Pre-season warm-up game."

Barry had noticed the number nine on the back of the man's jersey. "Scrum-half?"

John Stewart nodded.

Scrum-half was a position not without risk. "Got a smack in the mouth? Hurt a tooth?"

"No, Doctor. I got tackled. Someone fell on my tackler. He must have had his mouth open." He pointed to his right calf.

Barry bent — and pulled back. Good Lord, there in all its muddy, pink, wire-looped glory, was a single false white incisor on a dental plate — embedded in the man's flesh. "I see what you mean, Sister." Barry looked at his patient. "I'm sure that hurts." Bernie, undoubtedly feeling as much sympathy for the man as Barry was, pursed her lips, probably in an attempt to hide a smile.

"I've had worse," John Stewart said.

"Truly I have." He grinned. "I feel like a fisherman, and if anyone asked, 'Did you get a bite today?' I could say yes."

Bernie and the nurses chuckled.

Barry managed a smile. This was hardly brain surgery, but it was an unusual case to add to his list of oddities. "I'm sure we can fix this," he said.

"And I'm sure I can thole it. You carry on, Doc." John lay back.

"Right," said Bernie, her curiosity obviously satisfied. "Come on, Nurse. We'll leave Doctor Laverty and Nurse Clarke to carry on." There was the merest suggestion of double entendre in her tones.

If there was, Barry couldn't be bothered to acknowledge it. His head was pounding, he still felt weak, and he had a job to do. With the initial surprise at the presence of a tooth in a man's leg over, removing it would be no different from taking out any penetrating foreign body.

"Let's get on with it, please, Nurse Clarke," Barry said.

"Yes, Doctor." Her eyes met his.

He thought he was going to drown in their green, and perhaps because he was under the weather he was resentful that the pressures of their work schedules meant he'd not been able to see more of her. He

231

straightened his shoulders and took a deep breath. As soon as he finished here he was going to the pharmacy to get something for his throat and headache.

He scrubbed at a wall sink and put on sterile gloves.

It would have been routine if, like many harried juniors, Barry had simply applied himself in silence to the technicalities of his work, but he made the effort to talk to the patient. "So, John? What are you studying?" Barry asked as he returned and took a syringe of local anaesthetic from Virginia.

"Chemistry. I'm going into second year."

"We had to take that in first year. Prof. Henbest taught us organic. Now hang on. This is going to sting." Barry rapidly froze the area around the tooth. "It'll take a minute or two for that to work."

"That's all right, Doc. You asked about Prof. Henbest. He's still there, and the reader in inorganic is a Lady Myrna, sister of the Marquis of Ballybucklebo. Great teacher, and her research is world class."

"We didn't have her, but all of us from North Down know of his lordship." Barry used the back of his forearm to wipe sweat from his forehead. He shuddered. Shook his head. He wasn't just tired. He was sick, and the sooner he finished this the better.

He wondered if he should ask Norma to come and take over, but he had always hated leaving a job half finished.

"You all right, Doc?" John Stewart asked, concern in his voice.

"Just a bit tired, John." Barry handed the plate to John Stewart. "Here, the owner might like this back."

"Thank you."

"Just needs a stitch or two." Barry tried to start suturing, but the wound swam before his eyes. "Oh Lord," he said, then shook his head and waited for his vision to clear.

"Is something wrong, Doctor Laverty?" Virginia asked.

"No," he said. He took another deep breath and let it out slowly, feeling the cloth of the surgical mask grow warm against his face. "No. I'm fine." He was not fine, and he was damned lucky he hadn't passed out. Right. He loaded the needle of the pre-swaged suture into a needle driver, used forceps to pick up one edge of the wound and, blinking sweat away, passed the needle through. It took concentration to get it through the opposite side and the knot tied. "Cut," he said, and Virginia snipped the stitch so the ends were short.

Come on, Barry, he told himself. One more. He had to struggle but it was soon in, knotted, and trimmed.

Barry stepped back as Virginia applied an adhesive dressing.

"You need a tetanus toxoid jag. Nurse Clarke will do the honours, John. Nurses give injections much better than . . ." The room was spinning around him. "I," he managed, "I . . ." before his knees buckled.

Barry felt rather than heard himself mumbling, but from his depths could not make out what he was saying. He shook his head to clear it and regretted it at once. His head felt as if a malicious gnome were pounding it with a hammer. He tried to sit up to get his bearings, but his arms didn't seem to want to lift him. The weight of the bedclothes was too much. He gave up, lay back, shivered, and wondered where the hell he was. Judging by the smell of disinfectant, he was in a hospital bed. But where? He remembered being with a patient and Virginia Clarke in room C. Something to do with a tooth, but then what had happened? He took a couple of deep breaths. Told himself not to panic. There had to be a rational explanation. One thing was certain. He was sick, and he resented that deeply. Getting ill wasn't supposed to happen to doctors. And what was he sick with? He knew he should try to make a diagnosis, but he couldn't concentrate. It was simply too much work to make the mental effort. "Damn it. Where am I? What's going on?" Dear God, but that hurt his throat.

A staff nurse, gowned and masked, stood up from where she sat beside his bed. "Nice to have you back, Barry."

He knew that gentle voice, but even with his eyes screwed up he could not recognise her features.

"It's me, Jan Peters. Remember? Rusky's daughter?"

"Oh. Right." Barry did remember her. Two weeks ago he'd been playing draughts with her dad just before the man had been discharged. It was pure reflex when he asked, "How is he?"

"Coming on well, but you're not. You'd just finished treating a patient when you passed out in casualty. You've a fever. This is the staff room on ward 22 where we look after resident doctors and nurses who are taken ill."

"Oh. What's, what's, uh, wrong with me?"

He heard a trace of concern when she said, "We're not entirely sure," and with a towel wiped sweat from his brow. "But don't worry. You'll be fine. Honestly."

Don't worry? Barry was wide awake

enough now to admit to himself that he should have reported in sick earlier today. He could have passed out in the middle of treating someone, rather than at the end. He may have been passing on whatever bug was giving him a temperature, which was? He screwed up his eyes. Opened them. All right. He made the effort to concentrate. Headache. Fever. Shivering. Weakness. Sore throat. Fainting. All on top of being dog-tired. At a pinch he'd call it flu, but it could be — Damned if he could remember, and he was just too tired to try. He asked, "Has anybody come up with a diagnosis?"

Jan shook her head. "Not yet." She raised his head with one arm and fluffed his pillow with her other hand before lowering his head back into its softness. "Doctor Swanson, the houseman, has had a look at you. He's calling it pyrexia of unknown origin."

Barry grunted. PUO? He'd made that diagnosis often enough himself. It was doctor talk for "the patient has a fever, but we don't know what the hell is going on."

"You know we treat doctors and nurses with a bit of extra care."

It was true.

"Doctor Swanson thinks it's flu, except it's August and we don't see too much flu this time of year. He wants to be on the safe side, so he's taken some blood samples and a throat swab. We'll have the results in the morning."

"Fair enough." Probably was flu. He'd be discharged as soon as the results were in. Get back to his own bed. Lots of fluids. Rest and a few days to shake it. Nothing to worry about. "Thanks, Jan." Barry sank more deeply into his pillow. "Thank you." And thought he heard her say, "What you need is sleep, and lots of TLC, and you'll get that from me, I promise."

Tender loving care. She was a lovely girl, was Jan Peters. Lovely. Barry's last thoughts as he drifted off were that he hoped some-one had let Virginia know how he was, and that he must be quite ill if he couldn't be bothered to recall what ailments, other than infections, could give someone the symp-toms that afflicted him.

13
MORE BUSINESS AFTER DINNER

April 21, 1969

"Please come in, Commander and Mrs. O'Reilly." Thompson, Lord John MacNeill's butler/valet, stood in the doorway at the top of a low flight of broad sandstone steps leading to the front door of Ballybucklebo House. Thompson, once gunnery chief petty officer aboard HMS *Warspite* and a shipmate of O'Reilly's, was a true gentlemen's gentleman, insisting on using Fingal's old rank while he and John, lately lieutenant-colonel in the Irish Guards, had dropped theirs years ago when they'd left the forces. "Would you like me to take your stole, Mrs. O'Reilly?"

"Thank you, Thompson," she said as he folded it over his left arm.

O'Reilly admired the way she filled her simple black knee-length long-sleeved evening dress over sheer black hose and patent leather heels. Her dark hair with its silver tips was neatly coiffed, avoiding the multi-layered extravagances favoured by younger women these days.

"His lordship, Lady Myrna, and Colonel Mullan are in the study," said Thompson. "If you'll follow me?"

O'Reilly was looking forward to seeing how the marquis was going to try to dissuade Colonel Mullan from interfering with the sporting club's plans to hold functions. "You look very smart, dear, in your dinner suit," she said to O'Reilly as he offered his arm. "I think it's so civilized to dress for dinner once in a while."

At least, O'Reilly thought, John had been informal enough to stipulate "black tie without decorations." Fingal's medals only came out on Remembrance Day. "And you, my love, look stunning." And by God she did. He patted her bottom and she stifled a giggle.

The parquet floor rang under her heels as the three walked beneath the high ceiling of the oak-panelled hall adorned with portraits of the incumbent Marquis of Ballybucklebo's predecessors, stern-looking gentlemen all, some alone, others surrounded by their families. O'Reilly stopped to admire a more recent watercolour, *Dying Storm,* by the Grey Abbey artist Bob Milliken. "Not often you see mallard and widgeon flying together, but it does happen in heavy weather down on Strangford Lough."

"I like the seascape behind the birds," Kitty said. "It can be tricky to render in watercolours."

"His lordship," said Thompson, "greatly admires Mister Milliken's work. That was a birthday present from Lady Myrna." He took two more paces, opened a door to his left, stood aside to let O'Reilly and Kitty enter, and announced, "My lord, Commander and Mrs. O'Reilly," then, as a good butler should, closed the door behind them and vanished.

The spacious room with its three walls of floor-to-ceiling bookshelves smelled of old books, leather, and the peat that burned in a huge fireplace. Lord John MacNeill stood in front of it, glass in hand and ramrod straight, his iron-grey hair neatly trimmed. He may have enjoyed Bob Milliken's watercolours, but behind him, hanging on the wall above the mantel, was a family portrait done in oils of a younger John, his late wife, Laura, and John's only son, his heir and successor, Sean. The family's old red setter Oisin, who had been succeeded by Finn MacCool, lay in the foreground. O'Reilly had always found the picture striking, but tonight it had given him half an idea about another matter that had been puzzling him. He'd think on it later, because now the formalities must be observed.

The marquis beamed. "Fingal. Kitty, how lovely to see you both." The sombreness of his barathea dinner suit was relieved by an immaculately starched white shirt, maroon bow tie, and maroon cummerbund. He shook Fingal's hand.

Lady Myrna Ferguson, the marquis's sister, holding a sherry, sat on a Chippendale-style mahogany love seat probably made in Dublin, and said, "Lovely to see you both."

Kitty inclined her head.

Mullan had already risen as befitted a gentleman when a lady entered. He set his glass on a nearby wine table.

"And Colonel Oliver Mullan, late of the Royal Ulster Rifles. Oliver —"

Interesting, O'Reilly thought. Typical of John MacNeill to be on Christian name terms with the man already.

"I believe you have met Doctor Fingal O'Reilly, but may I present Mrs. Kitty O'Reilly?"

Kitty offered her hand, which Mullan took and in the continental manner raised to within an inch of his lips. "Enchanted," he

241

said, a smile lifting his pencil moustache as he spoke, but somehow, O'Reilly thought, the smile avoided the man's deep-set blue eyes.

"How do you do, Colonel?" Kitty said as he released her hand. "And please, it's Kitty, and do sit down."

"Oliver," he said. "Thank you." He sat on the love seat beside Myrna and picked up his drink.

O'Reilly hid a smile. In Alexandria during the war they used to laugh at the formal politeness of the Arab nobility, but it appeared that civility was alive and well in this Ulster drawing room. Yet he also knew John MacNeill was the courteous master of setting folks at their ease.

"The usual, Fingal, Kitty?" John MacNeill had already turned to a sideboard laden with decanters and glasses. "And do please have seats."

"Yes, please," Kitty said, taking an armchair beside Myrna, who, looking a little severe in a silk mustard-coloured trouser suit, immediately admired Kitty's outfit before John MacNeill gave her a gin and tonic.

O'Reilly nodded and sat himself down on the upholstered seat of a simple, rectangular-backed chair. "Thank you,

John," he said, accepting a neat Jameson in a Waterford whiskey glass. *"Sláinte,"* said John, raising his glass.

The company returned the toast.

"So, Oliver," the marquis said, "you were in the middle of telling us how you're enjoying your new home here among us in Bally-bucklebo?"

"Very much," Oliver said. "I'm settling in well. As a bachelor I've always enjoyed the simplicity of rural life. The peace and quiet." His smile was self-deprecating. "When I've had the chance."

O'Reilly waited to see if anyone was going to pursue that hint about details of the man's as yet undiscovered background or whether the reference to peace and quiet might give John the cue to enquire about Mullan's noise complaint.

"It is pleasant in the country," Myrna said, "especially after the bustle of Belfast. I find riding a great relaxation. Do you ride, Oliver?"

"I'm afraid not," he said.

"Pity," she said.

O'Reilly knew that Lady Myrna regarded anyone who did not ride, particularly to hounds, as odd. Many of the landed gentry did. She'd even tried to interest O'Reilly's older brother, Lars, during their brief affair some years ago.

"Do you get up to town often, Oliver?" John asked.

"Not if I can avoid it," Mullan said.

O'Reilly felt he should contribute to the conversation. "I agree," he said, "too many crowds and smells. Much prefer the country." He was impressed by how John and Myrna were keeping on neutral ground, neither discussing the topic that had led to his invitation here in the first place, nor prying into the newcomer's background. Nor had anyone — yet — alluded to the recent upsurge in sectarian violence that had been the prime topic of conversation for several days. Perhaps it was time, but obliquely, to test the waters a bit. O'Reilly said, "Are you originally from Ulster, Oliver?" He sat back and sipped his Irish. "A lot of the Rifles were."

"I am," said Oliver, "and proud of it. My folks were from Cookstown. My family was in linen."

O'Reilly saw a little moue cross Myrna's brow. He'd bet his boots she was thinking: Linen. The family was in trade. No wonder the man doesn't ride.

John was nodding. The town in County Tyrone was the largest linen centre west of the River Bann, and considerable fortunes had been made in the past century.

"They educated me locally until I was thirteen, then off to Dulwich in London."

"A very fine school, I believe," Kitty said.

That, O'Reilly thought, would certainly account for the man's upper-class accent, and also confirmed that the family had been moneyed. Fees were high at public schools of that calibre.

"Thank you. I was in Drake House."

O'Reilly sat back when he saw the slightest suggestion of a frown flit across John MacNeill's face. Something wasn't right.

"And if I'm not prying, Oliver," Myrna said, "I know you were a military man." She smiled at her brother. "John was Irish Guards and Fingal the Royal Navy. So, you were with the Royal Ulster Rifles."

"That's right. First battalion."

Myrna said, "John told me the first served in India before the war. We should introduce you to Miss Alice Moloney. She grew up there during the Raj. You and she will have a lot in common."

O'Reilly wondered what Doctor Ronald Fitzpatrick would think about that. Might be good for him to have a potential rival for Alice's attention.

"I should enjoy that very much," Oliver said. "I do want to fit in here."

"I'm sure you will," Kitty said.

Not if you keep interfering with the sporting club, O'Reilly thought.

John, now clearly wanting to pursue Oliver's military background, said, "Your battalion was converted to glider-borne light infantry during the war, I believe. Horsa gliders. Landed in Normandy on the afternoon of D-Day, 1944. Operation Mallard."

Nice segue, O'Reilly thought. John knows his British Army history, and that simple observation on the surface doesn't seem like a probe, but I'll be interested to see how the Colonel responds.

" 'Fraid I missed that party. Detached duties, don'tcha know? Bit hush-hush still. Official Secrets Act?"

That had been twenty-five years ago, O'Reilly thought. The act would be in effect — just — but would expire by next year in its application to events of the early '40s.

"Quite," John said, "we'll say no more." He sipped his drink. "Except to say that I once attended when your regimental pipes and drums were on parade. I'll never forget them, saffron kilts, a most stirring march past. They were playing 'The South Down Militia,' as I recall. I still remember a line or two of the lyrics . . .

From Greenland's icy mountains to
   India's coral strand
The South Down Militia is the terror of the
   land."

"Will you listen to that lovely tenor?" said Myrna, smiling at her brother.

"That's a tune I'll not forget in a hurry," Oliver said. "And not one you'd soon be hearing on the Falls Road."

O'Reilly was probably the only one to notice that puzzled frown reappear on John's face, a tightening of his shoulders. "Ah, quite. But," John said, "enough old soldiers' memories." He sighed. Smiled. "Once in a while though I do get a bit sentimental about my old regiment. My son Sean's just got his majority with them. Funny thing, your Rifles and my Guards have the same regimental motto, *Quis Separabit?*"

"True, 'Who shall separate us?' "

O'Reilly thought he saw the tenseness leave John.

"And my congratulations to your son," Oliver said. "I believe, sir, the MacNeills have a distinguished history of serving their monarchs, but to be honest I've not gone to any regimental reunion dinners or kept up since I retired." He sipped his drink. "I have, however, kept up with the news. I'm worried about the recent outbreaks of violence."

Oh-oh, O'Reilly thought. Was the man not going to heed this morning's advice to keep his Loyalist leanings to himself?

"It is troubling," John said. "I heard on the six o'clock news tonight that, after this recent rash of bombings of water and power installations, British troops on garrison duty here at Palace Barracks are going to be used to guard such places from now on." He set his empty glass on the sideboard. "And you are right to be concerned, Oliver. We all are, and there are no taboo subjects in this house, but I think we should probably drink up now and go in to dinner."

"Quite," Oliver said, finishing his drink. He smiled. "And I agree, sir. No more politics tonight."

The door opened. Thompson coughed as if sensing the tension in the room. "My lord, ladies, gentlemen, Cook has asked me to tell you that dinner will be served in ten minutes."

"Thank you, Thompson," John said as the butler withdrew. "No need to rush your drinks, everybody, but we'd better be on time. Cook will not be pleased if we let her mock turtle soup go cold."

Kitty smiled. "Your cook and Mrs. Auchinleck — she was Fingal's full-time housekeeper for years and still works part time with us," she explained to Oliver, "that pair are friends and sisters under the skin. Hell hath no fury like a good cook who thinks her efforts are not appreciated."

As they all laughed, Oliver Mullan muttered something about "fellow countrymen" that O'Reilly couldn't hear. The man may have said no more about politics, but he appeared to be having the last word.

And so it had been throughout the meal. Conversation had ranged widely on non-sensitive subjects. It seemed Oliver had a particular interest in live theatre in London, something he shared with Myrna. They both had seen Agatha Christie's *The Mousetrap,* which had been running since 1952. Neither thought much of *Hair,* which had opened at the Shaftesbury Theatre last September. Oliver's interest went back a long way. As a pupil at Dulwich, he'd become very fond of the comedies of the Whitehall Theatre.

O'Reilly had given up wondering when the topic of the noise bylaw was going to be broached. He had known John MacNeill for twenty-three years and had watched him play the long game often enough. O'Reilly had settled back and had, as always, enjoyed the delights of the marquis's table.

Now Cook and Thompson had been relieved of their responsibilities and had retired. O'Reilly was happy to have returned to the study for postprandial coffees and liqueurs. He was content with another Jameson, but had made a note of Oliver's preference for a 1941 Taylor's port. The man did have expensive tastes.

And the excellent wines John had provided had had their expected effect as social lubricants. Oliver Mullan had revealed himself to be an accomplished raconteur. He was now saying, "I remember one visit from an E.N.S.A. troupe."

"Excuse me, Oliver," Kitty said, "E.N.S.A.?"

"Sorry. Entertainments National Service Association. It was an organisation set up in 1939 to provide entertainment for the troops. All kinds of performers would appear. Folks like Beatrice Lillie, Sir Harry Lauder, Sybil Thorndike, Al Bowlly."

"And much appreciated," John said. "Let us, all ranks, get together, relax, and enjoy an evening's fun. Bring the troops together. Foster regimental spirit, wouldn't you say, Oliver?"

Aha, O'Reilly thought. Here we go. Enjoy

an evening's fun together. Bring the troops together. I see where this is leading, but John said, "Sorry. Didn't mean to interrupt. Please carry on."

Oliver warmed to his work. "We had a particularly overbearing sergeant major and he didn't mean to be amusing but — I was there when he addressed the enlisted men." Oliver's Oxbridge tones vanished, and he sounded like a man from Belfast's slums. "Right, youse lot. Right. Pay attention. Pay attention. The night youse is very lucky. A learnèd man is coming from Oxford University and he's going for til give youse a talk about Kipling. Kipling."

O'Reilly admired the way Oliver timed his pause to perfection before saying, "And when he finishes. When he finishes youse will all applaud like billy-oh" — another pause — "even though I know not one of youse ignorant Bs has the faintest idea, not the foggiest notion, of how til kipple."

Myrna clapped her hand over her mouth, pulled it away. "How to kipple." Her laughter rang to the rafters. Tears appeared at the corners of her eyes. "Oh my." She subsided into a series of stifled throaty chuckles.

Kitty too, was in stitches. "Oliver," she said, "you missed your calling. That's priceless."

He lowered his head in acknowledgement.

O'Reilly too chuckled, and wondered how this seemingly cultured, well-educated, socially charming man could be the one who had lodged the sound bylaw complaint.

John MacNeill smiled as he spoke. "Oliver," he said, "it has been a pleasure having you come to dinner, and I know I can speak for Myrna when I say I hope we will be seeing more of you in the future."

"Thank you, both," Oliver said. "It has been a wonderful evening, and a delight to meet you too, Kitty."

"Thank you, sir," Kitty said.

"There is one thing," John said, "and I hope you won't take it amiss, but . . . ."

Here we go, O'Reilly thought.

"Fingal and I are much involved in the Ballybucklebo Bonnaughts Sporting Club. You alluded earlier to the recent outbreak of sectarian tension. We don't have any of that in Ballybucklebo, and we would like the club to start holding nonsectarian functions on Saturday nights." He smiled. "I said E.N.S.A. brought the troops together. We'd like to think we could achieve something similar. Show the rest of Ulster that the communities can get along together."

Oliver Mullan was no longer smiling. His voice was level when he said, "I don't quite see what this has to do with me."

"Come on, old chap," John said, "surely you understand that your noise complaint to the county council could completely scupper our efforts."

"I see." Oliver rose. Finished his port standing with a quick toss of the glass's contents. "It has been, up to this moment, one of the most pleasant evenings of my life, but I came to Ballybucklebo for peace and quiet. I am working on a book about my wartime experiences, which can be released once the Official Secrets Act no longer applies. I have a tight writing schedule. Every weekday, one o'clock to four then six o'clock to ten. I do not need noisy neighbours. If tonight was intended to make me withdraw my complaint" — he shrugged — "I'm afraid I must disappoint you." He bowed to Myrna and Kitty. "Ladies. My lord. Doctor O'Reilly, it has been a pleasure, but now if you'll excuse me?"

John MacNeill rose. "Of course. Perhaps it was insensitive of me. Let me get you another port."

"Thank you. No." There was ice in the words.

John took a deep breath. "In that case, please let me show you out." He held out a hand to indicate the door.

"Thank you," Mullan said, and left ahead of the marquis.

No one spoke.

Oops, O'Reilly thought, but that wasn't helpful. Looks like the club's out of luck. Clearly the man's not going to withdraw his complaint voluntarily. Might there be some other way to exert pressure? O'Reilly would be damned if he could see it, and the next council meeting was in mid-May.

John reappeared. "Ha-hm, awfully sorry about that. Not very polite of me, I suppose. I didn't mean to upset the fellow."

"It can't be helped, John," Myrna said. "You were, as always, the perfect host. You were entirely within your right as president of the club to try to protect its interests." Her smile was wry. "And present company excepted, Kitty and Fingal, I'm usually right not being too keen on people who don't ride."

O'Reilly felt a pang. His brother, Lars, with whom Myrna had had a real falling-out about his preference for motorcars, had eventually fallen into that category, but O'Reilly smiled. Myrna's little joke, as he was sure she had intended, had lowered the level of tension in the study. It only rose a little bit when John said with a thoughtful look on his face, "Today's the twenty-first.

How is Bertie's subcommittee coming on, Fingal?"

"Final report is ready to present to the membership."

"Good. Council meet on?"

"May 19."

John nodded, spent a moment in thought, then said, "There's no point calling a meeting before that in case Mullan's request is granted, and clearly an appeal to the man's better nature has no chance of success, but while I don't share my sister's views on people who don't ride, there is something not entirely right about our Colonel Mullan."

O'Reilly frowned. "What isn't, John?"

"I'm going to be in London in the next couple of weeks. I want to have a word with a friend of mine in the Ministry of Defence. You see, my old school used to play rugby against Dulwich." He smiled. "Last time I played against them, we won six to three, by the way." The marquis laughed. "Like most public schools, the boys are assigned to a house, a social group looked after by a house master. I can't remember all their names, but at Dulwich they were all named for famous Englishmen. Mullan said he was in Drake House. Funny, that. If his family were in Cookstown, he'd have to have been a boarder. Drake and Raleigh were the only houses for day boys. Not boarders. See what I mean?"

O'Reilly nodded. "Unless he'd been living with family or family friends in London, John. He could have been a day boy then. That would have saved a fair bit of money."

"That is true, Fingal. I hadn't thought of that, but it's not all though," John said. "He knew what the Rifles' regimental motto meant, but their march-past is the Ulster Rifles March 'Off, Off, Said the Stranger.' I tricked him with 'The South Down Militia,' you see. It's their slow march. The rawest recruit would know that."

O'Reilly took a thoughtful sip of his Jameson's. "I'm beginning to think, and to quote *Hamlet* act one, John, you believe 'something is rotten in the state of Denmark'?"

"I do. And I intend to find out exactly what."

"And if you can find something and we can get him to withdraw, we can call the extraordinary meeting right away and make a start on running our events." O'Reilly raised his glass. "I drink to the hopes of your forthcoming quest, John MacNeill. I really do."

14
FEVER AND THE FRET

August 30, 1963

"Awake now, are we, Sleeping Beauty? What some people will do to get a couple of days off. I've been sitting here for a good five minutes. If you weren't going to wake up soon, I'd've been off."

Barry had woken moments ago, eyes unfocussed. His throat was not as raw, his headache was controlled by aspirin, but he was weak and only vaguely aware of someone, a man in mask and gown, sitting by his bedside. He screwed up his eyes but still couldn't make out the man's features. "Who — who is it?"

"Me, you goat. Mills. I had to know if you were dead or alive. Nurse Peters is here too."

"Jack." Barry finally recognised the voice and realised that his best friend, as was typical of an Ulsterman, was hiding his concern behind a mask of facetiousness. He noticed Jan at the far side of the room. "Thanks a million." Barry's reply had no hint of thanks in the inflection, but he was still pleased his pal had come to see him. "What time is it?" He vaguely remembered drifting off yesterday evening, being woken once or twice to have his pulse and temperature taken and being given his tablets and a warm salt-and-water gargle, but he had no idea how long he'd been asleep.

"Ten to noon. Today's Friday."

Barry struggled to sit up and Jan immediately helped him, placing two pillows behind his back, and lowering him onto them. "Thanks, Jan," he said. "Nearly twelve o'clock? I've been out for —" he blinked, found his concentration was better than it had been, and did the arithmetic "— about eighteen hours."

"And you needed your sleep, Barry," Jan said. "How are you feeling today?"

He managed a small smile. "A bit better. Thanks."

"And your temperature was down this morning."

"Good," he said, but he was aware of an urgent sensation. "But I really need to —" The pressure swelled in his lower belly.

"One or two?" Jan asked.

"One," he said, and if his cheeks weren't already flushed, he knew he would have blushed.

"Here," she said, opening his bedside locker and handing him a wide-necked glass bottle that was flat on its lower side and had its neck cocked up at a shallow angle.

"Thanks." Barry took the bottle, slid it under the bedclothes, fished himself out from under his light blue hospital night-gown, and into the bottle's neck. He strained, felt as if his bladder was going to burst — and nothing happened. Bloody hell. He couldn't pee because he was ashamed to in front of Jan. He had what as students they had laughingly referred to as a "bashful bladder." There was nothing funny about it.

She must have sensed his embarrassment. "I'll leave you for a while," she said, washed her hands, hung her gown inside the room, and left.

Dear God, the relief. The pressure subsided, and Barry felt the bottle grow warm between his thighs. He threw back the bedclothes, and taking care not to spill, pulled it out. "Jack, would you?"

"I will." Jack took it. "Got a load off your mind?"

Trust Jack to make light of this too. He went to the door. "Nurse," he called, handed the bottle over to one, and returned. "It's off to the sluice," he said. "Better an empty house than a bad tenant."

Barry had to agree, but it struck him how helpless sick people were. How — the best word he could think of was "degrading" — how degrading it was to rely on others to help you perform basic bodily functions. Even in his muddled state, he realised he was experiencing medicine from the other end of the stethoscope. And he didn't much like it.

The door opened, and Jan came in, accompanied by a young man. They both put on gowns.

Jan returned a clean bottle to Barry's locker. Rearranged his blankets. "This is Christopher Finn. He's one of our clinical clerks," she said.

That was what medical students attached to nonsurgical wards were called. On surgical units they were referred to as surgical dressers, because in the old days they were responsible for changing dressings.

"Doctor Laverty," said the young man, "I'm sorry to disturb you. Doctor Swanson did some blood tests yesterday, but he wanted some more as soon as you were awake."

Bloody hell, Barry thought. "That's all right." It wasn't young Finn's fault. He was only doing as he'd been told. Barry held out his left arm, outstretched, fist clenched. He knew the routine.

The clerk tied a red rubber tube tourniquet above Barry's elbow to block the return of venous blood. A fold of skin was entrapped by the tight rubber and nipped his flesh. "Ow." Barry pumped his fist to distend the vein in the hollow of the elbow, the antecubital fossa.

Chris Finn dabbed the skin over the vein with cotton wool soaked in pungent-smelling methylated spirits. Barry tried not to flinch when the needle bit as it pierced his skin and hit the vein wall to produce a dull ache. "Damn," said the young man after moments of wiggling the tip of the needle. "Sorry, I can't quite get into the vein." He pulled the needle free. "Sorry."

Barry clenched his teeth. The lad was learning, and Barry could well remember the number of times he himself had failed in his first attempts to draw blood, but back then he hadn't been the one hurting. Now he was.

Finn confessed failure a second, no less painful, time.

Barry gritted his teeth, grimaced, and controlled an urge to tell the student to bugger off and go and practice on someone else.

Jack, who had moved back to give the young student room, now drew closer to the bed. "Tell you what, Chris. Let me do it."

There was relief in the young man's voice when he said, "Thank you very much, Doctor Mills."

This time it still stung, but in no time Jack had filled the barrel of the hypodermic, pressed a cotton wool ball over the puncture site, told Barry to hold it firmly there, undid the tourniquet, and withdrew the needle. "Gonna have a bit of a bruise, chum, but it can't be helped." Jack injected the blood into three rubber-stoppered glass tubes, which he handed, along with the hypodermic, to Finn.

"Thanks, Jack," Barry said, grateful his friend was here. An ordinary patient would have had to submit to the less than skillful ministrations until he finally succeeded. To his shame Barry recalled the very worst of his attempted bloodlettings, six tries on one patient before success. It was all very well saying you learned by your mistakes, but you were making them at someone else's expense. He'd remember that.

Finn collected his gear and the samples, uttered a quick "I hope you're better soon, Doctor Laverty," bobbed his head to Jan

Peters, and fled.

Barry lay back. Three punctures instead of one. His entire left arm still throbbed, but he could feel the tension begin to leave his body. To be fair, although the bloodletting had been painful, the duration and intensity of the pain came nowhere near that of a toothache. His discomfort probably had more to do with a primitive resentment against the violation of a needle piercing his skin. Perhaps it went back in some ancient group memory of being skewered by a flint-tipped spear.

He frowned. Why had another set of samples been required, and what had the first ones shown? "Jan," he said, "I know you're not supposed to say anything, but have you any idea what's wrong with me?"

She shook her head. "Sorry, Barry, I honestly don't. Sister Lynch asked me to tell her when you woke up. She wants to have a word."

A word? With the senior sister. What the blazes was she going to tell him? "I remember her, from when we spent time on this unit being instructed in neurology, remember, Jack? She comes from Ballynahinch in County Down."

"Just a wee thing, about the same age as Bernie O'Byrne, but grey-haired? Yes, I

263

remember her. She played cricket for the Irish women's team as a girl."

"I'm sure she can explain," Jan said, "but before that, my instructions are to give you a bed-bath."

"Don't mind me," Jack said, getting out of her way. "I've seen young Adonis in the shower."

Barry was grateful for his friend's presence while submitting to Jan's gentle ministrations with a sponge, warm soapy water, and a towel.

He did everything she asked as she worked, but all the while the question nagged. Why more tests, and just how sick was he?

Jan finished. "I'll get you a clean gown. You really did sweat a lot, so we'll have to get plenty of fluids into you." She dressed Barry and tucked him in. "He's all yours, Doctor Mills," she said. "I'm off to speak to Sister Lynch."

"Thanks, Jan," Barry said. "Thanks for everything." He watched her go, hoping Sister would come very soon to answer his questions. He hated, hated, uncertainty, particularly when the subject of it was himself. It was time he forced his tired brain to concentrate.

Jack turned the bedside chair round, sat

with his arms draped over the back. His flippant tone vanished. "I'm sorry for your troubles, Barry. Sounds like you have a pretty nasty flu."

"Mebbe," Barry said, "but I didn't know there were any blood tests for flu. It's usually a simple clinical diagnosis based on symptoms and signs. And Jan could have told me that."

"But from what she told me while you were asleep, you have them all, in spades. What you need, Barry, is lots of kip, plenty of fluids, and tincture of time. I'll bet they discharge you home to your folks in Ballyholme as soon as the results of that bloodletting are in."

"I hope you're right." Barry did take some comfort from his friend's confidence, but still something nagged, and he couldn't quite put his finger on it. Och, to hell with it. He was too tired to think about it now. Later he would, after Jack and Sister had gone and he'd had another sleep. Barry wondered what was keeping her.

A squeaking of trolley wheels came from outside the door. Jack shook his head. "You'd think someone would have the wit to oil the things. It's noisy enough in a hospital. Anyway, on a more practical note, I phoned your folks last night, told them you had flu or just possibly some other bug." He chuckled. "I think your mum was about to drop the phone and head for the car until I explained that we're not sure exactly what the bug might be, so you're not allowed to have visitors. She says I've to tell you to do exactly what your doctors tell you to do, keep warm, keep out of draughts — and don't forget to brush your teeth. They'll be up to see you the minute they're allowed. She and your dad send their love."

Barry managed a weak smile. "That's Mum. How'd she sound?"

"Worried. That's mums the world over. Anyway, she made me promise to give them regular bulletins."

"Thanks, Jack."

"I'm sure you'll be able to set her mind at rest once you get home."

"Aye. Once I do get home," he muttered. Where the hell was Sister Lynch? She must know he'd be waiting for news.

"From a practical point of view, you know ward 21, neurosurgery, usually has two housemen? Well, they've pulled one off the ward and sent him to casualty, so we're coping in your absence."

"Good." Barry hated to admit it, but, at the moment, that was the least of his worries.

"And," said Jack, "I've been saving the best to last: your friend Virginia sends her wishes for a speedy recovery and her love — and, brother, judging by the light in those green eyes when she said it, I don't think it was one of those casual greetings. I don't know how you did it, but I think you've scored a winner there."

For a moment Barry wondered if he were imagining what he had just heard. "Do you mean that, Jack?"

"My old son, if I don't know girls, who does?"

Barry closed his eyes and relished the thought. Now he really had to get better and get the hell out of here. "Thanks, Jack. Next time you see her — give her mine."

Jack rolled his eyes. "Head over heels again? Don't say I didn't warn you." He stood. "Anyway, it's time for me to run away on back to casualty, but I'm off duty tonight, and you know the little redhead from Antrim Town?" He winked. "You get better soon. You need anything? A book? Luco-zade? Grapes?"

Barry shook his head. "What I need is for someone who knows what's going on to let me in on it. I don't like uncertainty."

"Nobody does, but I'm sure you've nothing to worry about." Jack stood. "All right.

I'll pop in tomorrow. See how you're doing."

"Thanks. Thanks a lot, Jack," Barry said to his friend's departing back. Dear God. Virginia sent her love, and the shiver that ran up Barry's spine wasn't because of his fever.

He was still smiling when the door opened and the ward's senior sister, Sister Lynch, came in. "Good afternoon, Doctor Laverty. How are you feeling today?" She put on a gown over her red uniform dress and spotless white apron.

"A bit better, thank you, Sister."

"Good," she said. "Now we need to have a chat."

Barry stiffened. It only took three words to say "You've got flu." Why a chat? "We thought you had simple flu —"

Barry didn't like the sound of that. If it wasn't flu, what could it be? Not all fevers were caused by infection. They could signify something serious.

"— but Doctor Swanson is a very thorough young man. We're fond of him here. When he examined you — and he went over you from head to toe — apart from your temperature and pulse being up and your throat a bit inflamed, he noted enlargement of your cervical lymph nodes."

268

Barry's left hand went to the left side of his neck and he could feel the rubbery things there. "I see. Yes, they are."

"We didn't think that meant much. They often get swollen with flu."

"That's true." Probably no need for concern. Then why was he feeling so nervous?

Sister continued, "He ran the routine blood screen for all admissions. Blood group. Haemoglobin, ESR, and white count. You are O positive. Your haemoglobin is normal. We all know the estimated sedimentation rate is very nonspecific. Yours is certainly elevated, but just about any fever will do that."

Barry nodded. She was, of course, right. "I wonder why we still bother doing it, it's so nonspecific."

She smiled. "Me too, but routine is routine, and once in a while we do pick up something." She hesitated, then said, "I'm afraid your white cell count was low — and that is unusual in cases of flu."

"Low white cells?"

"That's right. Probably nothing to worry about."

Probably? What did that mean? Damn. Wasn't there an infectious disease that suppressed white cell production at first before the count soared as the disease progressed?

269

He shook his head. Usually he could see the pages of a particular book in his head when searching for a diagnosis, but today his mind, fuddled by his temperature, aching muscles, and slight headache, could not find them. Taking in what she was saying was all he could do. Simple fevers like flu or a cold were hardly ever seen in a major hospital. They were mostly looked after by GPs, and Barry was not ashamed to admit his knowledge of them was less than perfect. That was true of most hospital staff. Barry closed his eyes and took a deep breath that ended in a bout of dry coughing.

Sister Lynch handed him a glass of water from the top of his bedside locker. "Here. Have a drink."

Barry drank and returned the glass. "Thank you."

"You all right?"

He nodded, but he wasn't. He was worried, but he wasn't going to make a fool of himself by questioning a senior sister. It was more important that he paid attention to her rather than struggle to make his own diagnosis.

"Good. That is a nasty cough. I'll get Doctor Swanson to order a cough suppressant."

"Thanks, Sister, but you were explaining about my white count."

"I was. Because it was low, we repeated it today, and also asked for a differential count."

And what would a differential count show? What were they looking for? The routine was to make a smear of the blood on a glass slide and count all the white blood cells present, the infection fighters, to see if the total count was up. That usually confirmed the presence of an infective agent. The differential was very consumptive of highly trained laboratory technicians' time. Each individual white cell had to be identified by type through a microscope and counted. It was expensive, so only ordered if something else was suspected. "I see," he said, but in fact he didn't. Barry wondered if instead of concern about infection, there was some suspicion that there was something not right — he couldn't face the word "wrong" — with the white cells themselves.

"Luckily for you, the Royal has one of the finest haematologists in Doctor Gerald Nelson. We've asked him to consult."

"Gerry Nelson? Head of haematology?"

"That's right."

Hell's gates, there was a problem with the white cells in his blood. All thoughts of other potential diagnoses fled. He was going to be under the care of the senior physician specialising in diseases of the blood and lymphatic systems, anaemias, leukaemias — cancers of the white cells — and another disease with all the symptoms he had now. Which blood disorder gave symptoms like flu? Come on. Think. He dismissed the idea that he could have another kind of viral infection. Doctor Gerald Nelson was not consulted for trivia.

Barry shuddered. Cough, fever, weakness, raised evening temperature and — he took a deep breath. Think, man, think. But he still couldn't remember.

"Unfortunately, Doctor Laverty, today's Friday, and Doctor Nelson's in London. Won't be back until Monday, his secretary says, but we'll keep you comfy until then. We'll probably not get the results of the new blood work back until then anyway. So, don't worry. Just get lots of rest and ask your nurses for anything you need." She bent and fluffed his pillow. "Now, before I trot along, have you any questions?"

Any? He had a hundred. Was there no one else who could give him a diagnosis? Silly question. Sister would already have thought of that, and the staff here had decided that Barry needed the haematologist's opinion, not someone else's. Barry'd have to wait, and he'd been working in hospitals long enough to know that any other queries would be fobbed off with "Try not to worry. Doctor Nelson will be able to answer that on Monday when the other test results are in." Instead he simply said, "Not really, but thank you."

"I'll be off then."

He put his first two left fingers on his right wrist at the base of his thumb. He could feel the pulse in his radial artery and see the second hand of his wristwatch at the same time. Twenty-seven beats in fifteen seconds. One hundred and eight per minute. Should be eighty-eight. It was racing, and why? Because of his fever, or because there was something sufficiently wrong with his white count to warrant doing a differential count? What else could be wrong with him? Calm down, he told himself. Get a grip. Wasn't it a well-known fact, and he managed a weak smile, that all medical students diagnosed themselves with at least one lethal disease during their clinical years? It probably was only flu, or as Sister had said, some other virus, but with Doctor Nelson on the scene, there must be cause for concern.

Monday, for Christ's sake, until Barry's fears could be resolved — or worse. Was he going to be told that he had something worse than an infection? Was there no way he could get an answer sooner? Harry Sloan had taken the fifth-year prize for microscopic pathology. Might he be able to read the blood smears?

Barry took a deep breath. Not bloody likely. He could not bring himself to ask Harry. Partly out of fear of Harry suspecting Barry had panicked, but more because he had no idea how his friend could legitimately get access to the smears of a patient who was not under his care.

Barry shook his head. He could think of no other options. No way to get an answer. He couldn't change anything. The old country adage "What can't be cured must be endured" not only applied to an illness. It covered unchangeable circumstances too. He mustn't let his anxiety show to other people. They'd think he was a worrywart. Barry took a long, deep breath. He'd simply have to tough it out.

15
HOPE SPRINGS ETERNAL IN THE HUMAN BREAST

April 24, 1969

Kenny made a throaty noise from the backseat of Barry's Hillman Imp when the car stopped at the traffic light. The two-year-old chocolate Labrador was accompanying Barry and Emer to the last home visit of the morning. Barry glanced across at the Duck and waved at Mary Dunleavy, the publican's daughter, as she stepped back to admire the window she was washing. Two days ago, he'd popped in for a pint and had run into Anne Galvin's husband, George, known to everyone as "Guffer."

"You mind, Doctor, when Anne first took bad you come out til see her," the man had said shyly, "and you brung Doctor O'Reilly's pup, Kenny?"

"I do. She fell in love with him."

"Right enough, she did. Well, could I ask you a wee favour, sir?"

"Certainly."

275

"If you're coming out til see my Annie once she's discharged, could you mebbe bring Kenny? I know how much it would please her."

Barry had smiled. "I'll ask Doctor O'Reilly. I'm sure he won't mind."

"Thanks a million, Doc. Now, I know you're off duty, like, and I didn't mean til intrude. I'll leave you to your pint."

The traffic light turned to green. "Last call of the morning, Emer," Barry said as they headed for the housing estate. "They sent one of our patients, Anne Galvin, home from Belvoir earlier today. She's had a recurrence of lung cancer and is getting radiotherapy. I want to see for myself how she's doing."

Emer inhaled. "Doesn't sound very promising."

" 'Fraid not. The relapse happened twelve days ago. She had her original diagnosis and surgery two years ago. Not one of our better efforts. Fingal and I both diagnosed acute bronchitis initially. We all get it wrong sometimes."

"I know." Emer smiled. "I'll bet you followed up right away, though, and got her into the Royal, but thanks for that, Barry."

As he drove onto the housing estate he wondered how Sue was getting on at Mac-

Neill Memorial Elementary School. She'd not been in good form when she'd left for work this morning.

Emer was saying something and he realized he hadn't been listening.

"Sorry, Emer. I missed that."

"I just asked if you were all right, Barry? You've been, I don't know, a bit distant today. It's not like you."

"I'm all right." But he wasn't. Sue's period was due today. She'd hardly spoken a word at breakfast. Waiting for the bad news, if it came, that would again confirm she was not pregnant, was killing her a little bit as each month went by. It wasn't doing much for his mood either. "Honestly, but it's kind of you to ask." It might have helped to talk to another woman, and a doctor at that, but apart from Sue's mum and Jack Mills, no one knew how worried Barry and Sue were about their apparent infertility.

He parked outside the terrace house. "Hop out." He grabbed his bag, let Kenny out, and they followed Emer.

Today was Ulster's spring at its best. The air was warm, soft, not a cloud in the thin strip of blue between the roofs of the houses on either side of the narrow street. Summer was on the way. A cock pigeon, his green-and-purple head shining, pursued a hen

277

along the gutter, and his burbling coos, while not having the purity of a skylark's song, helped even the gloomy old housing estate to seem brighter and more cheerful. The only gloom was inside Barry's head.

He knocked on the front door and Guffer answered almost immediately. His completely bald head shone in the sunlight.

"Doctor Laverty, and this must be Doctor Emer. I've heard good things about you, lass. How's about ye? Thanks for coming, and for bringing Kenny. It's dead on, so it is. I never told her you might, in case Doctor O'Reilly said no, so it'll be a grand surprise. Come on on in."

He led them into the familiar parlour where Anne, wearing a tartan dressing gown over her nightie and pink fluffy slippers, sat in one of the armchairs of the maroon three-piece suite. Barry noticed at once that her grey-blonde hair was neatly brushed, she was having no difficulty breathing, and her facial colour was good.

"Hello, Doctors. Nice of youse til drop by. And it's nice to be home too." Her face lit up. "And youse brung Kenny. Och, that's lovely, so it is. Come here, boy. Come here."

The big Lab, tail wagging, trotted over to Anne and, needing no bidding, sat.

She patted his head. "Who's a good boy, then?"

Kenny grinned his Labrador grin and his tail never stopped.

"And here's me forgetting my manners. Would the pair of youse sit down?"

Barry took the other armchair close to and half facing Anne, while Emer sat at the end of the sofa closest to the patient.

"Now, I know it's near lunchtime, but would youse like a wee cup of tea in your hand? Guffer's a dab hand at the tea-making, so he is."

"That would be grand," Barry said. "Thank you."

"Away you and see til it, Guffer, love, and bring some of them McVitie's chocolate digestives." She ruffled the fur on Kenny's head.

The dog looked at her with adoration in his big brown eyes.

"I'll attend til it." Guffer left.

"You're looking well, Anne," Barry said. "We just wanted to see how you are getting along."

"I'm doing a lot better than the last time you was here, sir. Mister Bingham's folks at the Royal was great, so they were. Give me a thorough going-over, X-rays and all, then got me straight to thon Marie Curie Centre and them folks there told me that their radiotherapy — that's what you call it, isn't it?"

"It is," Emer said.

Barry heard the high-pitched whistle of a kettle coming from the rear of the house. Like many Ulsterfolk, the Galvins would keep a kettle near to boiling for moments like this when people dropped in.

"Anyroad, they said it would shrink the growth in my chest that had made my lobe collapse, and, by jeekers, it must've." She smiled. "Mind you, it's scary when they get you all lined up in front of thon big machine with a kind of nozzle that looks like it's staring at you and they all run off and hide before it starts to hum and buzz. You don't feel nothing. Not then, anyhow. And glory be — I can breathe again, and I don't feel anything wrong with me, except I'm tired."

"That's to be expected, but otherwise I'm delighted with how you are," Barry said.

She smiled and patted Kenny's flank. "And I'm going til be even better on Saturday. Our oldest lad, Pat, and his family's coming up from Dublin."

"You'll enjoy that," Barry said.

Guffer came in with a tray that he set on a table. "What do youse take in your tea?"

"Just milk for me, please, Mister Galvin,"

Emer said.

"Milk and sugar," said Barry.

As Guffer fussed with cups and saucers, Barry said, "Anne, if you are feeling all right, I don't think me or Doctor Emer examining you is going to change anything, so unless you're worried?"

"Not at all. There's no need for that, sir."

"Here y'are, Doctors." Guffer handed a teacup to Emer and another to Barry.

"They've it all organised for me. Told me I'd need more courses of treatment, that I'd get queasy and maybe take the skitters, but I have medicines for both." A hand strayed to her head. "I might lose some hair too, but, och." She shrugged. "I have all my dates til go back and the ambulance is booked already to take me there."

Guffer gave her a cup and a biscuit.

"Doctor Laverty," she said, "could I give half of this biccy to Kenny?"

"You may, but he won't eat it until you snap your fingers. Dogs have been known to be poisoned by eating things lying about, so Doctor O'Reilly has Kenny trained not to eat anything unless he's given permission."

"Boys-a-boys," Anne said, "that's quare nor smart."

As she busied herself with the dog, Barry

thought about the woman in front of him and how modern medicine was treating her disease. He knew about lung cancer and its probable course, but he was out of his depth when it came to radiotherapy. They'd had three lectures as students on the effects of nuclear fallout from atomic bombs, but none on the medical applications of radiation. That was left to the experts. "It seems your specialists have pretty much everything taken care of, Anne."

"Pretty much, and Guffer and me's dead thankful, so we are, for everything they're doing." She reached out and took Barry's hand. "But we're grateful til youse Ballybucklebo doctors too." She looked up at him. "It's just nice to know you're always there if we need you, and that you all do, I don't mean to be forward, but you all do care for your patients." She let go his hand. "There now. I've said it. Thank youse all."

The lump was so big in Barry's throat he hoped it wasn't going to strangle him. He smiled at her. "Thank you, Anne."

"Aye," she said, "and I've other news too." Her smile was radiant. "Seamus's building business in Palm Desert is doing very well — that's our younger lad, Doctor Emer — and he'll be coming home from California in a wee while."

"It's dead on, so it is," Guffer said. "We don't have any dates yet, we're waiting until we see how the rest of Annie's treatment goes, but I got a letter from him yesterday. With them there jet aeroplanes now, he can be in Belfast in less than a couple of days, so if we need him in a hurry" — and from the look in Guffer's eyes, Barry understood exactly what the man meant — "he'll come at once."

"I'm glad," Barry said. "It'll be another homecoming for him, and you two'll be happy to see him."

"We will that," Guffer said.

Barry finished his tea, took a quick look at his watch, and stood. "I'm pleased you're making progress, Anne. Now Doctor McCarthy and I should be running along. You know we're country GPs and it's your specialists who will be looking after you for a while, but if you or Guffer are worried?"

"Doctor, dear," she said, "you're very kind, but sure we know that." Then her voice cracked, but she stiffened her shoulders. "And anyroad, Guffer and me both understands that it's more likely the Reverend Robinson we'll be calling, so don't you worry your head, sir." She bent and gave Kenny a huge hug, and he licked her face.

And for the second time in twelve days,

Barry stood in awe of this woman's courage. "You look after yourselves," he said. "We'll be off. Come, Kenny."

Back in the car with Kenny aboard, Emer said, "I'm glad she's getting such good care and that the radiation has helped. As a GP, though, it reminds me how useless you can feel in cases like this."

Barry put the car in gear and drove off. He knew the feeling all too well.

"And I worry," she said, "the other effects of radiotherapy are going to be much more unpleasant than Anne seems to believe."

Barry turned on the Belfast to Bangor Road. "I agree, but I've had a couple of other patients looked after at Marie Curie. They're very good at controlling the worst complications. I admire all of those oncology folks, but I couldn't work with patients when practically all of them are going to die while under my care." He shuddered.

"I've watched you and Fingal for nine months, and I know that's because you do care about your patients. Anne Galvin was right." She chuckled. "And how do I know? After what I've learned here, it takes one to know one."

"You, Doctor Emer McCarthy, are going to make a very fine GP." Barry smiled.

She sighed. "If I can find a job."

"Still no luck?"

She shook her head as Barry parked at Number One Main Street. "Not yet, but Nonie's still not mentioned what she may have up her sleeve, and it's only eight days since we all had that lunch together. Fingal and Connor are working on it too." The engine subsided, then ticked into silence.

"You talk of feeling useless on these more specialized cases. Have you thought about specializing? You're great with the kiddies."

"Thank you, Barry, and it might be an option, but I do love it here. I'd still like to find a rural practice if I can." She chuckled. "Maybe I could start a new specialty. Two weeks ago, I went out to see Norman Devine. Colin Brown was there with his dog, Murphy. We brought Kenny today. Both patients seemed comforted. How about physician with canine comforter?"

"Why not? But those two are taken. And you'd not want our Max. That eejit would give a nervous patient hysterics. You'll have to find your own." Barry laughed. "Now, enjoy your lunch. I'm heading home. I want to be there when Sue comes back from school for lunch. I'm off this afternoon and she has a half day."

"Thanks, Barry. Enjoy your afternoon." Emer shut the door behind her.

As he drove off he sighed. He'd been told twice today that he cared for his patients, and yes, he'd known since his houseman's year that getting close to them could cause him grief. How much more so, he wondered, when someone who wasn't his patient might at this moment be wrestling with enormous disappointment, and that someone was his wife?

Barry went through to their neat dining room/sitting room. Through the picture window, the panoramic view of Belfast Lough to the west and Whitehead and the Irish Sea to the east still startled him with its beauty two years after they'd moved in. Beautiful, and the weather of this morning had held. Blue skies. Plenty of sunshine. One of the side windows was open and through it Barry could hear the waves hitting the rocks, the cries of gulls. He inhaled the salty sea tang. A helicopter was landing on the foredeck of a twin-funnelled Royal Navy warship. The lough was always busy, always interesting, but today Barry had more on his mind.

Their springer spaniel, Max, was fast asleep on the three-seat settee. He wasn't meant to be there, but Barry couldn't be bothered to chase him. Who said, "Let sleeping dogs lie?" Barry shook his head. It didn't matter.

He walked back to the kitchen and turned on the transistor radio. Barry sat at the table and began to work on the rigging of his model of Lieutenant William Bligh's HMS *Bounty*. He'd done a bit after supper last night and they'd not needed the table at breakfast today. The three-masted square-rigger was already mounted on her stand and would be easy to move before lunch.

He'd finished *Victory* nine months ago and she now kept *Rattlesnake* company in the living room. Barry was grateful to have something to do that required a high degree of concentration. It would keep his mind off his worries for her.

He tied the knot attaching the port main backstay to the mast. "Got it," he said to Tigger, the adopted stray tabby cat who was sleeping in her basket beside the stove. A well-modulated voice was coming from the radio. "Earlier today, explosions at Lough Neagh and in Belfast damaged the pipeline bringing water from the lough to the city. No one, as yet, has claimed responsibility, but it is now suspected similar attacks four days ago were carried out by militant Loyalists in the hope that the blame would fall on the Irish Republican Army. The British

Home Secretary, Mister James Callaghan, has announced that five hundred more British troops will be arriving in Ulster tomorrow to take up peacekeeping duties."

Barry leant across from where he sat. He'd switch the bloody thing off and hope Sue hadn't heard the news at school or on the car radio coming home. She was still as committed to her civil rights work as she had been when he'd met her, and her concern about the deteriorating political situation here in Ulster seemed to mount with her own concern about not falling pregnant.

Max charged into the room and stood staring at the back door. He barked once.

The dog's hearing was so acute it bordered on the psychic. Only now could Barry hear Sue's car coming. He stood, set aside the fine forceps and scissors he'd been using, and opened the kitchen door to hurry along the short path through the back garden. He and Max met her at the gate. Max, as usual, tried to put his forepaws on her tummy, but she brushed him away. The tear tracks down her cheeks made any question Barry might have superfluous.

She nodded once and said, "Yes. It's come."

"Damn," he said. "I'm so sorry." And he

was, for both of them. He put his arm round her shoulders. "Come on inside and we'll have lunch."

She shook her head. "I'm not hungry. Let's walk. I need some fresh air. And no. We'll leave this one at home. Sorry, Max." She took the dog by his collar, put him in the kitchen, closed the door, and took Barry's hand.

They headed off east along the sea walk.

For a while neither spoke. It was now four months since they had decided to consult Doctor Graham Harley, fifteen since Sue had stopped taking the pill. And so far, no tests had shown a reason why she still had not conceived. The last four months had been a roller coaster of raised and then dashed hopes. Barry knew it was the not knowing, the unspoken fears, the uncertainty above all that was getting to her. He'd had his own bout with that six years ago.

"I'm sorry, Barry," she said. "But I was so hoping it wouldn't come." She inhaled through her nose. "It started about an hour before classes finished for the morning, and I managed to bottle up how I felt until I was in the car, but then the dam burst."

"Nothing to be sorry about, love. I know you're disappointed. I'm disappointed too." It had taken a while for Barry to become comfortable with the prospect of being a father, but now he wished for it as much as Sue wanted to be a mother.

She made no reply, and Barry knew that sometimes it was better to say nothing. He kept pace with her as they walked along the coastal path, passing dog walkers, being passed in both directions by cyclists.

Sue stopped once to let a young woman walk past pushing a pram. Barry watched as Sue deliberately looked out to sea, where eight snowy-white mute swans with black faces and red bills stretched out their black paddles and, like a team of water skiers, made successive landings, ploughing watery furrows in the stillness of Belfast Lough. They stretched their curved necks and twitched their feathers into position.

Sue stopped and faced him. "All right. That's it. No more self-pity." She braced her shoulders back. "I have to keep reminding myself, it's only been fifteen months since I went off the pill. I know you told me we didn't really have to worry until two years had gone by. I never realized how impatient I can be until —" She gulped, and Barry knew she was swallowing back tears. "Until — until now. We're not pregnant yet, I must accept that." She even managed to smile at him. "I can accept it. I can."

She took a deep breath. "It's — it's not the end of the world. It's not." Her voice trembled. Barry's heart wept for her, but he too managed a smile.

"You're very brave." He wondered from where this well of courage sprang to sustain women like his Sue — and Anne Galvin. "And the important word is 'yet.' We know what's going to happen next. I'll phone the Royal when we get home. See if I can have a word with Graham." As a colleague, he knew he would be put through, or at least Doctor Graham Harley would return Barry's call. "He said he'd arrange the next step, your laparoscopy, for early May."

"Thank you, Barry," Sue said. "Thank you for being so understanding. Thank you for attending to the practical details." She shook her head, ignored the other folks around, and kissed him. "And thank you for being Barry Laverty. I do love you so, you know. I really do."

16
HAUNTS OF HORROR AND FEAR

September 1 and 2, 1963

Barry woke. Except for a glimmer of light creeping in under the closed door, the room was dark. His luminous watch face read three twenty. For a moment he was unsure of where he was. He listened to the noises coming from outside the thin-walled room. Snores, feet on linoleum. The mattress under him was lumpy, and its rubber undersheet, a routine precaution against a patient wetting the bed, creaked as he moved.

Now he recognised where he was — the staff room off ward 22 where he'd been admitted on Thursday evening with an initial working diagnosis of pyrexia of unknown origin.

Sister Lynch's words crept into his mind, amplified by the silence in the room. "Luckily for you, the Royal has one of the finest haematologists in Doctor Gerald Nelson.

292

We've asked him to consult." Barry sat up, wide awake now. That consultation was still two days away. He could feel his stomach tense as he remembered desperately trying, and failing, to puzzle out his own possible diagnosis. Like a wasp attracted by a jam sandwich, he could not stop himself making another attempt now, despite one of his father's pieces of advice: Never try to work important things out in the muddle of the night.

Cough, fever, weakness, raised evening temperature, and — his left hand went to his neck — enlargement of the cervical lymph nodes. He could still feel the rubbery lumps. Flu to be sure could cause all of those things; so could other viruses. But now he did remember. So could Hodgkin's lymphadenoma, a lethal cancer of the lymphatic system. The kind of condition that would require the attention of a haematologist. Barry felt the shock of that sudden knowledge vibrate through him.

If that diagnosis was in the minds of the young houseman and Sister Lynch, he wouldn't be told yet — it was received wisdom that, until the answer was crystal clear, suggesting a patient might have a potentially lethal disease would only cause needless worry for the victim. It was kindly meant.

He still remembered a scene from *The Pride of the Yankees.* He'd seen it on TV when he'd been in first year. A dying Lou Gehrig asks his doctor, "Is it three strikes, Doc?" The physician didn't answer his patient, but told Lou's wife the truth. At that time Barry had thought keeping the patient in the dark was considerate. And maybe that was still the correct approach for the laity, but after six years of medical training, Doctor Barry Laverty had arrived at a very unpalatable conclusion on his own. He hoped he was wrong, he prayed he was wrong, but the possibility had suddenly concentrated his mind. The remembered words from *A Short Textbook of Medicine,* 1962 edition, now leapt from the page. "In Hodgkin's disease, occasional patients survive for ten or more years, but the great majority are dead within four or five. In rapidly progressive cases, the total course may not exceed six months."

Barry shuddered. You are jumping to conclusions, he told himself. Don't. What was the line one of his teachers used when there was a possibility of a poor outcome? Hope for the best but prepare for the worst. And the worst was he was going to die.

Barry Laverty felt the tears prick his eyes, pool at the back of his throat. No. Not me. And not now. I'm only twenty-three. I'm almost a fully licensed doctor. Not now when I've just fallen in love with this wonderful girl. He was barely aware of shouting "Not now," before he buried his face in his pillow and sobbed and sobbed.

Pull yourself together, man. He lay still on the bed and took a deep breath. Never had he felt so alone in his life. It was quite a while before Barry Laverty dropped off into an exhausted sleep.

"Sorry to wake you up, Barry," Jan Peters said, "but I have to take your morning pulse and temperature."

Barry opened his eyes. Light streamed in from the skylight overhead. He blinked. Sat up. "It's all right." He rubbed his eyes.

"How are you this morning?"

"A bit better, I think." Like hell. The feelings from last night rolled through his weary body like a tidal wave. He told himself to try to put them away. He managed a smile for Jan.

"Here," she said. "Pop this under your tongue." She handed him a clinical thermometer. He did as he'd been asked, remembering that whereas in cases of flu it would still be up, in Hodgkin's, the temperature was usually normal in the morning. He felt Jan's fingers on his wrist and watched her consult her pocket watch. All nurses wore one pinned to their apron's right shoulder strap.

The two minutes it takes for a mercury thermometer to register seemed like an eternity.

Jan removed it, said, "Nice and normal," and shook the mercury down. She lifted a clipboard from the rail at the bed's foot and made entries on a piece of graph paper. "Anything you need?"

A reprieve would be nice, he thought, but said, "No thanks."

"I'm off, then" — she took off her gown at the door — "but breakfast will be here soon, and I'll be back later to make your bed and give you a sponge bath." She left, and Barry barely had time to tell himself that no one had actually confirmed what he suspected — he could be entirely wrong, and getting himself up to high doh wasn't helping anything — when the door opened.

Jack, Harry Sloan, and Norma Fitch, all masked and gowned, trooped into the tiny room with a chorus of "Morning, Barry," bringing their energy, rude health, a dog-eared copy of Arthur Hailey's *Airport,* and a

296

jar of calf's foot jelly. Norma's mother swore it could cure any ailment.

"Morning."

None questioned the diagnosis of flu. It was considered bad form, apart from asking general questions about how the sufferer was feeling, for colleagues to pry into signs and symptoms. That was what the patient's doctors were for. Illness was considered a private matter between patient, family, and medical staff. Many Ulsterfolk had been shocked back in 1955 when the American press had announced to the world that their president, Dwight Eisenhower, had suffered a heart attack.

In front of his friends, Barry had hidden his concerns until they were getting ready to leave. "Thank you all very much for coming. Much appreciated. Jack, could you hang on for a minute, please?"

"Sure." Jack sat down again.

Norma and Harry left, Norma saying, "And don't worry, Barry, you'll be back in the salt mines with the rest of us soon."

He dearly hoped that were true.

"What can I do for you, my old son?"

Barry, fearing they might be overheard, glanced round the room and said in a low voice, "You and I go back a long way."

"Ten years."

"There's no one else I'd tell this to, but I'm worried."

Jack frowned. "Oh? What's up?"

"Jack, you were there when young Swanson came to repeat my blood tests. You took the sample. After you'd left, Sister explained that my total white count was low. You know that's not usual in flu. They wanted to do a differential, that's why they needed more blood, and they've arranged for me to be seen by Doctor Nelson on Monday."

Jack's frown deepened. "Why has that got you worried? Gerry Nelson's a good head."

"His specialty includes blood and lymph cancers."

"And you think you've got one?"

Had he heard a hint of laughter in Jack's voice? He pressed on. "I have a lot of the symptoms of Hodgkin's." Barry looked down and repeated them for Jack's benefit. He looked up. "I know I'm probably blowing this out of proportion —"

"You could say that."

"You think I'm an eejit."

"No, I do not." Jack frowned.

"I can't think of anything else."

Jack scratched his head. "I'm sorry, mate. As your friend, I can understand why you'd worry." He smiled. "But, remember Tom Williams? Thought he had bone cancer because his left knee was really sore. Consulted an orthopod. Orthopod examines Tom and says, 'Don't waste money on a coffin yet. You've knock knees — and you're way overweight.' " Jack chuckled.

Barry smiled. He did remember Tom Williams. But this was different. "I don't want to make a fool of myself by confronting Doctor Swanson or Sister Flynn, but I had to talk to somebody. Get it out of my system. It's the uncertainty, the having to wait, the not being in control that's getting to me. I know the prognosis for Hodgkin's. It's not good."

"I understand. Uncertainty is tough." Jack pursed his lips. "Maybe some facts might help? As a physician, and a green one at that, I can't help you with viruses. I missed some of those lectures. You know I've always been way more interested in surgery. But I do remember one thing about Hodgkin's. The disease only affects one in about thirty thousand people annually in the United Kingdom. Compare that to the fact that everyone has had flu or some other viral fever. Remember what Professor Bull used to say? 'If there are two birds on a telegraph wire here in Belfast, they're more likely to be sparrows than canaries.' Rare things are rare. My guess is that applies to you too."

"Rare things are rare. Thanks, Jack. That does help. And thanks for understanding."

"I believe," said Jack, "that is what friends are for. And you can buy me a pint when they tell you not to worry and let you out of here."

The orderly had just taken Barry's lunch tray away when the door opened, and a masked and gowned Bernie O'Byrne walked in, accompanied, glory be, by Virginia. His jaw dropped when he recognised those green eyes above her mask. The two women, wearing their uniforms under their gowns, crossed his room and sat on plain chairs at the head of his bed. He hoped he didn't look too much like a gormless mooncalf.

Bernie studied his face. "And how are you, Barry Laverty? You're looking tired."

"I am tired, and achy, and a bit feverish, but not too bad, thanks. And thanks for coming."

"We've been worried about you since you took ill, so we thought we'd pop by. It's a golden opportunity for Nurse Clarke to learn more about caring for infectious patients." Bernie winked at him. "We hear it's probably flu. There's a kind of sisters' union, and Margaret Lynch and I were in the same class when we were students here.

As long as we observe the barrier nursing protocol and don't tire you too much, she'll be happy for Nurse Clarke to be here."

He let Bernie chat for a while, but in truth he wasn't paying close attention. His gaze never left Virginia's face.

". . . anyway," said Bernie, "life goes on in casualty, and we're looking forward to having you back, Barry." She stood. "I'll be running along. Nurse Clarke. Hear me now, ten minutes, not a second more."

Barry couldn't wait for Bernie to wash her hands and take off her gown, but he didn't want to say anything personal yet. "It's lovely to see you, Virginia. How have you been? I must have given you an awful shock passing out like that."

"You did," Virginia said. "You certainly did. Norma was great. She sorted everything out and got you admitted here."

"Your ten minutes is running," Bernie called just before she closed the door behind her.

Victoria looked into his eyes. "Barry. Barry. My heart stopped when you collapsed on Thursday. I should have been concerned for that rugby player. I should have been working out what to do, but all I could think of was what if there was something seriously wrong with you, and how

301

much I would hurt if I lost you. I was being selfish, I know, but it hit me then that I was in love with you."

"And I've been falling in love with you since the day on Cave Hill," Barry said. "Thank you for sending your love with Jack. It helped. It really did."

"I'm glad." She smiled.

"I really want to kiss you, hold you," Barry said, "but" — he shrugged — "Whatever I've got I don't want to pass on to you."

"It's all right. I understand. There'll be plenty of time when you're better."

Barry hoped to God that Jack was right about sparrows and canaries. "Yes, there will be. I do love you, Virginia. I really do."

Monday had come at last. Barry sat propped up on pillows and sighed. He'd had the better part of three days of trying to cope with the unknown. It was ten thirty now, and still no sign of Doctor Nelson. Barry was at a point where, despite Jack's reassurance, repeated again yesterday when he'd visited, a firm diagnosis of Hodgkin's might be preferable to not knowing.

The door was opened, and Sister Lynch came in, accompanied by Doctor Swanson and a short, fair-haired older man. With a shock, Barry realized that none was masked or gowned. Whatever diagnosis had been made, the condition was not highly infectious. That wasn't good. Barry knew his pulse rate had risen and his anxiety had increased.

They marched over to his bed. Sister said, "Doctor Laverty, we've brought Doctor Nelson to see you."

Barry sat bolt upright.

"Morning, young Laverty," Doctor Nelson said. "Not feeling so hot?"

Barry recognised the haematologist. He'd been a superb bedside teacher when Barry was a student. "No, sir."

"I'm not surprised. Swanson here has told me your symptoms and signs. Sounded pretty flu-like, but the lab work doesn't agree."

Barry waited.

"While your total white count was low when we first measured it, it was high on the second count."

And it was high in Hodgkin's.

"The differential showed mostly monocytes and lymphocytes." Doctor Nelson smiled.

What the hell was the man smiling at? And what did that mean?

"I looked at the slides myself this morning. The little devils had a very characteristic

303

abnormality." Doctor Nelson tapped his fingernail on his front teeth before saying, "And your Paul-Bunnell test was positive, so you certainly don't have flu." He cocked his head to one side. "Care to take a guess at what's wrong?"

Damn it, this was no time to make Barry his own teaching case. "No, I don't." Barry knew he'd spoken sharply, but would somebody please tell him what was wrong?

"No? Pity. You were always such a good student. All right. I'll put you out of your misery."

Barry shook his head. Nicely phrased, I don't think.

"The funny-looking white cells are called 'glandular fever cells.' The Paul-Bunnell test is positive in eighty percent of patients with glandular fever, also called infectious mononucleosis. Those who have the disease have a factor in their serum which has the ability to make sheep's red cells agglutinate."

What Doctor Nelson was saying was beginning to sink in. Dear God, Hodgkin's hadn't even been mentioned. Mono? Did he have mono?

"Your serum did, at a very high titre."

Barry said, struggling to keep his voice calm, "Sir, you're telling me I've got mononucleosis?" He knew that despite his efforts

304

he'd gone up an octave on the last word, which he repeated. "Mononucleosis? That's all?"

"Correct."

Barry wasn't sure if now his worries were relieved he'd like to kiss the haematologist, or having been left in uncertainty over the weekend, to hit someone. Not Doctor Nelson. It wasn't his fault he'd not been available. One thing was for sure. Doctor Barry Laverty would never, never, leave a patient of his to stew that way.

"Yes, and its infectivity is very low. There's no specific treatment except rest and fluids, so there's no reason you can't go home for a while. Rest there."

"Thank you." And the realisation took root. He'd worried, shed tears, convinced himself he was going to die for nothing. Nothing.

"Get well," Doctor Nelson said. "I'll square things with the dean, so you'll not lose credit toward your year of preregistration work. You'll be fully licensed by next August."

"Thank you." Barry hadn't even thought about that until just now. Yes. That was important.

"So, Doctor Swanson and I will be getting back to our duties. Swanson will write to your GP. Go and see him on Friday next. He can decide when you're fit to come back to work."

"I will, sir. And thank you very much."

"You hurry up and get better." And with that, the senior consultant and houseman left.

"I'm sure you'll not be sorry to be going home," Sister Lynch said. "Can someone drive you? You really shouldn't be behind a wheel until you're stronger."

"If I can use the ward phone, my mother will come and get me."

"Good. I'll send Nurse Peters to give you a hand to get ready, and if you give me your mother's number I'll phone her while you're getting organised. Speed up your discharge."

"Bangor two one double five. Please tell her to come to The Huts, our quarters. She knows where they are. And please explain to her it's glandular fever, not flu, and it's not serious." Even without knowing what had bothered Barry so much, Mum would have been worried sick too.

"I'll ring straightaway." She smiled. "We don't want to rush you, but we do need your bed."

He was still chuckling when Sister left, but he had controlled himself by the time Jan Peters appeared.

"Hello, Barry," Jan said with a smile. "I hear it's only mono. That's great. Here are the clothes you were admitted in, and the sponge bag your friend Jack Mills brought for you." She laid them on the foot of his bed and opened a screen on wheels, so he could have privacy to change.

Barry got out of bed. "Mono, that's right," he said. "I must say I'm relieved to hear it." He slipped off his split-up-the-back gown and smiled. Jack Mills had been right years ago when they'd started walking the wards as students. "They take away your dignity, and in return give you a split gown with your arse showing." Barry dressed quickly. He left his long white coat on the bed and let himself out from behind the screen, which he pushed aside. "Thanks for looking after me, Jan."

She smiled at him. "It's what they pay me to do, and you were no trouble. You did talk in your sleep, though. You were frightened, you poor thing." Her eyes were pools of sympathy, her voice gentle.

Barry smoothed down his tuft of fair hair. He always did that when he was embarrassed. He didn't know Jan Peters well, but already he felt she was someone he could trust. "You're right. I — I was frightened. I was stupid enough to try to make my own diagnosis. I'm a little embarrassed that you knew, but happy to tell you I was wrong."

She shook her head. "Barry, us nurses see more of the human side of the patients. Most of them feel they have to be on their best behaviour when the doctors are around. You know what Ulster folk are like. Don't show your feelings in public. But they'll confide in us, and we're trained to listen. You could have too, but I'll bet it's tough being a doctor and a patient at the same time."

He nodded, and thought about what she'd said. None of the teaching he'd received as a student in six years of medical school had ever touched on this. What patients were feeling emotionally, not just physically. It dawned on him that everything in a hospital that he took for granted was new and frightening to the laity. And if as a physician he'd been worried by uncertainty, how must the patients feel? "Your dad said something like that about nobody answering his questions when his father was ill. About nurses not being allowed to in case they contradicted the specialists."

She nodded. "It's true, but it doesn't stop us being sympathetic, comforting. You were very kind to Dad when he needed it."

After the last few days, Barry understood

that much better now. "How is he?"

"Getting better slowly. Worried about whether he'll ever get back to work. He was up here to outpatients last week to have another pint of blood removed, but dad's a tough old bird. He'll be all right."

Barry lifted his sponge bag and thought, Polycythaemia does not have the best prognosis. Surely Jan knows that? Perhaps for some people, not facing the truth was a comfort after all? "Tell him I was asking for him, and please give him my regards."

"I will. He'll appreciate that."

Barry headed for the door. "Thanks again, Jan." He looked round the room. "I'm off. I want to get a shave and a bath before Mum comes to take me home." As he lifted his white coat with his left hand, he winced. The botched bloodletting. Jack had been right. The result of that extra blood test had led to the decision to consult Doctor Nelson, and given Barry three days of emotional torment and a large, aching bruise. And it wasn't as if Barry needed any other reminders of what uncertainty could do to an anxious patient.

17

OBSERVATION WITH EXTENSIVE VIEW

May 2, 1969

Barry sat at Sue's bedside, holding her hand. "Won't be long now."

"The sooner the better. I really want to get this over with, Barry. Get some answers at last."

Sue had been admitted last night to the gynaecology ward of the Ulster Hospital in Dundonald and was the first case on this morning's list. As a professional courtesy, Barry had been invited to observe.

"That's why we're here. To get some answers. We're going to get through this, you know."

"I like the 'we.' I'm the one who's getting poked and prodded." She'd said it lightly, but Barry could detect the tinge of bitterness in her words. He couldn't blame her.

"Sorry. I didn't mean to snap." She squeezed his hand. "Must be all the stuff they gave me. I'm just nervous, that's all.

Thank you, Barry, for coming today."

Barry smiled. "And where else would I be?" he said, leaning down to drop a gentle kiss on her forehead.

"Thank you for understanding. Such a comfort to have you here." Her free hand smoothed the sheet at her side. "To know that even while I'm asleep, you'll be there. I'm sure Doctor Taylor will find something and fix it. I just know it." The pressure of the grip of her hand increased.

Barry was not so sure. He had some understanding of what a laparoscopy might detect, but wondered if it would be the answer Sue was looking for. "We'll see."

Barry knew Pat Taylor from Bangor. The young gynaecologist had been a year behind Barry both at Campbell College and as a student, sailed out of Ballyholme Yacht Club, and had passed the examinations of the Royal College of Obstetricians and Gynaecologists in London to qualify early this year. He'd been sent to Oldham in England to be taught the technique by Mister Patrick Steptoe, one of the pioneers. Here in Ulster Hospital, Pat was a registrar, still a junior because of the slow rate of promotion to consultant, but the most experienced laparoscopist in Ireland.

The curtains were pulled back. "Time to

take you to theatre, Mrs. Laverty." The white-clad male orderly who had spoken was accompanied by a nurse.

Barry disentangled his hand, stood, bent, and kissed her forehead again. "Good luck, love," he whispered, then stepped outside the curtains to let the orderly and nurse carry on. As Barry headed for the operating theatre he hoped Sue was right about something getting fixed, but he had his doubts.

He sat down on a bench in the surgeons' changing room. He was already wearing surgeon's trousers and shirt and began pulling on ankle-length white rubber boots. Beside him, Pat Taylor was pulling a white stockingette cap over his fair hair. "Thanks for letting me come, Pat."

He was a slight man, five foot eight, slim, clean-shaven. "My pleasure. You know the drill. There's no need for you to scrub. Keep back until I tell you to come to the table. Don't touch anything. I'll give you a running commentary, and when I've seen all I want to see, I'll hold the scope and let you take a gander through the eyepiece." He put a hand on Barry's arm. "I know this is going to worry you, with your Sue the patient. Try not to let it. It really is a simple technique and I'm not going to be removing any bits. Just having a look."

"Fair enough." Although Barry would worry. The last time he'd been in an operating theatre, Jack Mills had been performing a gastroscopy on Bertie Bishop. Barry had never been comfortable with surgery during his short time as an obstetrics and gynaecology trainee. He found it difficult to forget that it was a human being he was cutting. It was one of the reasons he had returned to general practice in Ballybucklebo. He admired the obvious self-confidence of surgeons like Jack and Pat.

"Right," said Pat, handing Barry a mask. "Let's do it." He opened the door to the operating theatre.

Barry followed his colleague, who greeted those already in the theatre. "Morning, all. This is Doctor Laverty, who has come to observe." Taylor turned on the taps over a wall-mounted sink and began to scrub.

The anaesthetist at the head of the table, the gowned and gloved scrub nurse who stood with her instrument trolley on the table's right side, and the circulating nurse, who was there to carry out nonsterile tasks, all greeted Barry.

"Good morning," he said, staring at the table, where Sue lay under a blanket. An intravenous line was running. She was hooked up to the anaesthetic machine. From over the table, the powerful beams of the light limned her belly in brightness. Her legs were supported in stirrups and the table was broken so her buttocks lay on its edge to give the surgeon access.

Barry watched as Pat and the scrub nurse painted the operative area with pungent-smelling antiseptic and arranged the green sterile towels. The sight of Sue as a surgical patient, looking like patients he'd seen during his time in medical school, was unsettling. This was his darling wife. He wondered if it had been wise to be here. Be at her bedside, yes, but here in the operating theatre?

"I'm putting a cannula into the uterus," Pat said from between Sue's thighs. "It allows me to manipulate the uterus. You're a sailor, Barry. It's like a tiller. If I push it to the right, the uterus moves to the left, and" — Taylor placed a large syringe of blue liquid on Sue's belly as if it were a convenient shelf — "I'll be using the syringe, which I've connected to the cannula with a plastic tube, to test tubal patency." He moved to the left side of the table and turned to the anaesthetist. "All set?"

"Go right ahead."

"Scalpel."

Barry flinched and looked away as Pat made a skin incision along the lower rim of Sue's umbilicus.

"Veress needle, please." He showed it to Barry. At the needle's top was a fixture for connecting it to a rubber tube. "I have to put this needle into Sue's belly and then distend the space with carbon dioxide to give me room to work." Barry closed his eyes and opened them when he heard Pat say, "And we're in. Gas line, please."

Barry swallowed.

Pat connected the gas line to the needle.

"Trendelenberg position."

The anaesthetist turned a crank and the head end of the table descended so that it was at thirty degrees to the floor.

"That lets her puddings" — typical surgeons' talk for bowels — "slip out of the pelvis and out of my way."

Sue's belly was now, Barry sighed at the thought, about as swollen as it would be if she were nine months pregnant.

"Trocar and cannula."

Pat accepted a cylindrical steel outersleeve with a trumpet valve at the top, the cannula. The trocar was a solid steel core with a wickedly sharp tip protruding from the lower end of the cannula.

Barry couldn't bear to watch. Pat was going to thrust that thing through the incision. Barry turned away again.

"Scope, please."

Barry turned back. Pat had removed the trocar and was depressing the trumpet valve to allow him to pass the telescope. He pointed to a cable running from the scope to a box on a trolley. "What revolutionised this was the work of three Frenchmen, Fourestier, Gladu, and Vulmiere, in 1952. They used fibreoptics, as I'm doing now, to bring powerful illumination from an external source. Now let's have a look." He bent and put his eye to the scope's lens. "Just where we ought to be. Now, watch."

Pat's examination didn't take long. He could see Sue's internal genital organs aided by the instrument in her uterus, the probe, and the injection of the blue dye. He stood up straight. "Take a peek." He held the telescope steady.

Barry hesitated. Felt his stomach roll and churn as if he'd just ridden a huge swell on a small boat. The thought of peering inside his wife with this scope suddenly seemed like some kind of voyeurism.

"I understand. It is strange. But she's doing fine. Just take a quick look."

Barry squared his shoulders, then bent and put his eye to the lens.

"What do you see?"

"The uterus in the midline. It looks like a pink, upside-down pear. Both ovaries, shiny, oyster-shell-coloured. Both Fallopian tubes and their fimbriated ends like little tentacles. And there's blue dye in the pelvis." He stepped back. That was enough.

"Now I've used the probe to turn things over, push things out of my way. The findings are this. Normal uterus, healthy open tubes with no signs of scar tissue that might interfere with ovum pickup, and no evidence of endometriosis."

Barry had seen several cases of the condition where for unknown reasons the endometrium, the tissue that lined the uterus, had grown in islands on the peritoneum that lined the pelvis. It caused pelvic pain and infertility.

Pat removed the probe and its cannula. Out came the scope. "Put her flat, please."

The table was returned to the horizontal.

Pat held the trumpet valve open and pressed on Sue's abdomen. "We like to get as much carbon dioxide as possible out. It has a nasty habit of combining with the peritoneal fluid and turning into carbonic acid. That's not dangerous, but it can irritate the diaphragm, which shares its nerve supply with the shoulder tips. The patients

317

often experience referred pain there." He stopped pushing and removed the cannula. "Sutures, and you can start waking her up."

One stitch closed the secondary cannula puncture, two stitches closed the primary incision. "Thanks, everybody." Pat nodded to Barry and headed for the door.

Barry followed.

In the changing room, Barry thanked his colleague, shed his operating room gear, and dressed. Pat did not. He had a full surgical list today. "She'll be back on the ward soon, Barry. I'm sure you'd like to be there when she wakes up. I'll send a full report to Graham. Can you take her stitches out in seven days?"

"Yes."

"Save her a trip up here."

Barry noticed that Pat used the impersonal "she" and "her." Typical surgeon. "I'll do it, and thank you for letting me watch." His smile was wry. "That way we don't have to wait for ages to get the report." He sighed. "But you didn't find anything, did you?"

Pat nodded. "No, I didn't. I'm not a reproductive specialist like Graham, but, speaking as a gynaecologist, if all the other tests were normal?"

"I'm afraid they were."

"Then you and Sue are going to have to

318

face up to unexplained infertility, and that's a tough one. On the other hand, if we had found damaged tubes, the pregnancy rate after surgery is only about twenty percent. We really don't know what to do for endometriosis, and those were the main things we were looking for. With no obvious lesions, there's probably a better statistical chance of pregnancy spontaneously happening."

"I know," Barry said. "Believe me, I know, but statistics is for a group of people. For Sue it's going to be all or nothing." Barry remembered Sue in February in Paris reading about the first successful fertilization of a human egg in a petri dish. "Pat, you worked with Mister Patrick Steptoe and I suppose Professor Edwards. They've been trying in vitro fertilization. They've reported one success."

"I know. Mister Steptoe let me recover some eggs laparoscopically when I was there in Oldham. When a patient was ready to ovulate, Bob would come thundering up the one hundred and seventy-eight miles from Cambridge University. We'd take the patient to a theatre that had a small embryo laboratory attached. Mister Steptoe or I would do a laparoscopy. When an egg is ripe it will be in a fluid-filled cyst in the ovary called a follicle. We'd put a needle into the follicle and suck out the fluid. It was exciting when Bob would call from the little lab beside the theatre, 'I've got an egg.' "

"And now they have been successful in fertilizing one," said Barry. "Do you think they'll ever be able to get the embryos returned to the mother to implant in the uterus and go on to grow into a healthy baby?"

Pat stroked his upper lip with the web of his hand and frowned. "Bob Edwards is an amazing enthusiast. If anybody can, he will. It could be tomorrow, but it would more likely be in five or ten years." He sighed. "I know you want to do everything possible, but don't pin your hopes on in vitro just yet. I do know how tough infertility can be when there are no answers. I'm sorry."

"No need to apologise. You did what you were asked. Thanks, Pat." He held out his hand, which Pat shook. "Thanks again. I'll trot off and see Sue when she gets back to the ward." Barry let himself out. He had to prepare himself to break the news and try to help Sue with what was bound to be disappointed frustration and awful uncertainty.

Relatives were only allowed on the wards

during visiting hours, but being a doctor had its advantages. Barry sat on the chair at the head of Sue's bed, the curtains round which were closed. She'd been groggy when she'd been wheeled back in her bed from the recovery room. Barry had held her hand and now he was satisfied that the anaesthetic had worn off and she was awake. Her pupils were constricted because the anaesthetist would have given her 100 milligrams of pethidine for postoperative pain. "How are you feeling, love?"

Sue grimaced. "Hello, Barry," she said. "My throat's a bit sore."

"That's because the anaesthetist put a tube in it."

"I see. And I've an ache in my shoulders, and my belly button and right side low down are sore, but none of it's too bad."

"And it's all over."

"Thank goodness for that." She looked deep into Barry's eyes. "And what did you find?"

Barry hesitated. "You've nothing wrong with your ovaries, Fallopian tubes, or uterus." There was no easy way to tell her, but he could soften the blow. "Pat says that's actually good news, because the kind of things we might have found are tricky to treat. I know this being in limbo is hard on

321

you." And, he thought, it's hard on me watching you suffer. "We'll get through. I know we will. I'll be there to help you. I promise."

"Thank you, Barry." It was a little voice made smaller by the tears that glistened in her eyes and began to spill over.

"I love you, Sue," he said, and took her in his arms, feeling her shake. Then the shaking stopped.

"Barry, we need to talk."

"I'm not sure that now, when you've been given a strong narcotic, is the best time to try to work out what to do next." He could remember her saying, the day her last period had started, "So, we'll just have to bide, and I'll try not to say any more about it until after it's done." They deliberately had not discussed a plan B. "They'll discharge you tomorrow. Can you wait until then?" He moved back. Looked at her face.

She pursed her lips, nodded. "I suppose so."

He kissed her forehead. "You should try to sleep now."

She lay back on her pillows. "I think I'd like to, but Barry, we do need to talk."

"Not now, pet. Wait until you're fully awake. Please."

"No, Barry. Now. We need to talk about

adoption. I don't know how we'd even start. Who we'd talk to."

"Sue, love, this isn't the time. You're still groggy." He'd been avoiding thinking deeply about adoption. He needed time to be certain of how he felt. This wasn't like taking in Tigger, the stray kitten they'd found in the storm. "Let's wait until we get you home."

"Well" — she yawned, blinked, rubbed her eyes — "maybe you're right but, Barry, I've tried to be patient, but we've run out of options."

"Not really. It's still not twenty-four months. Come on, Sue. Let's get you over the anaesthetic, get you home. That'll be tomorrow. You've waited for months. Give it a few more hours."

"All right. I really am sleepy." She closed her eyes.

"I'll wait until you've dropped off. I'll have to go back to Ballybucklebo for a while, but I will come back and see you this evening." He bent, dropped a gentle kiss on her closed eyelids, and sat. He hoped he'd handled that gently, given her time to come to terms a little, but the physician in him knew that the next step would be to consult with Graham, and that Sue and he soon must begin a serious conversation about how both of them felt about adoption. Her words now had left him in no doubt how she felt, and he knew she would want to get the discussion going even before their next consultation.

Barry looked at her now relaxed face. Her worry wrinkles were gone, but so was her smile. She began to make little whiffling noises as she often did at home as sleep overtook her. He whispered, "Sleep well, my love. Sleep well," rose softly, and tiptoed away to nurse his worries alone.

18
THERE'S NO PLACE LIKE HOME

September 2, 1963
Barry lay in one of the two bathtubs that
served sixteen young men in single rooms,
eight housemen, and eight medical students,
in a simple wooden structure officially
known as "The Huts." The rest of the
juniors, men and women, were housed in
the hospital's East Wing, which was also the
location of their dining and common rooms.
He could feel the warm water soothing his
physical aches, speeding his cure. After three
days of sponge baths, it was a luxury to lie
back and soak. The deep internal ache from
what he'd been sure was a death sentence
could not so easily be salved. It had been
like the sudden recoil of a tightly stretched
rubber band against a thumb. The tension
was gone but the sting remained. He knew
he'd learned a valuable lesson about patients' anxiety when facing uncertainty.

A couple more minutes soaking, then he'd

better get a move on. Mum would be showing up soon to take him home.

A phone rang from across the corridor, then he heard the bang of a door closing, and footsteps receding on their way to the hospital. Someone had been called to duty.

Barry got out, towelled himself dry, chucked on a dressing gown and slippers, grabbed his sponge bag, and headed for his room, whistling the Searchers hit, "Sweets for My Sweet," off-key. He was still tired, but he'd consulted his texts and refreshed his memory on the details of mono before heading for the bath, and now knew that was to be expected. At least his temperature had returned to normal and his neck was less swollen.

He let himself into his room and half filled a basin with hot water. The mirror's silver backing was missing in places, so his reflected face had dark patches. Copper pipes ran up to the taps and from the plug hole down through the linoleum-covered floor. Barry shaved at speed, nicked himself, dabbed styptic pencil on the tiny wound, and flinched from the sting.

He dressed in the clean clothes he'd laid out on the iron-framed hospital bed parked against the wall opposite the basin and beside a built-in plywood wardrobe. A wooden chair and table on which were set books and the medical texts he'd just been reading, his record player, and an easy chair with its stuffing peeping out completed the furnishings. And the Spartans thought they'd lived a simple life of hard work and sparse comforts? He smiled. Try being a houseman here in Mortuary Mansions, as it was usually known because the morgue was next door. Living with his folks would be like staying in the Grand Central Hotel.

He fished a small suitcase out from under the bed. In went enough clothes for a week, his sponge bag, and his copy of *The Sand Pebbles.* He stared at the hefty book about a U.S. Navy gunboat on patrol in China just before the civil war there in 1926. He wondered if his father had read it and whether talking about the book might help the two break through the reserve they often seemed to feel in each other's company. Commander Tom Laverty (RN retired) was typical of men of his generation. Barry had been five when he'd first met his father in 1945 and, according to his mother, had been "terrified of this strange man."

"Barry?" The door was opening.

It opened fully, and Barry saw his mother, Carol Laverty, standing there, a small, neat-figured, auburn-haired woman of fifty-one who had given Barry his blue eyes. "I knocked, son. Did you not hear? Has the virus affected your hearing? We've been worried sick."

"Sorry, Mum. Just daydreaming. Come in, come in. Still a bit groggy, but I'll live. It's only glandular fever." Boy, the relief in being able to say that. "I'll be better in a few days."

"I should hope so. Now come on. The car's outside. Let me get you home and coddle you. Am I allowed to hug you?"

"Yes."

She did so, and looked him up and down. "Have you had lunch?" She cocked her head and said, "You've lost weight. You need feeding up."

Barry dumped his suitcase on the single bed in his old bedroom on the first floor of the four-storey 1890 terrace house on Ballyholme's Esplanade. He looked out his sash window over the creeper-covered walls round the back garden. Mum loved pottering about there, tending to her flowers and vegetable patch.

The walls of his room were adorned with two triangular pennants, souvenirs of the times his dad had taken a much younger Barry out to visit HMS *King George V,* a fourteen-inch gun battleship, and HMS *Il-lustrious,* an aircraft carrier, when the huge ships were anchored in Belfast Lough near Bangor. Framed photos of his final-year classes at Bangor Grammar School and Campbell College kept company with his graduating class from Queen's. Barry stood beside his pal Jack Mills in the last two.

A framed copy of Kipling's "If" hung above the bedhead. He knew the poem by heart. Dad had given it to Barry the night before he went off, a scared thirteen-year-old, to boarding school for the first time. "It's a good code to live by," Dad had said. Barry pursed his lips as he read the first line: "If you can keep your head when all about you are losing theirs." He'd certainly lost his head last weekend. Dad would not have approved. He could be less than sympathetic on occasions.

Barry glanced at the other wall. A chest-high bookshelf was stacked with old favourites like *The Wind in the Willows, The Jungle Book, Treasure Island, The Gorilla Hunters, Kidnapped,* and the five volumes of the original Horatio Hornblower series. Those books of his childhood sat beside several leather-bound volumes of his dad's pre–World War I *Boys Own Paper,* the Empire-promoting monthly magazine. The magazines had helped shape his father's late-Victorian attitudes and expectations embodied in Kipling's poem, some of which Barry had not always been able to attain.

On top of the bookshelf was his first model ship, a simple, three-masted square-rigger that Dad had helped him build and then put into an empty whiskey bottle. His split-cane fly rod, unused for the last six years, was propped in a corner beside his creel and net. He smiled. It was comforting to be back again, and yet he realized with a pang how much of his young self he had left behind here.

He put his clothes away and trotted upstairs to the sitting room on the second floor, where he parked himself in an armchair. He'd pictured this view of Ballyholme Bay and beach from his hospital bed, drawing strength from its beauty and familiarity. The tide was out at slack ebb. Ranks of groynes, low, barnacle-encrusted walls, descended like a series of narrow steps at a thirty-degree angle from the high-water mark to the water's edge. They were there to prevent erosion of the sand by the tides. Two green-painted diving boards with coir matting on their flat tops stood at the water's edge. In the summer the beach was a popular place for swimming, although becoming less so as air travel and package holidays tempted more and more Ulster folk to Spain's Costa Brava. Now, on a Monday in early September, there were few holiday-makers.

He looked out to Ballyholme Bay to see a forest of masts close to the left-hand shore — the larger yachts of the Ballyholme and Royal Ulster yacht clubs. Across Belfast Lough, the hills of Antrim bulked large against an azure sky. And past the village of Whitehead to his right, away in the distance and blue in the heat haze, was the Mull of Galloway in Scotland.

He heard Mum come in. "There you are," she said. "I've brought your lunch." She set a tray on a sideboard, went to a settee, lifted a tartan rug, and tucked it round his knees. "Can't have you getting a chill."

"Thanks, Mum."

She put the tray on his lap. "It's my own pea and ham soup. It's nourishing, and it's hot, so don't burn yourself." She tucked a napkin under his collar. "And I've made you an egg salad sandwich, your favourite, with a treat for dessert."

With fondness Barry thought, I'm still a little boy in her eyes. The wisps of steam from the soup bore its scents of ham, cloves, and onion upward.

Mum sat on a chair opposite. His framed graduation portrait taken this July outside the redbrick façade of Queen's University stood on a low table beside her. It was one of her most treasured possessions. She looked concerned. "So, you told me in the car you were on the mend. Are you sure?"

Barry nodded. "I'm sure, Mum." He thought they had discussed his illness enough on the drive here. He had deliberately refrained from mentioning how he was still coping with the quantum leap from the anguish of being convinced he was dying to the surge of relief after realising that he was not. As he started to eat his soup and sandwich he realised that, apart from Jack and perhaps Jan Peters, no one had any inkling of what he had put himself through. Dad was definitely one of the "stiff upper lip" fraternity, but Mum was someone in whom Barry had always been able to confide his worst fears. And he wanted to now.

"All right, I promise I won't ask again." She smiled. "Now, son, finish your soup while it's hot."

He did as he was told, then put down his spoon and sat back. "Mum," he said, "you asked if I was sure if I was on the mend, and I certainly am from mononucleosis, but," he hesitated, "I gave myself an awful scare."

She hunched forward and frowned.

"Before I was given a diagnosis today I was convinced — now please understand, I was wrong, thank God — but I was convinced I had a fatal disease."

Her eyes widened, and her hand flew to her mouth. "What did you think you had?"

"Doesn't matter. I was rattled. Tried to diagnose myself, and scared myself to death."

"Oh, Barry, I'm so sorry."

"So, it's not just recovering from the mono, I have to get over the fear, too."

Mum leaned forward and put a comforting hand on his. "How awful, and I do understand. It's the not knowing, isn't it?"

Barry frowned. "How did you know?"

"How do you think I felt during the war when the BBC announced, 'One of our ships was sunk today'? I was a young bride with a baby to bring up. I immediately convinced myself it was Dad's *Warspite,* and hardly slept until I got his next letter. So, I know how the floods of relief feel too." She smiled. "I know it's horrid, but you'll get over it, I promise."

Barry felt the warmth of her hand on his, the warmth of the soup in his belly, the warmth of her words. She knew just how he felt. "Thanks, Mum. Thanks a lot. It always helps to have someone to confide in."

"It does." They sat in silence for a moment, both looking out on the bay.

"Now, finish your sandwich." Mum sat back.

Barry took a bite.

"You've always been able to talk to me, son, but you find it more difficult with Dad, don't you?"

He nodded, spared from having to answer because his mouth was full.

"It's not surprising, really. His father was from a townland outside Ballymena in County Antrim. He died just before the war and I only met him once or twice. He was very strict with Tom, I think. Couldn't abide any display of weakness. Your dad finds it hard to show affection. Add to that, you were five in 1945 when you first met him." Her smile was wistful. "You were terrified of him, you poor wee dote. There are more casualties of war than those on the battlefield. I think that five-year gap kept you and Dad from being close."

"I do love him, Mum."

"I know. I do know, and I know how very hard you've tried to please him, but he's not a man who wears his heart on his sleeve.

He's very proud of you but finds it hard to tell you."

"Thanks, Mum."

"I always worried it was a lonely life for you with no brothers or sisters. After the war, when Tom left the navy to study engineering, money was so tight and there hardly seemed enough time after his studies for a child."

Barry thought about the times he'd spent with his father as a boy. The outings had been memorable — precious, but rare.

"Once he'd finished his engineering training, Dad and I decided that a nine-year gap would be too much for me to be having more children."

"I had you, and my friends. But I've often wondered. Thanks for telling me."

She took a deep breath. "I'd have liked more, but — the bloody war. I missed you so much when you went off to boarding school."

"I'm so sorry, Mum."

She pulled a white handkerchief from her apron pocket and dabbed quickly at her eyes. "Can't be helped. I was lucky to have you, and lucky your father came back from the war. Plenty didn't. Now." She stood and kissed her son's head. "Tom Laverty's a good man and so are you, Doctor Barry

Laverty."

He smiled and so did she.

She lifted his tray. "I'll be back in a jiffy with your dessert."

Barry looked round the familiar, comfortable room, the high, wide marble fireplace with two ceramic black-and-white Dalmatian dogs flanking the grate and Mum and Dad's wedding photograph in the middle of the mantelpiece. Dad, a keen sailor, had acquired three pencil sketches of yachts by the Ulster artist Cresswell Boak. They were hung one above the other on the chimney breast. The suite sitting on a rich green carpet was arranged to capture the warmth from the fire in the winter and that splendid view through the bay window of Ballyholme Bay year-round.

Mum reappeared, bearing a bowl of her homemade vanilla ice cream and toffee sauce. "Here," she said, "eat that up. You said your throat had been sore."

"Thanks. That really is a treat." Barry tucked in.

"So, how are you enjoying being a houseman?"

"It's fair enough," he said. "I'm working in casualty at the moment. Some serious illnesses. We start any urgent treatment and tests and get them admitted. I never see them again. Then there's a long procession of walking wounded who have to be processed as quickly as possible."

She frowned. "But you are happy at your work? I always want you to be happy."

Barry nodded, smiled, and finished his ice cream.

"More?" He heard the hope in her voice.

He smiled. "No thanks. I'm stuffed," he said, and was rewarded with a smile. "And yes, I'm happy, but I'm really looking forward to my next three months on the medical wards."

"That's good," she said, "and you are getting enough to eat? Enough sleep."

"Of course." Which wasn't quite true, but why worry her more?

She leant forward. Her tone was serious. "I'm very glad to hear that." Laugh lines came back to the corners of her eyes. "And any lady friends?"

He laughed. Trust Mum. She always asked. "As a matter of fact, there is. Her name's Virginia Clarke. She's a student nurse." And he relished the thought of her.

"If you like her then she must be nice."

"She is. Very."

"So why don't you bring her home soon, so Dad and I can meet her?"

Barry raised his eyes to the heavens. "I've

337

taken her out twice. Twice. I'm not fully qualified until I've finished this year. I don't know what kind of career I want, general practice or speciality, so I'm not thinking about getting —"

"Married? I know, son, but I'd like to meet her anyway."

Barry shook his head and smiled. "All right. I'll ask her for dinner. But let me get better first."

"Of course, Barry, but now, how would you like a nap? You must be tired."

"I'd like that a lot." And indeed, even though the excitement of being home had given him extra energy, he did feel drowsy. He might be mending, but he wasn't completely better yet. He stood, put the rug back in its place, and as he headed downstairs wondered how soon it would be before he could invite Virginia to Ballyholme.

"Hang on," Virginia said. "I love to walk through sand in my bare feet." She sat on the grass at the edge of Ballyholme Beach and began to remove her shoes.

"I'll keep mine on," Barry said. He looked around. "Mum was right suggesting we go for a walk." And, he thought, she understood I'd like to be alone with Virginia.

The September sun had lost the scorching heat of August. A soft onshore breeze chased fluffy clouds before it cast small, rippled shadows on the waters of the bay. Grey-and-white glaucous gulls, and smaller black-headed gulls, soared, glided, and squabbled overhead.

When she stood up holding her shoes in one hand, Barry said, "I'm going to take you to Ballymacormick Point. Mum took me there a lot when I was little. The National Trust acquired it in 1952 to preserve it."

"Come on then. Let's get going."

Together they crunched over the dry sand.

She took a deep breath. "I love the salty smell of the sea."

Barry chuckled. "Actually, that wonderful salty smell, and I love it too, is coming from decaying seaweed."

"What a romantic man you are, Barry Laverty." She laughed, then became serious. "But I'm so glad you're feeling much better."

He reached out and took her hand. "I went to see my GP, Doctor Bowman, on Friday. To my great delight he pronounced me physically fit to return to duty on Monday. Tomorrow. There's only one snag. He said that to be on the safe side, I've not to kiss anybody for another ten days. Damn it. But I'm so happy you were off today and able to come down for dinner." He squeezed her hand and she returned the squeeze. God, it was good to see her.

When they came to a narrow freshwater stream tinkling over its stony bed, Barry released her hand and jumped across. "Come on. I'll catch you."

She jumped, and he enfolded her in his arms, feeling the softness and warmth of her through her silk blouse. "I do love you, Virginia Clarke."

"And I love you, Barry." She laughed. "And it took you collapsing to make me recognise that."

He held her at arm's length and looked into her eyes, knowing that for him all was well with the world; well, pretty much all. The nagging discomfort after his emotional shock was still there in the background, but rapidly fading as with each day he felt stronger.

"I like your mum."

"She's not hard to like."

"She certainly seemed pleased to meet me. And not a bit shy. It was sweet what she said."

"About you being very lovely and having beautiful green eyes?"

"Yes, that," she said, blushing. "It's the truth."

"Flatterer." She smiled. "And she's very protective of you, telling you not to overtire yourself — 'like a good boy.' "

"She's always been like that." He shook his head but smiled. "I think all mothers are protective of their grown-up sons." He chuckled. "My dad's not. He reckons, and I quote, 'You're big enough and ugly enough to look after yourself. He expects me to be self-reliant. You'll meet him later. He plays golf every Sunday afternoon, so don't feel slighted that he wasn't here when you arrived. I reckon if the queen herself came to tea on a Sunday afternoon at 21B Ballyholme Esplanade, Dad would be playing golf. I hope you'll like him too."

He led her through two rough stone gateposts that marked the start of the footpath. "Better put your shoes on. The path gets rough from here on."

She sat, dusted her soles with the flat of her hand, slipped on her shoes, then reached out her hand so he could pull her to her feet and, briefly, into his arms again.

They started along the path that followed the shore between grasslands, and patches of yellow-flowered whin bushes and scrub.

Two birds like small geese with pink nebs

341

and dark green heads pitched with a splash into the shallows inshore, showing off the black, chestnut, and green patches on their wings.

"Shelduck," Barry said. "Pretty birds." He chuckled. "And so are you. Very pretty. No, that's not good enough. You are beautiful. God, I wish I could kiss you."

"So do I, but there'll be plenty of time for that later." She squeezed his hand.

He remembered her saying on Monday, "There'll be plenty of time when you're better." Then, he'd been convinced there would not. Now? Now, they had all the time in the world. "Yes," he said, "yes, there will." And he grinned from ear to ear.

The short waves splashed against the rocky shoreline.

A swirling in the water close inshore caught Barry's eye. He lowered his voice. "Keep still and turn your head slowly."

Virginia obeyed.

"Wait."

Moments later a shiny grey head with twitching whiskers and enormous limpid eyes the colour of polished mahogany surfaced not ten yards from where they stood. The creature stared at them, snorted through its wide V-shaped nostrils, breathed in, and slipped below the surface.

"Grey seal," Barry said.

"Are you sure it's not a selkie?"

"A what?"

"You know, a selkie, a magical half seal, half woman. If she comes ashore she sheds her sealskin and becomes a beautiful woman. If a man steals her sealskin, she can't go back to sea and has to become his wife."

"I've never heard of that. When Dad sometimes told me Irish stories, he talked about the giant Finn MacCool and his followers, the Fianna or Cuchulain, who led the Red Branch Knights of Ulster."

"Typical man. No time for stories about girls." But she was smiling.

"Perhaps, but I have time for you. A lot of time."

"When we can both get free together." She sighed. "The first time you tried to ask me out I gave you my usual brush-off line about having a class and that getting qualified was important to me."

"True, and when we walked up Cave Hill you told me about wanting to go on and be a midwife. That you hadn't gone into nursing to snag a doctor. 'To marry up.' You were serious about it."

"And I didn't expect to fall in love with you, Barry, but I did, and now I want to see a lot more of you."

Barry glowed inside. He started to walk again. "Me too, but the next two months are going to be tricky. Our shift system in casualty doesn't leave much room for swapping, but come November I'll be on 5 and 6, and Jack or Norma can cover for me when you're free in the evening."

"I am a nurse," she said. "I do understand what life can be like for young doctors. I'll try to be patient."

He stopped and hugged her. "What are you doing next Monday?" He let her go.

"As far as I know, I'll be off duty."

"And come hell or high water I'll be too. I'm going back to work tomorrow, so Mum will run us both up to the Royal after dinner, and by the following Monday I can kiss you." He hugged her again. "And if I have to wait any longer, I'm going to burst."

19
WROTE MY WILL ACROSS THE SKY

May 10, 1969

"So, this is where you'd pose then, Julie, when that Mister Hunter, Mister Bishop's cousin, had you do hair modelling for him?"

O'Reilly watched Donal Donnelly's eyes widen. He was wearing his Sunday-best suit, white shirt, and blue tie. His carroty hair was neatly trimmed. He whistled. "Boys-a-boys, but there's a quare clatter of equipment just for til take a few snaps." He was staring at large cameras on tripods, arrays of floor-and ceiling-mounted spotlights, and white reflecting umbrellas on stands.

Julie held little Tori's hand. "He's real professional, so he is." Her long blonde hair was shining, and she had on an aquamarine and polka-dot sleeveless dress and white boots. "And thank youse both, Doctor and Mrs. O'Reilly, for this. Imagine us getting our family portrait done to hang over the fireplace once we get moved into Dun Bwee on Monday."

"It's our pleasure. We wanted something to mark the occasion, now that all the work is done on the cottage." O'Reilly chuckled. It felt satisfying to be outsmarting Donal Donnelly, Ballybucklebo's arch schemer.

Kitty was standing at O'Reilly's shoulder, rocking the identical-twin Donnelly girls, Abigail and Susan Brigit, in their pram. He glanced at Kitty and pictured his elegant wife nearly choking with laughter earlier this week when O'Reilly told her his plans for today.

They'd been having their preprandial drink upstairs in the lounge. "You know, Kitty, I've been thinking about that family portrait hanging over John MacNeill's fireplace ever since we were there for dinner three weeks ago with that Mullan fellah."

Kitty sipped her G&T. "Go on."

"Bertie Bishop says he and his crew can move all Donal and Julie's stuff from the cottage on the marquis's estate to Dun Bwee this Saturday morning and then have the hooley in the afternoon. But he has to be certain Donal and his family won't be in there." O'Reilly let a puff of smoke from his pipe drift upward. "You and I, my dear Kitty, are going to give the Donnellys a housewarming present of a family photo-

346

portrait, to be shot on Saturday morning in Belfast."

Kitty's pealing laughter woke Lady Macbeth from where she had been sleeping in front of the grate.

"That's brilliant, Fingal. You are the Wily O'Reilly."

"I am, my dear, and so's Bertie Bishop. Donal needs the company van for the move, and Bertie's told Donal it won't be available until Monday. Flo and Kinky, Cissie Sloan, and Maggie MacCorkle will have all the catering done and ready to take to Dun Bwee, and all the hush-hush invitations have gone out. John and Myrna will be coming. Lars is coming too. He phoned me last night. Says he's ready to see Myrna again."

"Good for him. It's time he and Myrna Ferguson at least try to get comfortable with each other."

A crash brought O'Reilly back to the photography studio in Belfast.

Four-year-old Tori, her blonde hair tied with pale blue ribbons, had knocked over one of the umbrellas, and Donal was setting it back on its feet. "No harm done, Tori, but try to be a bit more careful, love."

"Yes, Daddy. Sorry, Daddy." She stuck her thumb in her mouth and clutched her dolly more tightly, the one she'd saved from last year's house fire.

The door opened, and in came Mister Hunter. "Sorry to keep you waiting, but I was on the phone. It is very good to see you again, Julie. It was fun when you modelled for me."

O'Reilly saw Donal's brow wrinkle. He cocked his head and looked sideways at Mister Hunter. Had Donal, who was initially unenthusiastic about his wife's modelling, been jealous of the photographer? "But it's different this time," said Donal. "You're working for us now — at least for Doctor and Mrs. O'Reilly."

"Indeed I am, and happy to be. Again, I'm sorry to have kept you waiting."

He wasn't one bit sorry, O'Reilly knew. Mister Hunter had been primed earlier to spin things out.

"Julie used to come home all made up back then. Will I need some now?"

"No, Mister Donnelly. We want you to look natural. Maybe a bit of powder if your nose is a bit red or shiny in the lights."

Donal clutched his nose. "There's nothing wrong with my nose. I haven't touched a drop, so I haven't. I don't need no powder. I'd never hear the end of it from the lads at the Duck. Me in makeup? They'd be calling me Danny La Rue, so they would."

348

O'Reilly chuckled. Danny La Rue was the stage name of the County Cork–born Daniel Patrick Carroll, a popular female impersonator.

Mister Hunter laughed as he fussed with positioning two spotlights at exactly the right angle. "Julie. I hesitate to ask, but your hair is particularly fetching today." He stepped back, cocked his head to one side, and studied it. "I don't suppose you'd consider sitting for me again?"

Julie smiled. "What do you think, Donal?"

"I, well, that is . . ." Donal's face did its usual whirling dervish act as he wrestled with the problem. "The extra do-ray-mi wouldn't hurt, but it's up til you, dear."

"I'd like to, Jimmy."

"Very good. Let's get this portrait taken, and then we can discuss it. Mister Donnelly, if you could sit on this Regency love seat and take one of your twins on your knee, and Julie . . ."

O'Reilly stopped at the Ballybucklebo traffic light and indicated for a left turn. "Donal, Mister Bishop called me this morning. I forgot to mention there's been a bit of a change of plans," he said. "He asked me to bring you to his place to discuss some building project."

349

"On a Saturday? Och, dear," Donal said from the backseat. "What about Julie and the kiddies?"

The light changed. O'Reilly waited for a gap in the oncoming traffic and turned onto Shore Road. "Mrs. O'Reilly will run Julie and the girls to our place from here." He turned onto the Bishops' drive. "And Mister Bishop will run you and me to Number One when you and he have finished, and we'll join the rest. Kinky has lunch ready for the seven of us."

"One of Kinky's lunches," Julie said. "Och, you are spoiling us. Thank you, Doctor and Mrs. O'Reilly."

Tori bounced on the seat. "And I can see the big doggy and the wee white pussycat." Her happy laughter filled the car as O'Reilly parked.

"Come on, Donal." O'Reilly and Kitty both got out, he to wait for Donal, she to walk round the car and get behind the steering wheel. "Drive carefully, pet. See you soon." He closed the door.

Lars's E-Type Jaguar was parked in front of the bungalow on the shore of Belfast Lough. He was going to have lunch with Bertie today, then run them both to this afternoon's housewarming party.

Bertie Bishop stood on the front steps.

"Good of you to bring Donal, Doctor. Flo's out with her friends getting something organised as usual."

O'Reilly knew bloody well what that something was.

"Come in, the pair of you."

O'Reilly followed Bertie, and Donal brought up the rear as they walked along the hall's Axminster carpet.

"In here." Bertie Bishop turned into the spacious lounge/dining room with its view through a picture window out over an extensive lawn to the waters of Belfast Lough. The Knockagh War Memorial, high on Knockagh Hill above the little town of Greenisland, stood dark against a clear blue sky.

Lars rose from where he was sitting at a dining table in front of the window. "Finn, and Mister Donnelly." He offered his hand. "I'm Lars O'Reilly. We've met when you've been looking after the bar at some of my brother's functions, and I remember you piping at Finn and Kitty's wedding, but we haven't been formally introduced. I'm sure you know I'm a solicitor. I've been doing some legal work that concerns you, for Mister Bishop."

Donal Donnelly, face working overtime in puzzlement, shook the hand and said,

351

"Pleased til meet you, Mister O'Reilly, but am I in some kind of trouble?" His gaze flitted from Lars's face to Bertie Bishop's.

"Not at all, Donal," Bertie said. "Come and sit at the table and Mister O'Reilly will explain. I asked Doctor O'Reilly to come as a witness of today's business. Thank you, Doctor."

O'Reilly inclined his head.

When Donal, O'Reilly, and Bertie were seated, Lars opened a file in front of him and beamed at Donal. He spoke in what O'Reilly had always thought of as Lars's legal voice. "The details are a little complicated, Mister Donnelly, so don't be afraid to ask questions, but Mister Bishop has asked me to draw up a contract between the Bishop Building Company and one Donal Donnelly Esquire, of Dun Bwee Cottage, 178B Bangor Road, County Down."

"Excuse me, sir, a contract? You mean with things like 'party of the first part,' and heretofores and thereafters?" He shook his head. "Look. I'm a carpenter by trade. A simple man. I'd never understand a thing like that, so I'd not. I —"

"Donal," Bertie Bishop interrupted, "you don't have to worry about all that stuff. That's what Mister O'Reilly's for. I don't care what you say. You're not as green as you're cabbage-looking. There's nothing difficult to understand. Mrs. Bishop and me has no family. You know I've been taken sick twice lately. I want to make sure if anything happens to me, my Flo will be looked after. So" — he counted on the little finger of his left hand with his right index finger — "point one. I want to make you a partner in my business. You can understand that, can't you?"

Donal blanched. His eyes widened. His lip trembled. He whispered, "You want to what, sir? You want to — ? Dear God." Donal frowned, turned his head off to the side, stared at Bertie Bishop, and said, "You're not having me on, are you, Mister Bishop?"

O'Reilly wasn't surprised that Donal's first thought might be to question Bertie Bishop's sincerity. Donal Donnelly was, after all, not above bending the truth himself. He was well known for occasionally pulling creative stunts on unsuspecting strangers to help provide for his family. Nevertheless, O'Reilly would never question the man's dealings when it came to folks from Ballybucklebo, and he knew Bertie wouldn't either.

"No, Donal Donnelly, I am not having you on. I want to make you my partner

353

because" — his index finger moved from his little to his ring finger — "point two, the way I want to set it up is you'll be helping Flo when I'm not here anymore, until she's not here anymore."

"I don't believe this, but Mister Bishop, apart from a wee misunderstanding about shares in a racehorse a while back, you've played fair with us, so I have to believe you." Donal's bucktoothed grin was vast. He held his hands up. They were shaking. "Would youse look at me. I'm all atremble." He lowered his hands. "Mind you, I really don't understand how I'm going til look after Mrs. Bishop." He turned to Lars. "Can you explain, sir?"

Lars's thin moustache rose as he smiled. "I can, and for the record, the Bishop Building Company is the party of the first part and you are the party of the second part."

Everyone laughed.

"Here's how it will work," Lars said. "You're going to buy a quarter share of Mister Bishop's business."

"Me, sir? Where would I get the dosh?" The excitement had gone from Donal's voice.

"From the bank," Bertie said. "It's already arranged with the manager, Mister Canning."

"A loan, like. Och, I don't know, sir. You don't hardly pay me enough to take on a loan. I've got three kiddies now and the new house and all."

"Are you asking me for a raise, then, Donal? Well, I'll tell you what —"

Bertie gave Donal a menacing look and Donal shrank back in his seat.

"I'll up your wages enough so you can repay a bank loan, you eejit. You can repay the capital and ten percent interest in fifteen years, and still be comfortable."

"Honest til God, Mister Bishop? You'd pay me to pay off a loan to buy your own company. Me?"

"Part of my company, Donal. Just part, mind."

"But what do I know about running a building company?"

"Look here, Donal. You're smarter than you look, and a lot smarter than you think. Who deals with all the men now?"

"Well, I do, sir."

"And who does the ordering and most of the scheduling as well as all the carpentry?"

Donal scratched his head and looked up at the ceiling. "Well, me, I suppose, sir."

O'Reilly glanced at his brother, who was watching the exchange like a ping-pong game, and trying, and failing, to get a word in.

"When I go, Donal, you'll still have to pay off the bank for your quarter share if you haven't already, but I'll leave you the other three-quarters of the company. No strings attached. You can have half the profits yearly, and the rest goes til my Flo for the rest of her time, then it's all yours. What do youse think of that?"

Donal said nothing, absolutely nothing.

Finally, Donal said, his voice low, "I'd not know how til thank you enough, sir. Nor can Julie and my weans."

"You can thank me by paying attention to Mister O'Reilly, who'll tell you about things like how you can get a reduction in your income taxes on the repayment of the loan, what happens if you die before Flo, how you can't sell the company until after Flo's gone. The learning won't take long, but we'll keep our partnership to ourselves until I've finished teaching you the business stuff like bookkeeping and quantity surveying that we've been working on, because as soon as I know you're able, I'm taking some of that twenty-five percent money and me and Flo's going on a world cruise and you can take care of Bishop's Building Company and tell the world why."

"I still don't believe this. Me, Donal Donnelly, I'm going til own a quarter of Bishop Building Company?"

"That's right, and we'll not be changing the name. People is used til it as it is," Bertie said. "No need to confuse them."

"Fair enough, and it still will be mostly your company anyroad, sir." Donal looked Bertie Bishop in the eye. "I'll do the paperwork with Mister and Doctor O'Reilly in a wee minute, but," he spat on the palm of his hand and offered it to Bertie Bishop, who replied in kind and said, "we have a deal, Mister Bishop. And thank you very much."

O'Reilly knew there was no more binding promise to an Ulsterman.

"We do indeed, Donal, and as from the minute you've finished signing with Mister O'Reilly, you can drop the 'Mister Bishop.' It's Bertie to my partner."

O'Reilly was sure he could see a moist glint in the eyes of both men.

20
FEEL THE PANGS OF DISAPPOINTED LOVE

October 31, 1963

Jack Mills was the last to join Barry, Norma Fitch, and Harry Sloan at a table in the busy housemen's dining room in the East Wing. Ten of the other twelve junior house officers were eating their dinners. The air was filled with the hum of conversation, the clink of cutlery on china, and the smell of boiled cabbage. For all of them, tonight marked the end of the first of the four three-month stints their preregistration year called for, two on medical units and two on surgical ones.

A phone mounted on the wall rang and was answered by the nearest young doctor. "Robin, they need you on 19. A plaster cast's too tight."

"Right." A tall redheaded white-coated man rose, pushed his chair back, and made for the door.

"He's on his way."

"No rest for the wicked, so," said Sean Barry, a Corkman with his dark hair in a crew cut, sitting at the next table. "Shame you're missing out on this gourmet repast, Robin."

"Away off and chase yourself, Sean," Robin said just before he closed the door.

"Indeed," said Harry Sloan, "but if any of us stick the pace long enough and get to be consultants, we'll have our lunches in the consultants' lounge and be home at night for our dinners while our juniors do the work."

"You remember that old legend," Jack Mills asked, as he plonked his plate of Cornish pasties, champ, and boiled cabbage down on Harry's table, "about how a freed galley slave would miss his chains?"

"You know I do, Jack Mills," said Barry, "because we were in the same class for English."

Jack laughed. "After these last three months in casualty, you're not going to hear me begging for a second rotation in the place. Or miss being on call for eighty-four hours a week."

Barry smiled. "I'm looking forward to having some freedom at night."

"Oh, aye, and I know why, too. Gives you a chance to see Virginia," said Jack with an exaggerated leer. "We're hardly ever called and we're allowed to cover each other after six and at weekends. Tonight, October 31, 1963, we've cast off them ol' casualty chains."

"Oh, come on, Jack," Barry said. "Casualty wasn't too bad. Bernie O'Byrne's a great sister. Very protective of her young doctors. Very tactful if she thought you were making a mistake. I reckon I learnt a fair bit in the month before I got sick, and even more when I came back to work after."

"All better now, I hope?" Norma said.

"Absolutely." And the internal tremors had long gone too. "In the two months since I got back, I also learnt how not to panic with tricky cases. How to get used to catching the occasional flea." He glanced at Norma Fitch. "I'd already been shown in August how to scare the living bejasus out of belligerent drunks."

Norma laughed.

"Anyway, it's over for us," she said, "except for Curly Maguire. He's got casualty shift until midnight when the next group takes over and we all move on to our next rotations and are on call for our new units."

"I start on 5 and 6 tomorrow," Barry said, relishing the thought of his next assignment.

"Don't worry, Barry," Norma said. "I'll

do that favour for you then. But you're not worried that it'll be your first day as a houseman there?"

"I've done two rotations there as a student. I know how the place runs. It'll only be for a few hours while I'm off-site. Thanks, Norma."

Harry said, "If you're looking for cover tomorrow, Barry, I'm going to sicken your happiness. Five and 6 are on 'take-in.' "

Barry's jaw dropped. "Shite."

Housemen were expected to be on or available to their units from eight to six, when the bulk of the work was done, and for the full twenty-four hours on "take-in days," to admit and help treat acutely ill patients from casualty. All junior staff had to be available. Although nominally always on call, it was often possible to snatch a few hours' sleep, and it was perfectly permissible to arrange evening cover with a friend on other evenings. Usually not much happened after six — except on those damn take-in days. He picked up his fork, then put it down and pushed the rest of the pasty aside. It was as tough as an old boot.

"Good luck to you, mate," Harry said. "I'll tell you what Franky P" — the juniors' nickname for the senior cardiologist at the Royal, the eminent Doctor Frank Pantridge,

361

MC, to whom the medal for gallantry had been awarded during the siege of Singapore — "said to me the day I started there: 'Welcome to 5 and 6, Sloan. Take a half day.' 'Thank you, sir.' 'And get a haircut. You won't have another chance for your three months here.' Typical of the man. Can't resist pulling people's legs."

Norma asked, "And did you get a haircut?"

Harry shook his head. "Didn't get a half day either."

Everyone laughed.

"You can laugh," Harry said, "but he has a habit of showing up at midnight and demanding, 'Where's my houseman?' "

Barry knew that. "But surely you can still get a houseman from one of the other medical wards to cover their unit and yours for a few hours in the evening if you want to go out? Then you repay the compliment when they want a bit of time?"

Harry nodded. "You can, but the boss won't let you away with it too often, and certainly not on take-in."

Barry sighed. In the last two months, he had tried to sustain his romance with Virginia, but it hadn't been easy. They were lucky to be able to meet once a week, and whoever had said, "Absence makes the heart grow fonder," may not have got it exactly right.

Harry toyed with his packet of cigarettes. "Actually, Franky P may come across as a bit of an ogre, but I think he's a shy man and his gruffness is a façade. He's a bloody good boss to work for. You'll learn a lot, and not only cardiology." Harry grimaced. "We've talked about this, Barry. You also have to get a pretty thick skin. Some of your patients aren't going to make it."

"So, cardiology's not for you, Harry?" Jack asked.

"Nyeh. Not bloody likely."

Jack rose and collected three empty plates and Barry's half-finished one. "There's apple pie and custard for dessert. Anyone?"

The rest passed. Royal Victoria custard could do double duty as wallpaper paste.

"Anybody mind?" Harry asked, producing a cigarette.

Two heads shook.

Jack returned with his dessert.

Harry lit up. Blew a smoke ring. "The thing I liked best when we were students was pathology. Now, I know the lot of you think it's doing postmortems, looking at removed organs, and staring down microscopes at tissue samples, all of which has nothing to do with helping patients —

363

'cause that's what I think attracted us all to medical school. Looking after people."

Three nods of assent.

"You'd be wrong. Every time I'd do a biopsy and say, 'That's a benign mole, not a melanoma,' or 'That section from an ovarian tumour is benign,' I would be helping a living patient. Telling a gynaecologist or a surgeon the exact nature of a biopsy or removed organ is critical to planning that patient's care. That's helping too. I'd just not know the patients closely. But the clinician's greatest support, particularly the surgeons', is the pathology department. They just don't get the pleasure of a grateful patient saying thanks."

"To each his own," Barry said, "but I find feeling I've done my best for a patient and then having them say thanks is very gratifying."

"Me too," Norma said.

"I think so too." Harry blew another smoke ring and watched the round blue cloud hover over the table before continuing. "But if I become a pathologist I won't have to deal with losing patients either."

"I'm with you, Harry," Jack said. "Now I've finished casualty, I'm going to 13 and 14, Mister Sinclair Irwin's surgical wards. I do want to help people, but I don't want to get too close. I'm pretty certain I'll be going for surgery. I really enjoy the diagnostic side of the work, I love working with my hands, but I don't want to be put off making a bloody great incision by thinking, I'm going to cut into Willy John, who plays centre-forward for the village team, is having a row with his girlfriend, and breeds rabbits. I want to ignore that, get in, whip out half his stomach, and sew him up."

Barry nodded. He'd known that about his friend for quite a while.

Jack pushed his empty plate aside. "Can I bum a smoke, Harry?"

Harry smiled. "Bloody cadger," he said, but handed over a Gallaher's Green and gave Jack a light.

"So, Harry and Jack seem to have picked," Norma said. "Me? I loved paediatrics when we were students, so I'm thinking I'll finish this year and then decide. I'm on 3 and 4, Professor Bull, the prof of medicine's ward next. It's a general medical unit like 5 and 6, but where Franky P. has a special interest in hearts, Prof. Bull's field is renal disease. Then we'll all have two more rotations, but I'm pretty sure I'll be applying for a six-month houseman's post at Sick Kids." She looked at Barry. "How about you, chum?"

Barry hesitated. "There's not a rotation I

didn't enjoy when we were students. I got a bit bored with a lot of the run-of-the-mill stuff in casualty —"

"I reckon we all did," Norma said.

Jack laughed. "I know I did."

"But, I still enjoy meeting people. Getting to know them. And I hope I'll be able to do that on my next three stints, starting tomorrow on 5 and 6."

Harry stubbed out his cigarette. "That'll be up to you, Barry. It'll mean spending more time with each patient, and you'll have to deal with losing some of them."

"I know, Harry, but I'm beginning to think I'd like to give general practice a crack."

"Nothing wrong with that," Norma said, "and if you don't like it, you can always come back into a junior hospital post for training in whatever speciality you fancy."

"Anyway," Jack said, nipping the end of his cigarette into the ashtray and rising, "we still have the rest of the year to decide. I'm heading for my room. Coming, Barry?"

"Right."

Barry left the room and joined his friend in the hall.

"You sounded pretty miffed about working tomorrow night," Jack said.

"I am. It's about the first chance I've had

366

to see Virginia for ten days. Now I can't get free, because 5 and 6 will be on take-in."

They turned onto the main corridor and headed for the stairs down to the passage past the cafeteria on the way to The Huts.

"She's off tonight and tomorrow, but I wanted to take her out to dinner tomorrow night. I don't want to take a drink on my first night on 5 and 6 in case I'm called after twelve and arrive on the ward stinking of it." He made a huhing noise. "I'm still daft about Virginia. In September I was thinking I might have a future with her."

Jack shook his head. "You're a glutton for punishment, Barry. You fall in love so easily. I feel for you. I really do."

"Says he who doesn't know the meaning of the word and thinks anything in a skirt except a kilted pipe band is fair game?"

"Unless it's the Dagenham Girl Pipers," Jack said, and laughed.

"Oh for God's sake, Jack, be serious. I think she's cooling off."

"Oh-oh." Jack frowned. "But if she is cooling off, don't forget your uncle Jack's advice about numbers of fish in the sea, or student nurses in Musson House."

"Are you ever serious?"

"Sorry, bye."

"I should bloody well think so. Here I am,

367

worried I might lose her, and your advice is there's plenty of fish in the sea. The first time I let her down was early October. I was meant to be off at six. I had a patient with a perforated ulcer so I couldn't just say, 'Right. It's six, I'm off duty now,' and leave the poor bugger. I was forty minutes late picking her up. She was miffed but said as a nurse she had to understand. It seemed all right for a while, but the same sort of thing happened ten days ago. She wasn't happy. Not one bit. I said I'd make it up to her. I promised I'd take her to the Causerie for dinner tomorrow."

"But the best-laid plans are scuppered by take-in," Jack said as they left the hospital and walked under dim lighting past the tennis courts and into The Huts. "Well, you heartsick Romeo, I'd suggest you nip over to Musson House. You're off duty until midnight." He looked at his watch. "Seven fourteen? You could explain about tomorrow and take her out for a coffee. Bring her back to your room."

"By God, you're right. I just need to get my coat."

Barry was still panting ten minutes later when Virginia appeared on the steps of Musson House. The night porter, Joe, clearly had succeeded in delivering Barry's message.

"Hello, Barry. Sorry I'm a bit of a mess. I'd just taken off my makeup. Can't stay long. I've staked out one of the bathtubs and I was going to wash my hair. I'm looking forward to tomorrow night and I want to look my best."

So, they'd not be going out tonight. That was obvious. "You look fine," Barry said. "I mean — you always look lovely to me."

She smiled. "Tonight, I think you need your eyes tested, but you're sweet. Anyway, what brings you here tonight?"

"To apologise."

"What for?"

"You know I start on 5 and 6 at midnight. When I asked you out for tomorrow I didn't know that 5 and 6 will be on take-in. I can't get away —"

Her smile fled.

"Look, I'm really sorry, but —"

"Sometimes your job has to come first. You told me that the last time you were late." She shook her head. "And I've just bought a new dress I thought you'd like."

Barry didn't know what to say. Another sorry would do no good. He tried to move closer to her, but she took a step back.

"I'll make it up to you, I promise. As soon as I can get free." He stopped talking as two

369

laughing student nurses in civilian dress trotted down the steps and one called out, "Goodnight, Virginia."

"Goodnight, Noreen. Phyllis."

Their laughter faded as they walked away.

Barry said, "I will make it up to you. I love you, Virginia."

It seemed an age before she said, "All right. And I love you too, but my bath's getting cold. I'm working on 9 and 10 starting tomorrow. Come and tell me when you'll be free, but please don't let me down again."

"I won't. I promise."

"Goodnight, Barry."

He could only stand and watch as she climbed the steps and closed the door.

21
BLESS THIS HOUSE

May 10, 1969

O'Reilly peered through the glass front door of Alice Moloney's dressmaker's shop. Inside he could see Alice standing behind a glass display case. Perhaps, he thought, cowering was a better word, because leaning across it, with his face close to hers, was none other than Colonel Oliver Mullan.

The red-lettered "Closed" sign swung on its cord and the bell tinkled as O'Reilly opened the door. He snibbed the lock and strode inside.

Mullan spun round. He was looking dapper in polished black shoes, grey flannels, and a dark green blazer bearing the Royal Ulster Rifles' harp crest on its left breast pocket. What O'Reilly would at first have described as a leer was now transforming into a welcoming smile. "Doctor O'Reilly, how pleasant to see you. In to buy something chic for your lovely wife, are you?"

371

"Not exactly." O'Reilly kept his voice level.

"I do hope you'll accept my apology. While I do not intend to withdraw my complaint to the borough council, I feel my abrupt withdrawal from his lordship's dinner the other night was less than courteous, but I was upset, you see." He offered his hand, which O'Reilly ignored.

Mullan frowned.

O'Reilly stepped past Mullan and asked, "Are you all right, Alice? You sounded very shaken on the phone."

"Oh, thank you for coming, Doctor O'Reilly. I'm sorry to interrupt your luncheon. I'm all right now you're here, but would you please ask this" — she stopped, then squared her narrow shoulders and continued in a lower tone — "this horrid man to leave and never come back?"

"I beg your pardon?" Indignation from Mullan.

O'Reilly ignored him. "Tell me what happened please, Alice."

She wrung her hands. "The colonel came to my shop two weeks ago. Introduced himself. Told me he'd been stationed in India. He knew I was an old India gal and asked me out for dinner. I refused, politely of course. I'm walking out with Ronald. I thought for the colonel, being an officer and a gentleman, that would be that, but he's kept on pestering me."

"Pestering," Mullan mumbled. "Is that what you call friendly overtures in Bally-bucklebo?"

O'Reilly looked at Mullan, who had stepped away from the counter and stationed himself beside a rack of women's summer dresses.

"I see," he said, turning back to Alice. "Yes, it was Lady Ferguson who suggested the colonel might like to meet you." He sensed movement and spun to see Mullan slipping toward the locked door. "Stay where you are." It was a voice he had little call for these days, but he was still able to summon the authority of his former title, naval surgeon commander.

Mullan froze.

"Please go on, Alice."

Alice looked at Mullan and then quickly looked away again. "This is the third time he's come and asked me out. Ronald's spoken to him, but he just laughed at poor Ronnie. 'All's fair in love and war,' he said. Now he's here again. And this time he tried to kiss me." She screwed up her face in disgust. "I didn't know what to do. I told him I had to go to the toilet. He said he'd wait. That he was a patient man. That's

373

when I phoned from my flat above the shop. Thank you for coming so quickly." Her voice was cracking.

"It was brave of you to come back down to the shop."

"I knew you'd be here in minutes, Doctor, and I wanted you to catch that man here."

"I see." O'Reilly turned on Mullan. "Quite the officer and gentleman, Colonel." O'Reilly curled his lip before the last word.

Mullan resorted to bluster. "I don't know what you're talking about, O'Reilly. Miss Moloney's a single woman. I find her very attractive." His smile was a rictus. "Faint heart never won fair lady, don'tcha know?"

O'Reilly stepped close to Mullan, and although they were of equal height, the man seemed to cringe and shrink slightly. "When a lady says no once, Mullan, she means no. Do you understand?" O'Reilly put an edge into his voice.

"Not always." His voice had lost its bluster. "Sometimes they're playing hard to get. Honestly. Come on. You're a man of the world."

Good God, had the man actually winked? O'Reilly raised his eyes in disbelief, then stared at Mullan. "Then I'll say it for her, and I'm not playing hard to get — although

I can play very hard indeed if pressed, so repeat after me: 'No means no.' "

"That is your opinion." Mullan stood more straightly. "And if I choose not to share it?"

O'Reilly took a step back. The trouble was that short of threatening violence, he held no trump cards if Mullan refused to back down, although perhaps John MacNeill might have found something. "I hoped a man with your background would have had the decency to leave Miss Moloney alone. Tender an apology."

A slow smile spread over Mullan's face. He made a mocking bow to Alice. "I do apologise, madam, for not being more charming." He turned toward the shop entrance. "And, now if the good doctor would open the door?"

O'Reilly had no choice but to comply.

"Councillor Bishop was kind enough to invite me, a newcomer to Ballybucklebo, to the party this afternoon, but I'm afraid I have a previous engagement. So I bid you both a very good day." Mullan left.

"What a horrid man. Thank goodness he's not coming this afternoon," Alice said. "But thank you, Fingal. You tried very hard. I do appreciate it very much." She smiled. "And if you couldn't convince him, I don't think

Ronald would stand much of a chance. He said last time Mullan came that he was going to speak to the man again. At least you've saved Ronald from embarrassment. Thank you."

"I'm sorry I wasn't able to do more. Perhaps he'll leave you alone now he's saved his bruised pride."

"I do hope so." She glanced at her watch. "Oh, my, look at the time. Ronnie's coming to take me to the Donnellys' and I have to get ready. Will you excuse me, Doctor?"

"Of course. We'll see you there. I'll be off." And as O'Reilly closed the door behind him he realised that John would be at the housewarming. Perhaps he would have some more compelling arguments with which to discomfit Colonel Mullan.

"I thought you was taking us home til our wee cottage on the estate," Donal said from where he sat in the passenger's seat of O'Reilly's Rover.

He had just driven past Ballybucklebo House's driveway where it met the Belfast to Bangor Road.

Lunch with the Donnellys was over. O'Reilly hadn't finished his, but there'd be plenty of grub where they were going.

"I'm sure Doctor O'Reilly knows what

he's doing, Donal," Julie said from the back, where she sat with Tori. The twins' double pram was in the boot.

Kitty was following in her Mini with the twins, along with Kinky as their babysitter and dog minder to Bluebird.

"More surprises," Donal said. "First the family picture. Then me going til be a partner with Bertie Bishop. I'm still in shock about that, so I am. I would not of had of believed it if I had not of would've been there."

O'Reilly chuckled. "It's true, all right. And it couldn't have happened to a nicer fellah."

"Thank you, Doctor O'Reilly," Julie said.

"And not a dickie-bird til no one," said Donal, "until Bertie gives me the go-ahead til tell people."

"So, it's Bertie now, is it?" said Julie, smiling.

Donal puffed out his chest as he turned to the backseat. "Mister Bishop said as I should call him Bertie now. I know it sounds strange, love, but we'll have to get used to mingling with our betters from now on."

O'Reilly said, "You two have no betters. Not in my book, anyway."

"But you're a learnèd man, sir. A doctor," Donal said.

"And so are you, Donal Donnelly. Making a perfect mortise and tenon joint takes skill and precision, much like surgery."

"I never thought about it like that."

O'Reilly indicated for a left turn at the crown of the hairpin bend. In his rearview mirror, he noted the Mini following.

"This is the lane til Dun Bwee," Donal said. "What sort of shenanigans are you up to, sir?"

O'Reilly parked in the front yard. "Everybody out."

The Mini parked behind him as O'Reilly lifted the pram out of the boot and set it up. He joined Donal, Tori, and Julie. Kitty, with a large brown-paper-wrapped parcel under one arm, Kinky, the twins, and Bluebird piled out of the Mini. Kinky put the twins in their pram.

"Mother of God, would youse look at that," Donal said, pointing to a banner hung along the eave line of the rebuilt Dun Bwee. Its new yellow thatch, red door and window frames, and blindingly white walls all sparkled in the early May sunshine. " 'Welcome Home the Donnellys.' "

The front door flew open and what seemed to O'Reilly to be the entire population of Ballybucklebo and the townland poured out. Led by Bertie Bishop and followed by Lord John MacNeill, Lady Myrna

Ferguson, Lars, Father O'Toole, and the Reverend Robinson, they were cheering, "Welcome home."

By now O'Reilly, Kitty, and Kinky had withdrawn a little so the rest of the Donnelly family could be the centre of attention.

Donal stared, looked at Julie, back at the crowd, and started to laugh.

"Quiet please. Settle down. Quiet." Bertie Bishop had taken on the role of master of ceremonies. He stood beside the family, facing the now silent crowd. "My lord, my lady, Father O'Toole, Reverend Robinson, and ladies and gentlemen. It is with great pleasure that we welcome the Donnellys back to their own home. I'm only going til say a few words of thanks til some very special people who helped make this happen, then we're going til have a hooley til beat Bannagher, a housewarming of the first magnitude."

Applause, cheers, and whistles filled the air.

Wide-eyed Tori, with one thumb in her mouth, clung on to Julie's leg. The twins both looked startled.

"Youse all know what a terrible thing it was when fire destroyed this cottage just after Christmas last year."

Low murmurings.

379

"Youse all know how lots of people chipped in the next day with clothes and grub and things, how his lordship and her ladyship loaned a cottage on their estate that was fixed up by volunteer work —"

"And donated materials from you, Mister Bishop." O'Reilly recognised Alan Hewitt as the speaker.

"That's as may be," Bertie said.

"It is not," Lenny Brown called from the front row, "for you donated your vehicles and tools at the weekends while volunteers was helping to rebuild Dun Bwee too. You're a sound man, Bertie Bishop." Lenny turned to face the crowds. "I want a big hand for his lordship and her ladyship, and Mister Bishop."

The applause was deafening and scared a clamour of rooks from the tall limes at the far end of the back garden to circle, cawing, before the shiny black birds settled back on their perches.

Donal's greyhound, Bluebird, barked once.

The marquis, his sister, and Bertie Bishop all bowed their acknowledgements.

"I am proud of everybody here, for every one of youse has helped in some way. Everyone, no matter what persuasion. And while there's rumblings in the rest of the wee

380

north, we're still a big family here. That's why we have two men of the cloth here the day til bless this house, and they will in just a wee minute, but a bit of housekeeping first. We've a marquee loaned by the Ballybucklebo Highlanders set up round the back of the house. Willie and Mary Dunleavy will pour the drinks —"

Paid for by your company, Bertie, O'Reilly thought.

"— and there's plenty til eat or snack on, thanks til my Flo, Cissie Sloan, Kinky Auchinleck, and Maggie MacCorkle."

A low groan from somewhere in the crowd — O'Reilly could not identify the critic — accompanied the mention of the last name. Everyone knew Maggie was unlikely to be representing Ireland at the culinary Olympics in Frankfurt.

"Please, when we've finished here, head for the drinks and grub, and give Donal Donnelly and his family a bit of space to have a look at their new home. Now, I've said my bit. Father O'Toole, if you please."

Father Hugh, wearing his cassock and biretta, turned and faced the crowd, his right arm raised, and three fingers held up.

Everyone closed their eyes and bowed their head.

"Oh Lord, we are gathered here today in

381

the spirit of friendship to bless Dun Bwee and the Donnelly family. We beseech you, may you hold them in the palm of your hand, but not close your fist too tightly, may peace and plenty be the first to lift the latch to their door, and happiness be guided to their home. In the name of the Father, Son, and the Holy Ghost. Amen."

"Amen."

Father Hugh's place was taken by the Reverend Robinson, in a black suit and white dog collar. He bowed his head and O'Reilly knew the man's eyes would be closed. "Dearly beloved," he began, "we are gathered here today in the sight of God to celebrate and give thanks for our friendship, our community, and the resurrection from the flames of the Donnellys' cottage, Dun Bwee. We humbly beg thee to bless this house and those who dwell therein. I now ask you all to join me in the Lord's Prayer. Our Father, which art in heaven —"

The crowd had got as far as "and deliver us from evil" when Tori yelled, "I want a wee-wee," but was shushed by Julie.

". . . forever and ever. Amen."

Reverend Robinson said, "Out of the mouths of babes and sucklings," and everybody laughed.

"You're dead on, Your Reverence," Bertie

Bishop said, "so I'll let youse all go in a jiffy, but first" — he stood close to Donal — "Mister and Mrs. Donnelly and family. Here's the key to the door." He gave Donal two keys on a large ring festooned with a red bow. Donal held up the key ring and waved it in the air as the crowd began to cheer and whistle.

"You can thank my missus for that there bow," said Bertie. "And you'll find the house all set up and ready to go, but we thought you'd like to hang your own pictures. Health to you all, to enjoy your home again."

O'Reilly could see the tears through Donal's smile. "My lord, my lady, ladies and gentlemen, I don't know what til say. I'm all choked up, but Julie and me and the girls want til thank everybody here from the bottom of our hearts, to thank Lord MacNeill and Lady Ferguson for gracing us with their presences, and Father O'Toole and the Reverend Robinson for their blessings, and youse all for coming, but now if you'll excuse us, me and mine are going inside. We'll be out with youse as soon as we've had a good gander, the twins have had their nap, and wee Tori is comfy again. Thank youse all very, very much." He took Julie's hand and she held on to Tori's.

A deafening round of applause disturbed the rooks for a second time.

Big motherly Kinky gave Bluebird's leash to O'Reilly. "Would you put the dog in her run please, sir?" Then she pushed the twins in their pram toward the now open front door.

The Donnellys were back in their own home at last.

22

WELL IF THAT IS SO, WE MUST GO OUT AND GET THESE PEOPLE

November 1, 1963

"Morning, Sister."

Sister Kearney, the senior sister of wards 5 and 6, looked at Barry over the tops of her half-glasses and smiled when he reported to her desk at eight o'clock exactly on Friday, November 1. He'd been officially on call since midnight but had not been disturbed. At least not by the ward. His worry about Virginia had kept him awake for quite a while.

"Nice to have you back as our new houseman, Barry. Just barely survived your three-month stint in casualty, I hear."

He could laugh about the mononucleosis now, and he did. "It's good to be back on your wards, Sister."

She handed him a chart. "You're in at the deep end today. As you know, we've four beds on ward 6 equipped with ECG machines for continuous cardiac monitoring,

385

but the rest are general medical beds, and we're on take-in all day."

"I'm ready." Maybe the work would stifle his nagging concern about Virginia, who had captured his heart, but did not seem to feel so strongly about him.

"Very good. They've sent us a Mister Dennis Carson, who's just had what sounds like a grand mal epileptic seizure. He's in bed 7. Off you go."

Barry grabbed the chart and hurried onto ward 6 with its familiar wooden floor, rows of iron beds evenly spaced along both walls, and plain wooden tables arranged up the centre of the long room. French windows at the far end led to a balcony from which, across a lawn, could be seen the redbrick Royal Maternity Hospital.

Staff and student nurses moved about, attending to their duties. A clinical clerk Barry recognised, Pat Taylor from Bangor, was drawing morning blood samples. The final-year student was a year behind Barry.

The man in bed 13 said in a loud stage whisper to his next-door neighbour, "Look out, Sammy. Here comes Count Dracula."

"Morning, Pat."

"Morning, Barry. Both of us starting together here today."

"I was here for three months as a clinical

386

clerk last year, doing the same thing you are now."

"And getting called 'Count Dracula' by the victims, I'll bet. Did you know the book was written by a Dublin man, Bram Stoker."

The overhead curtains round bed 7 were closed. Barry let himself in. A staff nurse was undoing a blood pressure cuff from the arm of a man Barry guessed might be in his thirties. The patient was awake and breathing easily, but pale. "Hello, Doctor Laverty," she said. "Mister Carson's blood pressure is normal, one twenty over eighty and" — she indicated a tear-stained young woman sitting on a bedside chair — "this is Mrs. Diana Carson. She was with him when the attack happened."

"Good morning, Mister and Mrs. Carson. I'm Doctor Laverty."

"Pleased til meet you, sir," she said.

The nurse handed Barry the chart. Dennis Carson was thirty-six years old, a plater by trade. The previous medical history referred to the usual childhood fevers, nothing to help make a diagnosis. The commonest cause of fits was epilepsy, and usually there were few if any diagnostic physical signs. Nor did doctors often get to observe the attack. "Can you tell me what happened, Mrs. Carson?"

387

"Aye. Him and me was in Smithfield Market and says he til me, 'Diana, can you smell fried onions?' He sounded all puzzled, like. Then he goes stiff as a board. Falls down like he's been poleaxed. I was scared rigid myself." She sniffed. "I was sure he'd hurt himself, he went down so hard."

Grand mal epilepsy was preceded by an aura that could be of smell, hearing, or hallucinatory. Then came the tonic phase, when all the muscles go into spasm.

"I knelt down and he starts til shudder and shake. I don't know how long that went on for. And now there's rubberneckers all round. And him's frothing at the mouth like a mad dog." She looked up at Barry and the tears started. "I didn't know what til do. Then a nice man kneels down and says til me, 'Missus, your man needs til be in hospital, so he does.' He whips off his jacket, sticks it under Denny's head for a pillow, like. He says, says he, 'I'll go into a shop and phone the ambulance.' And off he trots. By now Denny's stopped having a fit, he's just lying there. By the time your man gets back, Denny'd woken up."

She had given a classic description of a grand mal epileptic seizure.

"He said he had a ferocious headache —"

"Still do, Doctor," Mister Carson said.

388

His voice trembled as he asked, "What the hell happened, anyway?"

"You had a seizure, Mr. Carson, and I'm sorry to hear about your headache. I'll take care of it in a minute," Barry said. "Thank you, Mrs. Carson. You've been very helpful. Now I'd like to examine you, sir."

Barry satisfied himself that, except for a bruised elbow, the patient had sustained no injuries from his fall, nor had he exhibited any neurological signs, nearly always the case once the attack was over. The next step would be to try to decide if the cause was some underlying lesion like a brain tumour or whether, more likely, the disease had no obvious cause. "This has been very unpleasant for you both, and I'm sorry I can't give you a definite diagnosis today." A diagnosis of epilepsy carried an enormous social stigma, and practical implications like not being allowed to drive. For once Barry was able to accept received wisdom that the word not be mentioned until a firm diagnosis of cause had been made. "But we'll get you something for that headache, I promise."

The curtains were being pulled back. Barry turned to see the stately progress of the ward round. The boss, Doctor Pantridge, was accompanied by his registrar;

his senior house officer, Doctor John Geddes; Sister Kearney; a student nurse; and half a dozen clinical clerks in their short white coats. Doctor Frank Pantridge was a colourful character and a pioneer in coronary care.

"Ah, Laverty," Doctor Pantridge said, "welcome back aboard, and what do we have here?"

Barry quickly recapped the history and physical findings and said, being deliberately obfuscatory, "My diagnosis is one of seizure of unknown origin, which will require an electroencephalogram and skull X-ray to begin to look for any underlying cause."

"Quite right." Doctor Pantridge's words were clipped. "And admission to ward 22 under the care of Doctor Millar. See to it, Laverty."

"Yes, sir."

The entourage moved on to the next bed.

"Mister and Mrs. Carson, that was the senior consultant. He has asked me to arrange for you to be transferred to the care of Doctor Millar, who specialises in diseases of the nervous system. We mostly treat patients with heart troubles here. I'll be making the arrangements now, then I'll have to join the ward round but, chart please, Nurse." Barry scribbled an order for Panadol. "We'll give you something for your headache, and I'll come back and give you a better explanation when I get a chance."

Barry returned from arranging the transfer to the ward where in September he himself had been a patient, and joined the retinue as it moved from bed to bed. Each patient's case was presented by one of the clerks in turn, and Franky P. grilled the student about the disease under discussion. The great man was not renowned for his tact.

One of the students applied the bell of his stethoscope to a man's left chest between the fifth and sixth ribs, frowned, clearly concentrating, removed the bell, and said, "I can hear a presystolic murmur, sir. Mitral stenosis."

"That is quite amazing," Franky P. said. "When I examined him yesterday he had the classic systolic murmur of mitral incompetence." He took a three count. "Tell me, young man, were you born stupid — or have you been practising?" It produced the required laughter from all except the unfortunate butt of the joke. Barry felt for the man, yet Doctor Pantridge was worshipped by his juniors, highly respected by his peers, and dreaded by the hospital administration. An earlier remark of his that "Either Matron goes, or I go — and I'm staying" may have been apocryphal, but it was part of the Royal's folklore.

When rounds ended, the students and junior doctors returned to their duties, and Doctor Pantridge and Sister Kearney headed to the clinical room for morning tea.

"Welcome back to 5 and 6, Barry," said John Geddes, a slight, bespectacled man with a soft voice who'd been a houseman here last hospital year. "When you're free, come and find me. If there's not much excitement, I'll be in the side ward of 6 and I'll give you a briefing about what some of your work here will entail."

"I'll get there as soon as I can."

"Good." Doctor Geddes went to join his colleagues. Barry knew these morning teas weren't social, but brainstorming sessions on cardiac resuscitation.

Barry admitted one more patient, a woman in congestive heart failure. Then, true to his word, he headed back to bed 7 on ward 6. But before he reached it, he met an orderly and nurse pushing a trolley onto the ward. The nurse was Jan Peters. "Hello, Jan," he said, "come for Mister Carson?"

She stopped and nodded. "You asked for him to be admitted to ward 22, the neurology ward, where I work. Doctor Millar will see him there." She inhaled deeply, then sighed as she began to push the trolley forward.

Barry frowned. "You all right, Jan?"

She shook her head. "Not really. Daddy was readmitted to ward 10 an hour ago. He's got more gangrene."

"No. Oh, Jan, I'm so sorry."

"Thanks, Barry. Any chance you could pop in on him? He's very upset."

"Just as soon as I'm free. I promise."

"Thank you. I'd better get back to work."

"Jan, I was going to try to explain a bit to the Carsons, but I'm running late. Can you make sure someone has a word with them on their new ward?"

"I will, Barry."

Damnation, Barry thought. Rotten luck for Jan's dad. Even if they were on take-in and Barry was probably going to be busy, he would get a lunch break. He'd go and see Rusky Peters then.

John Geddes was not on 5 nor on 6, so Barry let himself into the side ward of ward 6, where John sat in a simple wooden side chair reading a reprint from a cardiology journal. "Have a pew." He indicated a second chair. "Nine thirty and no more new admissions yet needing my attention."

"I admitted a woman in heart failure. The registrar was on the ward. He approved of

393

my investigations and proposed treatment."

"That's why you didn't need me?"

"Mmmh." Barry sat facing a trolley covered with a dust sheet.

"You're a very lucky doctor to be on this unit at this time, Barry. After three months of the walking wounded down at casualty, you're going to be part of one of the most exciting advances in medicine of the twentieth century." His eyes lit up. "And — so you can be — it's my job to give you some teaching about your new responsibilities. I know you learned cardiopulmonary resuscitation, CPR, last year as students. This year we decided to teach your year of housemen, starting in August, how to use the defibrillator as well as a refresher in CPR. You all have to live in the hospital, so we've been building a rota to have twenty-four-hour cover for any cardiac arrests in the hospital. You missed your turn to be instructed when you were sick. The boss, ever practical, said, 'Laverty's coming here in November. We've enough juniors trained now for inside work. Teach him when he gets here.'"

"I remember the CPR training. I like the bit of medical history you chucked in."

John smiled. "I could see eyes widen when I told your lot that 'mouth to mouth' respiration began in 1767 but fell out of favour because it was aesthetically unpleasing." He cleared his throat. "The idea of a strange man kissing a woman was simply not acceptable in 1767, and kissing another man? Good Lord."

Barry chuckled and said, "I thought CPR had worked for a chap called Robbie Martin on my first day in casualty, even if he didn't last long after he was admitted here. But I really felt I'd done something useful."

"And by the time we've finished with you here," John said, "you'll be doing even more good. You might even decide to become a cardiologist. It is a very satisfying speciality, even if we can't save them all."

"I'll have to see about that," Barry said, "but I'm always eager to learn."

"All right, now, the nearly final aspect of care after cardiac arrest concerns reversing ventricular fibrillation. There is a completely disorganised contraction of the individual muscle fibres of both ventricles, so the heart stops pumping blood. It was uniformly fatal until 1947 when a Doctor Beck successfully defibrillated a fourteen-year-old boy undergoing open heart surgery."

"So long ago? I thought it was brand new."

"You're right about it being a recent development. The breakthrough came last year. Doctor Lown, an American, in part using information provided by Russian scientists, produced a portable DC defibrillator. Doctor Pantridge went to hear him lecture and" — John whipped the sheet off the trolley — "hey, presto, a few months later —"

Barry saw the portable defibrillator that John Geddes had used on the patient he had helped Harry Sloan perform CPR on back in August.

"— our very own Lown model. It lives in here, and we can rush it to the bedside when necessary and plug it into the mains." He beckoned. "Come on and I'll show you how this thing works."

When John had finished teaching Barry the steps and they were sitting in their chairs again, John said, "Now, I'm going to tell you the final and most exciting bit of the cardiac resuscitation story, and some of it involves me, but I'm only telling you the facts. Please don't think I'm boasting."

Barry smiled. John Geddes had always been a self-effacing man. Boasting was the last thing Barry would accuse him of.

"Back in April of this year, when Brian Pitt and I were both housemen on ward 21, a hospital worker stuck his head in and told us a man was lying on the ground outside the building. Brian and I yelled for help and ran outside. A pulseless middle-aged man lay on the pavement. I started CPR. Dennis Coppel, an anaesthetist registrar, charged up, pushing an anaesthetic trolley. He intubated the man and connected him to oxygen. Anand Garg, a neurosurgical registrar, helped us load the man on a trolley and we got the patient to a side ward and took an ECG. Ventricular fibrillation.

"Doctor Pantridge was on ward 5. He brought the new portable defibrillator and plugged it in. It only took two shocks to restore a normal heartbeat. That was the first case of successful defibrillation at the Royal."

"You must have been excited."

John smiled. "I was." His smile faded. "But the man died later that night."

"That would have been an awful letdown."

"It was, but only for a little while. I'd already decided to specialise in cardiology and I'd come to terms with the possibility. A lot of patients do succumb. I don't mean to sound callous, but for your own sanity you have to develop a fairly thick skin. Do not get personally involved."

Barry thought of Rusky Peters. Although sorry that he had been readmitted, Barry was looking forward to seeing his friend and could already imagine the pleasure he

397

would feel in helping him weather this latest setback. He would take John Geddes's words under advisement.

"And that was the acorn from which I believe is going to be a mighty oak. We have a team of on-call medical staff who carry bleepers, a staff nurse on duty on wards 5 and 6, and two defibrillators. They can get to every ward in the hospital. Now you're part of the cardiac team on 5 and 6 and I've trained you on the defibrillator, you join the on-call rota. It's not very onerous. Here's your bleeper." He handed a pager to Barry. "You and I are going to be part of something that's going to be implemented worldwide one day, but had its beginnings right here. I'll explain the details in a minute."

"Me?" Barry was flattered. "That's an exciting thought, but how?"

"I'm working for my doctorate. My thesis will concern itself with recovery after coronary thrombosis. I came across a paper by Doctor Wallace Yater and his team, which found that sixty percent of those who die from a coronary do so within one hour of the onset of the symptoms. I told Doctor Pantridge that one morning when we were having our after-rounds cup of tea." John laughed. "You know how he, no pun intended, cuts straight to the heart of any matter."

Barry smiled. "I do indeed."

"He said, and I quote, 'Well if that is so, we must go out and get these people.' "

Barry nodded. "You mean like the obstetric flying squad that takes a registrar, a midwife, and a medical student to the patient's home if there's a complication to a delivery?"

"Exactly. On-the-spot defibrillation's going to be one of the greatest medical achievements of the twentieth century. We're working on a defibrillator that can be charged from car batteries. Our cardiac technician, Alfred Mawhinney, has discovered that if we use a thing called a static inverter, we can do just that. The engineer in the cardiac laboratory, John Anderson, has added more refinements."

Barry was out of his depth. He was a complete bollocks when it came to physics, but just as one didn't need to understand the workings of an internal combustion engine to drive a car, all the doctor would have to do was know how to use the defibrillator.

"We've already trained some nearby GPs in CPR, and to give the patient fifteen milligrams of morphine and an antiemetic. The

GPO have set up a cardiac telephone hot-line, telephone number two double four, double four, that will be connected directly to a red telephone at the main desk here. Doctor Pantridge is getting funding for a dedicated, specially equipped cardiac ambulance which should be able to reach the medical and nursing pickup point at the back of the hospital in forty seconds from receipt of the call to the ambulance depot.

"The team will be a junior cardiologist, me initially, and you if I'm not available, during the day, and all the other housemen on a rota from six P.M. to eight A.M., a staff nurse, and a medical student attached to 5 and 6."

"Me?"

"At least until you finish your three months with us. We'll be the only cardiac flying squad in the world —"

"In the whole world?"

"That's right, Barry. I told you, you're going to be part of one of the most exciting advances in medicine of the twentieth century."

Barry took a deep breath. "A small part. And that's quite the honour and responsibility."

John Geddes smiled. "It is, but I'm quite

sure when you have to, you'll rise to the occasion."

23
TO CELEBRATE THE EVENT

May 10, 1969

Judging by the increasing buzz of conversation coming from the Donnellys' back garden, the housewarming hooley was already well on its way. Before Kinky had returned from delivering the twins, Bertie Bishop had joined the O'Reillys, John and Myrna, and Lars where they had stood at the front of the welcoming crowd.

"You made it, Lars," O'Reilly said.

"Only just," said Bertie, who had been driven to the party in Lars's Jaguar E-Type. "Your brother, Doctor, drives thon hot rod like your man Stirling Moss used to in Formula One races. I think we were flying beneath the legal limit. I'm not sure if the tyres actually touched the ground. It's a fine car, though, Mister O'Reilly."

"It is, Mister Bishop. Sorry if I had you worried."

Myrna said, with a sardonic smile, "Still

mad about speed, Lars. I thought you might have grown out of it by now."

"I make no apologies, Lady Ferguson. I'm too set in my ways now."

O'Reilly, sensing the tension, changed the direction of the conversation. "Kudos to you, Bertie Bishop. Your crew must have worked like blazes to shift the furniture, set up the marquee, and put up the tables and chairs. It was a brilliant surprise."

"Och, sure it's praise to everyone, not just me, particularly Dapper Frew. It was really his idea."

"It was. I was there that night in the Duck. Remember?"

John O'Neill asked, "Will you join Mister O'Reilly and us at our table, Mister Bishop?"

"I'd be delighted to, sir."

"Good. And O'Reillys, after you've seen to the dog? We'll get our food and keep seats for you."

"Thank you, John," O'Reilly said. He turned to Kitty. "I'll get a bite to make up for my missed lunch."

"I thought I heard your tummy rumble in the car." Kitty laughed.

"And do you fancy a drink, Mrs. O'Reilly?"

"It's early for a G and T, but it's a warm

day. Lager and lime would be nice."

Kinky came out through the front door and joined the O'Reillys. "Wasn't that grand altogether? The two families all content."

"Two families?" O'Reilly said as he and Bluebird, Kitty and Kinky started to walk round the house toward the back garden.

Kinky's chins wobbled as she laughed. "The Donnellys and our village."

"You've got that right, Kinky," Kitty said.

They passed the Neolithic burial mound, stopped at the dog run, put Bluebird inside, and closed the gate. The greyhound charged round with head down, sniffing, and, clearly remembering, gave a contented yip, glad to be home.

Beneath a canvas canopy, a small crowd clutching paper plates and cutlery moved from left to right past a table covered in plates of sandwiches, smoked salmon on wheaten bread, slices of cold roast ham and chicken, sausage rolls, hard-boiled eggs, and salads.

Cissie Sloan and Flo Bishop stood behind, advising diners, handing out portions, and, when asked, carving.

O'Reilly heaped his plate. Ham, chicken drumstick, smoked salmon, a couple of sausage rolls.

"Before you sit down to eat your lunch,

sir, can you come to the dessert table with me?" Kinky said. Maggie Houston, née MacCorkle, stood behind a second table, three blue cornflowers in the band of her hat. She grinned at them and O'Reilly noted that, as was her habit on formal occasions, she was wearing her false teeth. Sonny Houston stood behind her.

Kinky offered O'Reilly a plate. "Please sample that, sir."

O'Reilly accepted Kinky's offering. "What is it?"

"Maggie's plum cake."

I'll kill you, Kinky, O'Reilly thought. I'm trapped. I'm trapped by courtesy. I'll have to eat the bloody stuff and spoil my lunch. He looked at his full plate, then closed his eyes and took a bite. Chewed. "Holy Mother of — Sorry, ladies. That's Maggie's, is it? It's —" He stopped. If he made too much of a point of how delicious it was, surely the woman would be hurt.

"What do you think, Doctor?" said Maggie. "Kinky has a different way of making it. It doesn't have as much texture as mine, but Sonny says his oul' teeth are getting a bit loose, like, and this cake's easier to chew. I still think mine is better, but I don't want my Sonny losing any teeth over a silly cake. So I'll do it Kinky's way from now on."

"I think that's a very compassionate thing to do, Maggie. It's a sacrifice, but it's for a good cause."

"Ah," said Sonny, holding both thumbs up where Maggie couldn't see. "If Kinky — I mean if Maggie was a Catholic, I'd be putting her up for sainthood."

Maggie turned to face Sonny, pecked his cheek, and said, "You could charm the birds from the trees — you oul' goat."

"Well done, Maggie MacCorkle," O'Reilly said. "Well done."

He was rewarded by another of Maggie's dry, cackling laughs as he headed toward the drinks table. The grass underfoot was springy, its newly mown scent filling the air. The surrounding hedge of lime trees sheltered the garden from a light breeze that shook the pale green new leaves and added a whisper to the low hum of many conversations. Folding tables and chairs borrowed from the sporting club were scattered on the grass.

Cissie's husband, Hughie; Gerry and Mairead Shanks; Lenny and Connie Brown; and Alan Hewitt occupied one. Each had a full plate and a drink. Alan stood up and touched his duncher. "Good afternoon, Doctor and Mrs. O'Reilly."

"Good afternoon to this table," O'Reilly

said, and was rewarded by a chorus of greetings. "How's your Helen getting on, Alan?"

"Bravely. She sits her finals next month." The man's pride could be heard in every word he spoke.

"I'm sure she'll do you proud."

"She already has, sir. More than I can say."

"Wish her luck from us," Kitty said. "And, Lenny, does Colin sit his national school exams in June too?"

"He does, Mrs. O'Reilly. And he's revising and cramming like billy-oh."

"Wish him luck too."

"Thank you." Alan sat and the O'Reillys moved on. "That table is Ballybucklebo in a nutshell. It's what Ulster should be. Hughie and Cissie Sloan and Alan Hewitt are Catholics, and the Browns and the Shanks are Protestants." He sighed. "If only the wee north could look that way at every table."

Soon they spotted John and Myrna, Lars, and Bertie Bishop. The men rose as Kitty approached. "I'm going to get drinks for us, love."

"Then please sit down with us, Kitty," John MacNeill said, "and I'll get another chair for Fingal when he returns."

"Thank you, John." Kitty set her parcel on the grass beside her and O'Reilly set his lunch plate on the table.

"Guard that with your life. Won't be long."
He was eager to find out what John Mac-
Neill might have discovered about Mullan,
but he knew the marquis was a great believer
in imparting that kind of news all in his own
good time. O'Reilly left and joined the end
of the queue. There was no mistaking the
tall gangly man and the shorter woman immediately ahead. "Ronald. Alice."

Both turned. "Hello, Fingal," Ronald Fitzpatrick said. "Alice contributed some
clothes after the fire, and when she was
invited to this do, Bertie Bishop said it
would be perfectly all right if I came along."

"It's better than all right. You're part of
the family now. I'm afraid you can't escape
us."

"I wouldn't want to. I thought the whole
little ceremony was extremely moving. It
reminded me how I can never forget your
kindness to me when I was in trouble."

"I —" But Ronald wasn't finished.

"And Alice told me what happened earlier.
Thank you, my old friend. Thank you very
much. I've become very attached to Alice. I
despise anything that hurts her. I know,
because Alice told me, that Mullan stood
on his dignity, refused to apologise, but we
can hope that when he's calmed down, had

408

time to think, he'll not bother Alice any-more."

"We can hope so." And I can hope John MacNeill's got something on the man.

The line shuffled forward.

The customer ahead of Ronald and Alice, Mister Coffin the undertaker, moved away carrying two drinks. "Afternoon all."

"Afternoon."

From behind the bar, a perspiring Willie Dunleavy asked, "What'll it be, folks? And the drinks are on Mister Bishop's company."

Ronald said, "A small dry sherry and a brown lemonade, please."

"Well, I can't vouch for how dry it is, sir, I never drink the stuff myself. But I do have some sherry. And for Doctor O'Reilly?"

"Lager and lime. Have you Harp?"

"I do."

"And a pint."

"Coming up." Willie bent to his work with glasses and bottles. "Here y'are, folks."

"Thanks, Willie."

"We're sitting with the doctors," said Ronald, pointing to Connor Nelson, Nonie Stevenson, and Emer McCarthy. "I gather Doctor Laverty couldn't make it today. What a pity. I would have enjoyed seeing him."

"It is a pity," O'Reilly said, but he knew

409

why. Barry had confided in his senior partner when he'd asked for time off eight days ago about Sue's surgery and the reasons for it. He'd begged off today because, as he'd explained, Sue didn't feel like partying. God knows, O'Reilly thought. I've dealt with enough apparently infertile patients in the last twenty-three years to know how much turmoil they go through. His heart bled for them, but he said, "Enjoy your afternoon," as their paths parted. He arrived at the marquis's table and put down their drinks. "Kitty, before we settle down, let's give the Donnellys their housewarming presents."

Kitty picked up the parcel and joined him. "Lead on."

In moments he was knocking on the front door.

Donal was beaming when he opened it. "Doctor and Mrs., come on in. The twins is having a nap in their bedroom, but Julie and Tori's here."

"Mrs. O'Reilly has little presents for you," he said, and followed her into the spotless kitchen/dining room. There were bright chintz curtains for the windows; the table from the cottage had a red tablecloth and a vase of blue-with-yellow irises. A Welsh dresser was adorned with willow-pattern

410

dinner plates. Julie sat on a love seat with Tori, her Christmas dolly beside her.

Tori said, "Hello again. It's nice to be home, but I didn't see the unicorn."

"I think she's back in the Lilac Wood," Kitty said, bending to be closer to the girl.

"With Schmendrick," Tori said, her small face serious. "I hope so."

Kitty straightened and handed the bulky parcel to Donal. "We hope you'll like these."

Donal laid the parcel on the table and carefully undid the tape securing it. "Och," he said as he revealed what was inside. "Youse remembered I said I'd lost my Gilbert and Sullivan records, and here's the *Gondoliers, The Mikado,* and *The Pirates of Penzance.* Thank youse very much. And look here, Tori. It's your very own kitty. He handed her a tabby-striped stuffed animal. "Say thank you."

"Fank oo very much, Doctor and Mrs. O'Reilly." She took the cat and hugged it to her. "It's a pussycat, just like the lady kitty at your house."

"And would youse look at that?" He held up what O'Reilly knew was a pure silk, semi-transparent spring green scarf. "That'll keep my neck dead warm when I go til cheer for Linfield."

Before O'Reilly could interrupt, Donal

411

laughed, handing the scarf to Julie. "I'm only having you on, love. You'll look smashing in it."

Kitty laughed. "The ever-practical Doctor O'Reilly wanted to get you an electric mixer. I thought it should be something pretty that would go with your hair."

Julie took it from Donal. "It's lovely, just lovely," she said, draping it round her shoulders. "Thank you so much."

"And look," Donal said. "Two wee pandas for the twins. Thanks again."

"So," said O'Reilly with a smile, "are you coming to your party?"

"Aye," Donal said. "Julie's going til look after the kiddies and I'm going til thank as many people as I can." His voice quavered. "That there December night of the fire, I never thought I'd be back in here. I thought the place was going to be just a heap of ash, and me and mine would be de-destituted, so I did. But I should have known better than to doubt. Before long I was singing a different tune, all right. I mind saying til you, sir, that maybe, just maybe, the new Dun Bwee would be better than the old." He gasped, swallowed, and said, "It is, and I swear til God you can feel the love of those good people out there coming through the walls."

O'Reilly clapped him on the shoulder. "Health to you and yours to enjoy it."

"We're the luckiest family in the whole omnibus."

O'Reilly had to think on that before saying, "Universe, Donal. Universe."

"Aye, right enough. Anyroad, come on." He turned to Julie. "When the twins wake up, please come out, love, and bring the girls."

"I will, Donal. But don't be worrying about me. I'm enjoying just sitting in my own kitchen again. Have fun," she said. "I'll see you later."

Donal stood aside to let O'Reilly and Kitty leave, followed, and shut the door. "I never thought I'd see the day when the whole village would pull a fast one on me, but they did. I never seen this coming — and it's sticking out a mile, so it is. Thank you, sir," Donal said, and wandered off with a grin on his face that would have made the Cheshire Cat's look miserable in comparison.

"Welcome back, O'Reillys," said John MacNeill when they arrived at the table. He held Kitty's chair and pushed it in to seat her.

"Bertie's off to mingle," Myrna said. "Never know when he might need a vote or two at the next council election."

"That's Bertie Bishop, all right." O'Reilly lifted his pint. *"Sláinte."* He started to gnaw on his chicken drumstick. "And speaking of elections, I was very pleased when our prime minister, Captain O'Neill, announced universal suffrage, one man one vote, for the next local council ones."

O'Reilly heard Kitty muttering under her breath. "It's such a great day, Fingal, could we not leave politics alone for once?"

"I couldn't agree with you more, Fingal," John MacNeill said.

Lars said, "Pity the poor man had to resign five days later because of the bombs."

"I believe," Myrna said, "it was because he had lost the confidence of his Unionist Party. You may be pleased by the suffrage thing, Lars, but I'm none too happy about James Chichester-Clark, O'Neill's successor. Granting amnesty for people who organised demonstrations? And then releasing Ian Paisley and Major Bunting four days ago? That's more trouble in the making."

"Perhaps they'll settle down," Lars said. "Having learned their lesson."

"Those two?" There was an edge in her voice. Myrna frowned at O'Reilly's brother and shook her head. "That's always been your trouble, Lars O'Reilly. Typical. You'd've

414

found a bright side on the blooming *Ti-tanic*."

O'Reilly saw Lars tense up, and ached for the man. Better perhaps that he and Myrna had gone their separate ways two years ago.

John MacNeill said, "It has been, from time immemorial, forbidden in the officers' mess to discuss politics, religion, and women. And I know you feel strongly, Myrna, but please don't cast a shadow on what has been a lovely day so far."

Myrna coloured and looked as if she might argue with her brother. Then her shoulders relaxed. "Yes, John. Absolutely right. Sorry, Lars. Didn't mean to snap. These are tense times."

Lars's moustache lifted in a smile. "All is forgiven, and you are right. I do have a habit of optimism."

"Takes after our late mother," O'Reilly said. "During the war she set up a local 'Buy a Spitfire' fund. We didn't think she'd raise the money — but she did." The ham, chicken, and most of the smoked salmon on his plate had disappeared.

Kitty, clearly sensing the need for more diversion, said, "Look at that," and pointed.

Dapper Frew, a longstanding member of the Ballybucklebo Highlanders, stood in his usual clothes but with a set of Great High-

415

land pipes, bag under his left arm, the three drones over his left shoulder, blowpipe mouthpiece between his lips, chanter held by his fingers. He smacked the inflated bag and the pipes howled. Bag under his arm, he squeezed, and above the roaring of the drones the slow melody rang loud and clear.

"Do any of you know that tune?" Kitty asked.

"Yes," said John MacNeill, "and it's singularly appropriate. It's a slow march called 'My Home.' And thinking of slow marches reminds me, Fingal, that I did see my friend at the War Office and a couple of other folks when I was in London." John MacNeill's gaze fixed on Fingal O'Reilly's eyes. "It's not something I wish to go into the details of today on such a happy occasion, but I promise you I have enough ammunition, to mix a metaphor, to spike Colonel Mullan's guns for good. Today's the tenth. The borough council meeting's not until May nineteenth. Could you meet me outside the clubhouse at two o'clock on the fourteenth? It's a Wednesday and there's an out-of-season game to be played."

"Of course. And we know he'll be home because he told us he works from one until four."

"I'll phone you tomorrow and brief you then."

"Fair enough." O'Reilly would have liked more information, but he could be patient because he knew John MacNeill always delivered on his promises. "Let's enjoy the afternoon." And he knew he could now, because he was suddenly flooded with the pleasing belief that, although Colonel Oliver Mullan had thought he'd won earlier today, on Wednesday, May 14, he was going to realise that it had only been a skirmish. O'Reilly and John MacNeill were going to declare war.

24
BRINGER OF UNWELCOME NEWS.

November 1, 1963

"Lunchtime. Off you trot, Barry. I'll hold the fort," John Geddes said.

"Thanks, John." That was typical of the man who, nominally Barry's senior, was not above picking up Barry's duties. "I'll get back as quickly as I can." He walked along the ward, pushed through the blue plastic flap doors, and turned left on the main corridor with its usual bustle of uniformed staff, patients, and visitors. It was time to keep his promise to Jan Peters.

It was only two weeks short of three months since Rusky's last admission. Barry was no haematologist, but he had read up on polycythaemia after getting to know the dockworker. It seemed the more severe the disease, the less time between relapses and the worse the long-term prognosis.

He entered ward 10 and immediately ran into Virginia, who was carrying a towel-draped bedpan and heading for the sluice. As always when he saw her, his breath caught in his throat. He smiled at her. "Hello. Sorry about tonight," he said.

"Are you not on take-in? I thought you'd be on your wards." He heard little warmth in her words.

"I'm on my lunch break. I've come to see an old patient." Oops, he thought. I can practically hear her thinking Oh? I thought you'd come to see me.

"Excuse me, Barry," she said, "this bedpan is quite ripe." She slid past him and into the sluice.

So she was still angry. He sighed. He wasn't going to pursue her into the sluice. He knew well what Jack's advice would be: "Give the bird time to cool down." He would stop worrying about her and see Rusky Peters as he'd planned. He headed for the ward sister's desk.

She smiled. "Hello, Barry. Come to see Mister Peters?"

"Jan told me he'd been readmitted, and he'd like a visit."

"He's really down in the dumps. Try to cheer him up, if only a little. And it won't be easy. The senior surgeon's already seen him." She inhaled. "It's not good. We're waiting for Doctor Nelson to consult, but if

419

he gives the haematological go-ahead, with respect to reducing the risk of possible postoperative bleeding, it'll be an above-knee amputation of the left leg sometime this afternoon. We haven't told him yet."

"Amputation?" Barry sucked in his breath. "No, not good at all. Where is he?"

"In the side ward. Like last time."

"Thanks, Sister." As Barry headed there, he remembered how, as a student, he'd assisted the senior surgeon, Mister Willoughby Wilson, in an above-knee amputation, helping the surgeon form two flaps from the skin and flesh in front of and behind the now-exposed nacreous femur. Barry knew it would probably take many years to forget the sounds he heard that day — the grating of the bone saw, the *thump* of the amputated lower leg into a bucket held by the circulating nurse. But the surgeon's speed and skill in sewing up the flaps to form a cushion over the end of the bone had been a joy to observe. Technically, Rusky Peters was in very good hands.

Barry went into the side ward to find Rusky propped up on pillows, lying in bed wearing his own blue-and-white-striped pyjamas. His face was plum coloured and screwed up in a grimace. "Sorry to see you here again, Rusky," Barry said. "Jan told me you'd been admitted."

A nurse had finished taking the patient's blood pressure.

"Thanks for coming, Doctor Laverty, and I'm the better for seeing you, sir, but I took a fierce headache, so I did, and keeled over again at home. Scared the missus half to death, and, well, I'm scared, too, sir."

"I can understand that. I'd be very worried too. Tell me what's been happening."

"Well, the missus sent for the ambulance like Doctor Nelson told us to if anything like that happened. They brung me til casualty and got me admitted here. One of the young doctors there ordered a wheen of blood tests and give me codeine to take the edge off my headache."

"Mister Peters's blood pressure is normal, Doctor, and so is his pulse," said the nurse. She entered them on a chart.

"Thank you, Nurse."

She left.

Rusky's eyes followed the nurse out of the room, then returned to look intently at Barry, but he said nothing.

"Blood pressure and pulse both normal. That's good," said Barry.

"Aye, well, the rest of the news isn't. I don't want to burden you with my troubles, Doctor."

421

"If all patients thought that way, you'd put me out of a job, Rusky Peters. Tell me how you feel. It always helps to get things out in the open."

"The whole thing, Doctor, it's worser than last time. From the knee down, I can't feel nothing, and the leg's the same colour my toes was. I've got gangrene in my left leg below the knee. Both the houseman here who admitted me and one they call the surgical registrar told me I'd have til see the consultant surgeon, Mister Wilson."

"I've worked with Mister Wilson. He's an excellent man."

"He's been and examined me and he wants an opinion from my haematologist, Doctor Nelson, but that was all they said." Rusky Peters's voice cracked. "I'm sure it'll have til come off." He took several deep breaths, banged his fist on the blanket. "They're just whittling me away piece by bloody piece." And he gazed up with the look of a man about to face a firing squad. Barry thought, Why is it so difficult to tell a patient what they suspect and give them a chance to try to come to terms instead of keeping them in suspense? Rusky's "I'm sure it'll have til come off," was really a question, not a statement. What harm would it do to tell him? Barry opened his mouth, but the door opened, and Doctor Gerry Nelson, accompanied by his registrar and another nurse, came in. "Hello, Barry," Doctor Nelson said. "You're looking a lot better than the last time I saw you. You the houseman here now?"

"Thank you, sir, and no, I'm on 5 and 6. Mister Peters is a friend. May I stay?"

"Of course." He moved to the bedside. "Hello, Mister Peters. Sorry to see you back." He inclined his head. "And you know my registrar, Doctor Muz Khan."

"Hello, Doctors."

"Once I've confirmed your history, Mister Peters, I'm going to examine you and tell the young doctors what I find, then the three of us are going to leave you alone for a while so we can consult."

Barry waited as Doctor Nelson made his examination. When Rusky pulled up his left trouser leg, Barry gritted his teeth. The lower leg was a dusky blue-black, darker in the remaining toes and in the stumps of the missing great and next toes.

Doctor Nelson put his fingers on the instep just below the ankle. "No dorsal pedal artery pulse." He pressed. Hard. "What do you feel, Mister Peters?"

"N-Nothing, Doctor. Nothing at all."

This was bad, but it was not unexpected.

"Please undo your pyjama cord." Doctor Nelson slipped his right hand under the material and felt in the groin. "I can feel the pulse of the femoral artery."

That was the main blood supply to the leg. There was no blockage there.

"Please roll on your right side." Doctor Nelson put his right fingertips into the hollow behind the left knee. "No popliteal artery pulse."

No doubt Willoughby Wilson had found the same. "Thank you, Mister Peters. Nurse, can you make Mister Peters comfy while we go and discuss the findings?"

Rusky stared at Barry, who caught the pleading in the man's gaze, a look that to Barry said, *Come back and talk to me.* Barry nodded.

He followed the two doctors out into the corridor and down the hall. Who was going to break this horrible news to Rusky? Since Barry's own bout with the unknown two months ago, he had believed as an item of faith that patients were entitled to the truth about their condition. How did anyone tell a man of only fifty-six, a man who Jan had told Barry over a coffee in the staff cafeteria had been overjoyed to be back at work a week ago? Rusky was as much a friend as a patient. How did you tell him he was going to lose his leg above the knee? Barry took a deep breath.

"Right," said Doctor Nelson as the three men headed into the clinical room and arrayed themselves around a small table. "You both know the clinical findings. No question. That leg has to go, and Willoughby Wilson has already made that decision. He wants us to comment on the patient's haematological status. The houseman in casualty ordered a complete blood count. I'll read each significant result and, Barry, as I recall, you seemed too distraught to tell me what a Paul-Bunnell test meant when you were sick. But I'd like you to comment on each result."

"Yes, sir."

"Red cell count: in excess of one hundred million per cubic millimetre."

"It should be less than six-point-nine million."

"Correct. White cell count: twenty thousand."

"Normal range four point three to ten point eight thousand, so twice normal."

"Yes. Platelets: five hundred thousand."

"Wow. Upper normal's three hundred and fifty thousand. And we already know he's got polycythaemia."

Doctor Nelson nodded. "But the question

is, is he fit for surgery?" He turned to Doctor Khan. "Muz?"

Muz Khan was a tall man from Islamabad who had won the hardly ever awarded first-class honours in finals three years ago. "No. With so many cells, the capillaries are congested and liable to bleed. It could be difficult to keep the stump from oozing."

That was the paradox of polycythaemia. Too many blood cells could and did form clots that blocked major vessels, which was why Rusky had a gangrenous leg. But as Muz had just said, it could also cause bleeding from the smallest blood vessels.

"And you'd suggest?"

"Reduce the count by bleeding him. Take off a pint, then he'll be fit for surgery. There'll still be a higher risk of capillary oozing, but I'm sure Mister Wilson will be well aware of the risk — he did the toes amputation — but the incision should be drained so no blood collects under the flaps. I'll speak to Mister Wilson's registrar, collect my gear from our unit, and come back to do the phlebotomy to reduce the red cell count."

"Fine, Muz. Thanks." Doctor Nelson turned to Barry. "Any questions?

"The medicine is clear, sir. I admitted the patient through casualty back in August, so

I read up about polycythaemia then. Mister Peters suspects he's going to lose his leg." And as is often the case, Barry thought, some junior on ward 10 would stop by, deliver the news, and move on. "I'm not on his ward, but —" He thought of John Geddes's words: "A lot of patients succumb. I don't mean to sound callous, but for your own sanity, you have to develop a fairly thick skin. Do not get personally involved." Well, John Geddes be damned. "He knows me. May I tell him what's in store?"

"Please do. But may I ask — you say the man is a friend. Did you know him before he was admitted?"

"No, sir."

"Then this friendship, as you call it, has sprung up while he was in hospital."

"That's right. I knew his daughter before. She's a staff nurse here."

"I see. Well, I'm happy for you to tell Mister Peters about the amputation, but I must caution you, Barry. There is a fine line between compassion and getting too close to your patients. Be sure you learn to walk it wisely."

"I will, sir. Thank you." It was conditional, but that was all the permission Barry needed.

"You carry on, Barry. Come on, Muz,

we'll have a word with Sister, and you brief the registrar."

The three men left the clinical room, Barry to go back to the side ward.

"Thanks for coming back, Doctor Laverty. I appreciate it." Rusky gulped. "Are you going to tell me what's going til happen?"

Barry nodded and took a seat by the bedside. "I am."

"So, what's the verdict?" Rusky's smile, which was clearly forced, must hide his fear. "Would you shoot me if I was a horse?"

Barry took a deep breath and steeled himself. "Rusky," to hell with formality, "you know as well as I do your disease has got worse."

"I was due for another bleeding next week. It seemed to be working, but . . ."

"Doctor Nelson wants to get that done today, so Doctor Khan's gone to get the gear. He'll be back soon."

"That's not bad. Just a wee jag in your arm, and I know the headache'll go once it's done." He shook his head then pointed down. "But I suppose the leg'll have to go?" His voice shook.

Barry nodded. "I'm afraid so. I'm truly sorry."

"Och, Jasus." Rusky Peters took a deep breath. "Life's not very fair, is it, Doctor

Laverty?"

"You're right. It's not."

Ulstermen weren't supposed to cry, but Rusky's eyes filled and tears spilled onto his cheeks.

Without thinking, Barry put his arms round the man's shoulders and felt him shake. There were no words of comfort that would not sound trite.

Rusky stiffened. Straightened his shoulders. "Sorry about that," he said, and wiped his nose on the back of his hand. "Thanks, Doctor Laverty. Thank you very much. It is better to know the truth, so it is, than lie here hoping it's not so and worrying yourself sick."

Barry had to agree, although in his case the truth had come as a relief.

"Does Jan know?"

"I'll nip up to 22 and tell her."

"Thanks, Doctor." Rusky's voice held supplication. "And you'll come and see me after the operation? Talk to the missus and me, like?"

"I will. I promise." He put a hand on Rusky's shoulder. "But I'll have to leave you now, see Jan, and get back on duty."

"Fair enough." And Rusky Peters rolled on his side and closed his eyes.

You poor bastard, Barry thought as he

walked down the ward, and you are right, Rusky. Life isn't fair, but I hope I've helped you a little, my friend. There was some satisfaction in that.

25
LET US HOPE FOR BETTER THINGS

May 12, 1969

Barry paid the cashier, picked up a tray on which sat two cups of coffee, and headed back to the alcove in the Royal Victoria's The Caves, the under-the-wards cafeteria. Sue was waiting in a partially enclosed semicircular booth, and as usual the room was humming with the conversation of nurses, medical students, physios, radiographers, and junior medical staff. Barry set Sue's cup and saucer in front of her, put the tray on the table, and sat beside her. He shook his head and laughed. "You and your 'I don't want to be a second late for our appointment with Doctor Harley.' "

"I know," she said, "but punctuality is the virtue of princes and we've only twenty minutes to kill. I'm anxious to hear what he has to say, you know that, but having a cup of coffee is better than sitting outside his consulting room."

431

Barry took a sip of his and looked around the familiar room. "Wish I had a pound for every coffee I had here between 1960 and 1964. The place never changes. Well, maybe one thing has. I'm sure the tobacco fug was much thicker back then. We were taught in my third year that the relationship between smoking and lung cancer was first suggested in 1950 by a British doctor, Richard Doll. And then confirmed by a massive study of forty thousand doctors reported in 1954. It was still pretty revolutionary thinking back then."

"Not anymore," Sue said. "Things like that are common knowledge now. The American Surgeon General's report in '64 was front-page news."

"It seems, at least among people in my business, the message is beginning to sink in."

"I'm glad you don't smoke, Barry. Maybe you should try to get Jack Mills to quit."

"Or try to get water to flow uphill."

Sue looked at her watch and then looked Barry right in the eye. "I feel that way — as if we're trying to swim upstream when conceiving should be as easy and natural as, well, making love with you. Why does it have to be so difficult?" Sue didn't wait for an answer. There wasn't one anyway. That was the problem. "Please, as a doctor, tell me again what you think."

"As a country GP, mind, not a specialist." Barry, to give himself a moment, took a deep swallow of his coffee, then put the cup in the saucer. "All right. Here's a summary of what we know from the technical point of view. We are a perfectly healthy young couple, both under the age of thirty, who make love with, well, what Graham would probably describe as 'satisfactory frequency.'"

"And now we don't have to perform on cue, most satisfactorily on all counts." Sue touched Barry's hand.

He smiled at her. "Thank you for that."

Neither spoke for a few moments, then Barry said, "My sperm counts were normal. You are ovulating. There is no hostility to sperm in your cervical mucus."

"I didn't like that postcoital test, Barry. Making love on cue and then me rushing up here for the test. I know Graham's a gynaecologist. He's done hundreds but" — she shook her head — "making love is a private thing between a man and a woman."

"It should be."

"And, what else?"

"We know from your laparoscopy that your Fallopian tubes are not blocked or

433

covered in scar tissue, and you do not have endometriosis." Barry sighed. "You've had the whole range of tests and nothing's shown up."

"And that's what I find so hard to deal with. The not knowing."

"I know." Barry wanted to give her something to cling to. "There is still hope, Sue. It's been fifteen months. Fifteen months between when you stopped the pill and your last period on April 24. That means that as far as the doctors are concerned, we still don't really qualify as having a problem. Not until another eight and a half months have gone by. It still may happen."

"I know, Barry," Sue said. Her sigh was vast. "Oh Lord. Another eight months of hoping for the best, then having your world come crashing down. And if nothing does happen, then what?" Her shoulders slumped, and she set her half-finished coffee down.

"I honestly don't know. That's why we're seeing Graham today. To ask him." If they'd been in complete privacy, Barry would have taken her in his arms. Instead he kissed her on the cheek, then looked at his watch. "It's a reasonable walk from here. We probably should be heading over. I know we both have reservations about rushing into adoption until we've spoken to Graham. So let's have that conversation and see if there's anything else he can offer." He took her hand to help her rise. And for the life of him, Doctor Barry Laverty did not have a clue what that "anything else" might be.

"I'm sorry you've had to wait ten days to see me since your laparoscopy, Sue," Graham Harley said. He was half standing with his left hip on the plain wooden table in his consulting room. Behind him the high-backed leather swivel chair on casters remained empty. He held a fawn-coloured file containing their chart, open in both hands.

"It's all right, Graham," Sue said. "Barry explained to me that you had to be in London at the Royal College last week." She glanced at Barry. "Pat Taylor let Barry observe and explained his findings. Barry explained them to me. At that point we knew we'd had all the tests and nothing had shown up. It gave us time to talk to each other about things."

"And we'd like your advice now," Barry said.

Graham opened their chart. "Happy to give it." He hitched farther onto the table-top.

Sue said, "I'm sure you're sick of being asked, as if it were your fault, Graham, why 'if everything's normal, I'm still not getting pregnant —' "

Graham Harley smiled and nodded.

"So, I'm not going to do that, but I'd really like you to tell us what our options are now."

Graham pursed his lips before saying, "Before we discuss options, can we talk about how you're feeling, Sue?"

Barry waited.

"Disappointed because there's nothing to fix. Frustrated because I wanted answers and there aren't any. Grateful to you for helping me understand at our second visit that it's nobody's fault. No need to apportion blame. Trying not to say, 'It's not fair.' Trying not to get angry or sad when my period comes. Trying not to take it out on Barry." Her eyes were damp, but she managed a smile in his direction. "Barry's been a brick, you know, and I know he's disappointed too."

"I am," Barry said, "and I hate to see Sue suffer."

"Does talking about it help?"

Sue took a deep breath. "Sometimes. I've told my mum. We're going to Broughshane to see her and Dad for lunch today. I'll tell

436

her what we've discussed this morning."

"Barry?"

"Yes, Graham."

"I'm asking you too, does talking about it help?"

"I — well, Fingal knows. I told him and he's sympathetic," Barry said. He decided not to mention the conversation he'd had with Jack Mills at the rugby match in March, because at that time he and Sue had decided to keep their troubles strictly to themselves, and Barry was a bit ashamed that, needing some solace himself, he hadn't kept his word.

"I'm glad you've told other people. And I do know what a horrible roller-coaster ride it can be. It does help to get it out of your system once in a while, so if you want to talk to me, give me a call or make an appointment."

"Thank you," Barry said.

"I keep thinking," said Sue, "that maybe it has something to do with being on the pill. Are you sure it doesn't cause infertility?"

Barry recognised that any reason was better than none in most patients' minds, and waited to see how Graham would respond.

He leaned back, smiled, and leaned forward. "Women have been using it in the

437

United Kingdom since late 1961. Initially, we thought women became more fertile in the six months after they'd discontinued its use. Subsequent research showed that we were wrong, but for a while we were prescribing a six-month course for women having difficulty and hoping to see that apparent increase, a so-called rebound effect, in pregnancies happening. It didn't, nor have we been able to establish any correlation between use and subsequent difficulty conceiving."

"Oh. Thank you." Sue sighed. "Deep inside I'm still blaming myself."

"Please don't, Sue."

"I'll try not to." She looked at Barry. "Barry has explained that the in vitro work of Mister Steptoe and Professor Edwards is exciting but may not be applicable for years."

"That's true, I'm afraid, but their work is enormously exciting — for the future."

Barry leaned back in his chair. "So, Graham, what would you suggest we do?"

"Yes," said Sue, moving forward to sit on the edge of her chair. "What about these fertility drugs I keep reading about?"

Barry leant across and took her hand in his.

She glanced at him and tried to force a smile.

"That's what the papers call them — and please don't think me cruel, but the two kinds are both for one specific kind of infertility, Sue. The kind that occurs in women who aren't ovulating — and you are."

"I see."

Barry heard her disappointment.

"Some gynaecologists believe that, as these drugs often cause more than one egg to ripen and be released, giving the fertility drugs might improve the chances of women like you. Sort of like using a shotgun instead of a rifle. The more pellets, or eggs, the greater the chance of a hit. I'm not so sure."

"So there's nothing we can do," Sue said. "All we can do is keep plugging away or adopt?"

"Not quite," Graham said. "In six months, we'll be starting a clinical trial comparing three groups of patients."

Sue said, "Can I be in the trial? I'll try anything."

Barry ached for her. He understood how desperate infertile women could be.

Sue looked at Barry before saying to Graham, "Please just help me have a baby, Graham."

439

Graham nodded. "I do understand, Sue, believe me, but I'm still going to have to ask you to be patient. Only women under thirty who have completed a workup like yours and been trying for at least two years will be admissible. One group will receive a pill called clomiphene, one injectable hormones, and one no treatment."

Sue frowned, turned her head half sideways, regarded Graham, and asked, "How can I be sure of a place in a treated group?"

"Because only current patients from my practice and the Royal clinic will be invited to volunteer for treatment. The data from the untreated group will be culled from earlier records."

"I volunteer."

Graham laughed. "Hold your horses, Sue. Let's give it a few more months. Statistically, it still is likely that good things will happen. And we may have a few results from the study by the time you are eligible, so I can give you better advice."

"God, I hope things do work out, but at least I have a straw to cling to if they don't."

"I sincerely hope by the time you are enrolled — if that becomes necessary — it will be more than a straw." Graham scribbled briefly in the file before saying, "Sue, I know you are disappointed, upset. Let me

440

say again, the odds are still in your favour."

She nodded.

"And I don't want to overwhelm you with details of the trial, which I hope you won't need to enter, but if you do start treatment with us I'll explain everything about it then. But for now, do either of you have any more questions for me?"

Barry shook his head. "Thanks for explaining what you have."

Sue nodded. "Thank you, Graham, for giving us hope." She rose. "I think we should be running along, but thanks. Thanks for everything."

Graham slid off the desk to put an avuncular arm round Sue's shoulder. "And I meant what I said. If you simply need someone to talk to between now and then, you only have to ask, and if things don't work out I'll see you in six months, give you both a detailed explanation, and we'll enroll you in the study, to start treatment three months later."

"We'll see you later, Selbert," Edith Nolan said to her husband when lunch was finished, and the table had been cleared. "Sue wants to visit Róisín."

Selbert rose. "Enjoy seeing your old horse, Sue. If you need me, Edith, I'll be in the barn. I have to tinker with that tractor, hey. It keeps stalling on me." His County Antrim accent made "tractor" sound like "trektur."

No coats were needed. The late-spring day was on the cusp of summer. The sun swung from a cornflower blue sky. As Barry opened the gate from the farmyard to the path leading to the paddock, the continuous melodious warbling of a skylark came from high overhead. He glanced up and was able to make out a tiny dark dot.

"Your father-in-law has a skylark plot, Barry." Edith followed his eyes to the sky, shading hers with her hands. "Their numbers have been going down, according to the Royal Society for the Preservation of Birds, because farmers have changed from autumn to early summer harvesting of cereals. So Selbert keeps a wee patch of later-growing cereal so the birds can nest and find food. The same pair or their weans come back every year and rear a couple of broods." She opened the paddock gate, let them in, and closed the gate.

"I can't imagine this farm without the sound of the skylark," said Sue, looking down to the ground. "Lovely to think of them rearing their families here each year." Sue leaned on the gate and was silent. The liquid warble continued to fill the warm, still air. "Mum, Barry and I saw Doctor Harley today."

"Oh? And?"

"All our tests are completely normal. He's finished the investigation."

"I see." Edith frowned. "So, what did he advise?" Before Sue could answer, Róisín whinnied, tossed her head, and trotted across the pasture. The Irish sport horse stopped in front of Sue and nudged her mistress. There was welcoming love in those deep, limpid eyes.

Sue stroked Róisín's cheek, muttered endearments, fished in a pocket, and produced a sugar lump, which was devoured with great smackings of rubbery lips.

"She's glad to see you, hey," Edith said. "She misses you, girl. We try to give her attention, but you're the one she loves."

"And I her." After another cube, Sue said, "Off you trot, girl. I want to talk to Mum. No riding today." She slapped the horse's rump and the animal ambled off.

Sue took a deep breath. "He said that medically we're not really considered in trouble until another nine months have passed. To be patient — which is what you advised too. And you said that things often had a way of working out." She sighed. "I hope you're right, Mum. I really do."

"How do you feel, Barry?"

Barry looked at his shoes and back at Edith. "Sorry for Sue, frustrated, still hopeful, and, Sue, Graham did hold out another glimmer of hope."

Sue looked at Barry. "You explain to Mum, pet."

Barry said, "We have to wait for nine months more before we can be subjects in one of Graham's research programmes, where Sue will receive one of two medications to stimulate ovulation."

"But I thought you did ovulate?"

"I do, Mum, but this treatment will produce more than one egg per cycle."

Edith frowned. "I'm not sure I understand, but will it be safe for Sue, Barry?"

Barry wasn't certain.

"There may be some risks, and I know we'll find out more before treatment — if we need it — but I trust Graham Harley implicitly."

"So do I," Sue said.

"Please take care of her, Barry." Edith looked at Sue. "Have you considered adoption?"

"We were both a bit uncertain about how we felt about it, so we decided not to talk about it until after we'd seen Graham today. We did discuss it on the drive down."

"And?"

Róisín had come up behind Sue and was nuzzling the pocket that had produced the sugar cubes.

"Hang on, Mum." Sue gave the horse another cube. Gentled her.

"I think Sue would like to get moving straightaway." He saw Sue nodding as she gave the animal another lump.

"There's a belief that couples who adopt a child often fall pregnant soon after. When we were students, all Graham would say was, 'Those are the ones you hear about. You never hear about the ones who don't.' I'm the stumbling block. I wasn't sure about having one of our own initially, now I want one very much." He inhaled. "But I'm not so sure about taking on someone else's. I told Sue."

Sue said, "I think you'll come around, Barry. At least I hope you will."

"I need a bit more time," Barry said.

"Barry, I think you're being very sensible —"

"Mother —"

"Sorry, Sue, but I do. But I have a suggestion if you'd like to hear it?"

Tactful, Barry thought. Very tactful. "Please go ahead."

"Would you be averse to making enquiries

445

about how to go about it should it become necessary? I think it can be quite a time-consuming business. It wouldn't hurt to get a head start."

"I agree, Mum." Sue had an arm draped over Róisín's neck, probably taking comfort from the nearness of a very old friend.

Barry took his time before answering. "That makes sense. I can ask our health visitor. She often helps couples get the process going."

Sue let go of Róisín, hugged Barry, and gave him a huge kiss. "Thank you, darling. Thank you."

And he hated what he was going to say next, but it had to be said. "I'm happy enough to get the ball rolling, as long as we understand I'll not be ready to accept a child until I'm comfortable that I'm really committed."

Edith said, "I think that's very wise, Barry. Your dad and I, Sue, raised you and your brother. Being a parent will take a lot of hard work — from both of you. It's not an easy job."

"I know, Mum." Sue hugged her mother. "Thank you for all you and Dad did, and still do, for both of us." She turned to Barry. "And thank you for being honest, pet. I know you don't feel ready for adoption now, but it took you a while to want to be a daddy. But you did. You do."

"That's right."

"And don't forget, you still have each other," Edith said. "I can see how much in love you both are, and that kind of honesty with each other, even if it's painful, is part of the rock-solid foundation of a strong marriage." She smiled. "You'll be all right. You'll see."

Sue took Barry's hand. Looked into his eyes. "Mum's right." She squeezed his hand. "We'll get through this together. I've had time to let what Graham has told us sink in. And now we have a plan, to explore adoption — even if we don't go ahead at once, to have a chance of trying a possible treatment. I feel that some of the horrid uncertainty, the not knowing, has been removed." She looked at her mother. "You're always a comfort, Mum."

Edith nodded an acknowledgement. "Any time you need to talk."

Barry put his arm round her shoulders. "And we've got each other."

"So, I'll do my damndest not to let this gnaw at me. To get on with our life together, Barry, and I know it sounds silly, but somehow, just somehow, I can't help but believe that things will work out."

447

26
CRUEL MADNESS OF LOVE

November 7, 1963

"I've my bleeper," Barry said to Sister Kearney, "and things are quiet here. I'm going to pop up to ward 10."

She shook her head. "Going to see Jan Peters's dad again?"

"Yep. He's a decent man and I think having me visit cheers him up."

"You're a decent man yourself, Barry Laverty, but you can't look after every single patient you see forever and ever."

Oh yes you can. In general practice, Barry thought, and laughed. "I do know that, Sister. I never try. It's too busy. But it's not so much me following patients. Mister Peters seems to follow me around. I admitted him from casualty on the very first day of my houseman's year."

"And we all know his daughter, Jan, of course," said Sister.

Barry nodded. "She asked me to talk to

him when he was settled in. I did. Played draughts with him. Got to know the man. Now he's been readmitted and lost a leg, it just seems natural to pop in on him once in a while. I'd do the same for any of my friends."

Sister Kearney smiled. "I understand. Off you trot then. I'll bleep you if I need you."

"Thanks."

Barry headed along the main corridor. He'd seen the Peterses three times since the surgery, and Rusky's physical recovery was proceeding perfectly. Emotionally? Rusky was brittle, but he was improving.

So was Barry's romance with Virginia. At least he hoped so. He'd taken Jack's advice and left her alone for five days, but when he'd visited Rusky on ward 10 two days ago he'd looked for her on the ward, found her, and asked her out for dinner tonight. She'd seemed pleased to accept.

He went through the doors, checked with Sister that it was okay to visit, and let himself into the side ward.

Dora Peters was sitting on one of the plain bedside chairs on the far side of the bed. The shoulders of her unbuttoned beige woollen overcoat showed traces of damp. Must be drizzling. He could go for hours in the hospital without the faintest idea what

449

the weather was doing outside. Dora was removing a head scarf from her shoulder-length auburn hair. When she smiled up at Barry, the laugh lines deepened at the corners of cornflower blue eyes. "Hello, Barry. Thanks for coming again."

Rusky was propped up on pillows. His marquetry gear lay on a narrow, cross-bed Formica-topped table. The bedclothes were arranged over a protective cage. A metal gantry curved from the bedhead and Rusky was able to pull himself up by using a horizontal bar supported by thin chains attached to its ends and the gantry above. "Good til see you, Barry," he said, and his voice had returned to its usual firm tenor. "Have a pew." His colour was better too.

Barry sat in the other bedside chair beside a locker, on top of which sat a bunch of green grapes and a bottle of Lucozade. "How are you, Rusky?"

The docker shrugged. "I'm getting a bit stronger every day. It's been a week since the — well, since the operation, and there's just a wee bit of an ache in the stump and I've no phantom pains this time."

"And he can't wait to get fitted for an artificial leg," Dora said. "Meantime, with a bit of help til get into it, you can get about rightly in a wheelchair, can't you, love?"

Barry heard the deep affection for her husband in the woman's voice.

"Aye." He smiled. "And one of them wee physios comes every day. Makes me do exercises for til strengthen my thigh muscles for when I get fitted with a peg leg, and learns me how til get around on crutches."

That was the first smile Barry had seen since Rusky's admission seven days ago. The man was starting to fight back. "Did you ever see that film, *Treasure Island* with Robert Newton?" he said.

Barry nodded. "I was ten when it came out."

"At the moment all I'll be needing is a crutch and a parrot, and hey presto, Long John Silver. Aaaar, Jim lad."

Barry and Dora laughed. "Good for you, Rusky," Barry said, admiring the man's courage. "Yo-ho-ho and a bottle of rum."

"Aye, I could use the bottle of rum, but I don't suppose Sister would approve." Rusky smiled then sighed. "Sure, I know it'll be a long ould road, I'll probably never work again now, unless mebbe I can get some kind of watchman's job, but, och, I am getting better. I still have my Dora."

She reached out and took his hand.

"And I wanted til say thank you til you, Barry." Rusky reached under the bedclothes

451

and produced a brown-paper-wrapped parcel. "Here." He thrust it at Barry. "I asked Dora for til bring it."

"Thank you." He stared at the wrapped package, unsure what more to say. This was a first for Barry. Students did not receive presents, and housemen rarely. Received wisdom was that as obstetricians usually had very happy patients, after a long relationship, their cupboards were often overflowing with bottles of whiskey. "Thank you very much."

"Go on," Dora said. "Open it."

Inside the paper lay the inlaid draughts board Rusky had made during his first admission, and a box presumably containing draughts. Barry felt the lump in his throat.

"There's a wee card, too, so there is."

Barry opened the envelope. The words *Thank You* were embossed in silver on the front. Inside a handwritten message read, *With many thanks for your kindness to us during all my troubles. From Rusky Peters to Doctor Barry Laverty, a doctor who cares.*

Barry reread the message. He looked from Dora to Rusky. "Thank you again," Barry said, "thank you very much. This is something I will always treasure." He slipped the card back into its envelope. He felt close to tears, at a loss for what to say next, when his bleeper went off.

"Duty calls?" Rusky said.

" 'Fraid so." Barry stood. "I'll have to go, but thanks again. Hurry up and get better, my friend."

"You run along, dear," Dora said. "Away you off and look after some other poor divil."

Draughts set and card clutched in his left hand, he opened the door, then looked back. Dora and Rusky were both still smiling at him.

Barry closed the door. He was far from being a religious man, but he had had religious instruction as a child. "Lord, please," he whispered, "be kind to Rusky Peters. He's borne enough."

"That," said Virginia, laying her knife and fork side by side and pointing directly across her plate, "was delicious." She dabbed at her lips with her napkin, leaving a tiny trace of coral pink lipstick on the white linen. "Coq au vin and a bottle of Châteauneuf-du-Pape aren't often on the menu in Musson House. Thank you, sir." She inclined her head in his direction.

"Nor the East Wing," Barry said, and smiled. Their initial conversation on the drive down to the Causerie, on the first floor of a terrace building on Church Lane, had been a little formal after her gracious acceptance of his apology for letting her down a week ago. She'd even said she was sorry for being brusque with him the next day when he'd come to see Rusky before his amputation.

Over an aperitif, starters, and the main course, she had become more relaxed, seemed to be the old Virginia again. Wonderful, Barry thought, what the universal social lubricant can do. He smiled at her. Just looking at her green eyes still made him feel weak.

"Excuse me, sir," the waiter said. "May I remove the plates?"

"Please. And please ask Chef to give us a few minutes before starting our desserts."

"Certainly, sir."

Barry looked round the familiar room. He'd been coming here since he'd been a fifth-year student. Their corner table kept company with six others, each with four chairs. All were occupied, and on each table a Waterford cut-glass vase held a single red rose. A pleasant low hum of conversation and the clink of cutlery on china rose to accompany a hint of garlic mingled with the inevitable aroma of tobacco smoke curling upward to the ceiling. The lighting was pleasantly dim.

"So," Virginia said, "how are you enjoying the cardiology aspect of your work?"

"It's a very exciting place to be just now. Doctors Pantridge and Geddes are developing the use of a special cardiac ambulance to take a cardiac care team out to patients who've had a coronary. Looks like it could reduce the initial mortality considerably."

She looked thoughtful. Nodded.

"It makes so much sense," Barry said, "going directly to the patient, rather than the patient coming to us. I mean, it wouldn't work for everything —" He noticed the way she was fiddling with her napkin and wondered if he dared ask if he was boring her by talking shop. Yet it was she who had introduced the subject. No, he'd press on. "But when a defibrillator could be the difference between life and premature death —"

"Excuse me, sir, madam. Shall I prepare your desserts now?"

"Please," Barry said.

The chef, in his white jacket and tall hat, had pushed a two-element portable burner on a trolley beside their table. He began to smother two yellow pancakes folded into triangles in a frying pan with a warm orange sauce from a saucepan sitting on the second burner.

"I know you've had crêpes Suzette before." He'd tried to impress her with them, a lass from a small town, the first time he'd brought her here. Then wide-eyed, she'd studied the chef's every move and had made little throaty, approving noises. He'd always liked girls who showed enthusiasm. Tonight he was trying to recapture the pleasure of that evening. "But I thought you might enjoy them again."

But Virginia barely seemed to notice what the chef was doing or when he lit a match.

The first time her hand had flown to her mouth as flames, blue at their base, danced, shimmered, and hovered over the frying pan before dying away. She'd applauded while grinning and laughing.

This time she said, "It was exciting the first time, but after a while?" She shrugged.

Barry winced. Was she trying to tell him something?

"Tell me more about your cardiac ambulance."

Before Barry could speak, the chef had spooned crêpes onto Virginia's and Barry's plates, bowed his tall-white-hatted head, said *"Bon appétit,"* with a thick Belfast accent, and pushed his trolley away.

"The Daimler should be arriving any day. I'll be the backup to John Geddes, during the daytime if he's not available. It's a bit scary, but exciting too. After six there's a fourteen-houseman rota, so at least I'll only be on that about once a fortnight, so we can easily avoid those nights when we're planning our dates." He smiled at her and took a mouthful of crêpe.

"Good. It's probably selfish, but I really don't like getting all gussied up, looking forward to a night out — and having to play second fiddle to your work. It's happened four times in three months. I know as a nurse I should understand, but —" She took another mouthful.

Barry left his dessert. He didn't like that remark. As a nurse indeed she should understand, but he said, still trying to be placatory, "I am truly sorry," although why he should have to apologise for simply doing his job was beyond him.

"I think sometimes, Barry, you take your responsibilities a bit far. When we worked together on 5 and 6 last year, most of your mates couldn't wait to clear off at the end of the day. I remember you often coming back when you were off duty to look in on a patient you were worried about. I admired that then, but I know your hours are brutal

457

now. I try to understand, and yet you keep on coming to see Mister Peters, and he's not even your patient."

"He's a friend."

She sighed and took another mouthful.

"And your seeing him is very commendable." She finished her crêpe, looked Barry in the eye, and said, "Have you made your mind up about what you'd like to do after this year?"

"Yes. I'm pretty certain I'm going to try general practice."

"Where you can get to know all your patients the way you've got to know Mister Peters?"

"Yes."

"I see." She sipped her wine. Nodded to herself and again looked at Barry. "Pet, that dinner was delicious. Thank you. Thank you for explaining about the cardiac ambulance. I'm sure we can work 'round it. I love you, Barry, and I'm sure we can make it work."

"And I love you, Virginia. I'm sure too." He was glad she'd said that, because he very much wanted it to work. Yes, perhaps she'd been a bit unreasonable, but she was getting over it. She was. And she was so, so lovely. So kissable. He gazed into those sea green eyes and found himself saying, "*Lawrence of Arabia* with Peter O'Toole, Alec

458

Guinness, and Anthony Quinn is showing next week. What nights are you free?" A gesture of good intentions.

She grinned. "I think Peter O'Toole is a dish. I saw him in *The Day They Robbed the Bank of England.* I'm off every night for once."

"Grand. I'll check my schedule, get cover, and I'll take you for a snack in O'Kane's pub across from the Royal and on to the cinema. And I promise I won't stand you up. Honestly."

"Good." She blew him a kiss.

And Barry grinned at her, pulling his dessert plate back. He felt hungry again and was really looking forward to being in a darkened theatre with this lovely girl. He'd make damn sure they'd get a seat in the back row so he could kiss and caress her, letting himself be transported by his love and his need for her.

27
AND GREAT WAS THE FALL OF IT

May 13, 1969

O'Reilly turned the collar of his raincoat up against the steady drizzle — the classic "grand soft day" — and listened to the intermittent shrill blasts of a referee's whistle and occasional shouts from the muddied players. Teams from two neighbouring schools without their own sports fields were playing seven-a-side rugby football.

Colonel Mullan's tidy two-storey redbrick house with its low bottle-green verandah dated back to the mid-1880s. It had been the farmhouse when the sporting club had bought the property in 1934. The necessary ground for playing fields and clubhouse had been kept, the arable land rented to a neighbouring farmer, and the house sold to a series of retired gentlemen, of which Mullan was the latest. The rugby pitch that it faced had been part of a ten-acre field. Mul-

460

Ian's home was within easy earshot of the playing field and clubhouse.

O'Reilly had arrived two minutes before the assigned two o'clock meeting and, hearing its engine, turned to see his friend's 1962 Ford Cortina come to a halt and the Marquis of Ballybucklebo get out. His Gannex raincoat, made from the same material that sheltered the Royal Corgis, would protect him. He waved and called, "Hello, Fingal."

O'Reilly waved back.

"Soggy day," John said. "Glad you could make it."

"Wouldn't miss this. From what you told me on the phone on Sunday about Mullan and the Royal Ulster Rifles, we're certainly going to cook his goose."

The two men began walking past the sevens game, then John stopped to watch. "You have to be fit to play a game like that. Great training for real life — getting knocked down and being able to get up again and carry on as strong as ever. From what I learned, Oliver Mullan got knocked down but he never really got up again. Pity." He continued walking and O'Reilly followed.

O'Reilly had thought he was going to be like a spectator waiting to watch a demoli-

461

tion crew make a building implode. He looked over at his friend's serious face. Now he wasn't so sure. "Let's get this over with." He opened the gate and stood aside to let John precede him, closed the gate, and followed.

John MacNeill lifted a brass lion's head knocker and rapped twice. The door opened almost immediately, as if Mullan had been watching them approach. He shook his head and looked O'Reilly up and down as much as to say, *You've got a brass neck coming here after I faced you down the last time,* then turned to the marquis. "And to what do I owe this pleasure?" By his tone and frown, the term was clearly nothing but forced politeness. "Particularly during my working hours?"

"Good afternoon, Colonel," the marquis said. "May we come in?" His smile was open and friendly.

"Well, I —"

"I think you'll find it to your disadvantage if we don't."

Mullan took a pace back, the frown deepened, and he cocked his head. "Please do come in."

The man had little choice, O'Reilly thought. It's simply not done to slam the door in the face of a peer of the realm, and

462

especially not one who has issued a veiled threat.

Mullan led them along a carpeted hall. O'Reilly was surprised that no pictures adorned the walls, but then Mullan had not lived here long, only three months. The living room was small but neatly furnished. The fire was not lit, despite the damp day. A portrait of a younger, uniformed Mullan with the two pips of lieutenant on the shoulder straps of his khaki blouse hung above the mantel. A picture window at the end of the room gave a view of the pitch and the game in progress and on out to Belfast Lough and the distant Antrim Hills.

"Take a seat."

So far O'Reilly noticed Mullan, a stickler for titles himself, had not recognised the marquis as such, never mind a mere physician.

O'Reilly sat in a red velvet armchair and John O'Neill took another, both facing the picture window. "I prefer to stand," Mullan said. "Now, if you'd be so kind, why would turning you away be to my disadvantage?"

"Please forgive me, Colonel, but ever since you were at Ballybucklebo House for dinner three weeks ago, I've been puzzled by some things you said, and I find I cannot get them out of my mind. I wondered if you might help me clear up the mystery, as it were."

"I will certainly try."

"Very good. I was surprised when you said, for example, that you'd gone to Dulwich School in London and had been in Drake House."

Mullan, who had taken up a position behind a wingback chair as if it might offer him protection, smiled. "That's easy to explain. I went to the local Cookstown College until I was thirteen." He puffed out his chest. "I won a scholarship to Dulwich. I attended from 1921 until 1925."

"But surely Drake is a day boy's house?"

"It is. The scholarship only paid for tuition and school supplies. I stayed with a London cousin of my father's during term time. On Pickwick Road near the Sports' Ground, and I don't see —"

"I'm sorry. Please don't think I'm hinting that you may have been untruthful."

Yet, O'Reilly thought. It won't be a mere hint when John does.

"I should hope not."

The marquis smiled. "Just a couple more things, please. You attended the Royal Military College Sandhurst next?"

"I did, but I fail to see what is so mysterious about that. Why have you and O'Reilly come to interrogate me? He and I are not on the best of terms."

"Don't worry about me, Oliver," O'Reilly said. "I'm just keeping his lordship company. Give him the answers and we'll be off."

"Oh, very well." Mullan stepped away from the wingback and pulled a straight-backed armless chair from against a wall, positioned it facing O'Reilly and the marquis, sat, and folded his arms. "Please be brief — sir."

"So you left Sandhurst when?"

"In 1929."

"When you were commissioned into the Royal Ulster Rifles as a second lieutenant?"

Mullan nodded, but he fidgeted on his chair.

"Fine regiment. You surprised me when you said their march-past is 'The South Down Militia.' "

Mullan shook his head and grimaced. "Did I actually say that? Silly me. I'm hopeless with music. It's our slow march. Our march-past is 'Off, Off, Said the Stranger.' "

He stopped fidgeting. He's getting cocky again, O'Reilly thought.

John MacNeill crossed his legs, glanced out the window and back to fix Mullan with an unblinking stare. "It's no good, Mullan. However you explain away these cracks in your façade, I'm afraid I know the truth. That under the Army Act, section 44, you were court-martialled, spared prison, but cashiered in 1936 for embezzling mess funds when you were stationed in Victoria Barracks in Belfast. That automatically debarred you from ever serving the monarch in any capacity. You could not reenlist in the ranks and try to regain your good name. You couldn't even be a postman."

"Absolute rubbish." Mullan got to his feet. He shouted, "If you are going to make such vile, unfounded accusations, I must ask you to leave my home at once."

The marquis kept his voice level. "Please, Mister Mullan, don't try to deny it. I have senior friends in the Judge Advocate General's Office of the Ministry of Defence. I can have a transcript of your court-martial mailed by making one phone call." The marquis, with complete ruthlessness, continued. "Impersonating a military officer as you are now doing is also a criminal offence."

"But you don't have the transcript."

Now there was steel in the marquis's voice. "No, Mullan, I don't, but unlike you, I am not a liar. You can trust my word on this."

Mullan's face crumpled and he collapsed

into the chair. "I'm ruined — again."

Much as he had come to dislike the man, O'Reilly squirmed for Mullan's humiliation.

When the marquis spoke, his voice again was one of reason. "*Mister* Mullan, if you will explain to us why you did it, we might be able to find some extenuating circumstance. If we can understand and if you promise to behave as we tell you, Doctor O'Reilly and I might be persuaded to turn a blind eye."

Mullan lifted his head, looked from the marquis to O'Reilly, and back to the marquis. He inhaled, shook his head, took out a hanky, and blew his nose.

O'Reilly said in his most consoling voice, "Come on, man. Spit it out. You'll feel better once you have."

Mullan half turned to look out a side window onto a gnarled beech dripping with rain. "Very well. It's nearly all been a lie. My father was in linen. I was honest about that." Mullan made a huhing sound. "He was a warehouseman at a mill." Mullan, when he looked at O'Reilly, had the eyes of a chastised Labrador. "I was smart, you see, perhaps too smart. I wanted a better life than my parents, living on a housing estate in County Tyrone. Our minister knew that some public schools did grant scholarships to working-class pupils so Daddy asked if he could help. He did all the paperwork. Arranged for me to go there and sit the exams. I won one. My daddy was so proud." Mullan inhaled deeply. "When it came time to go, I was sad about leaving Ulster, but I grew out of it."

"You got off to a good start," O'Reilly said.

Mullan shook his head impatiently. "There was no future for me until I won that scholarship to Dulwich. I joined the Combined Cadet Force there, the infantry subunit. The CCF didn't play at soldiers. We took training just like the adult regulars, went to summer camps. I loved the life. I was promoted to cadet colour sergeant in my last year. I loved everything to do with it."

O'Reilly was impressed. Very few boys gained that distinction.

"In fifth form I asked the careers master how I'd go about joining the Regular Army as an officer. They put me in the army class that groomed boys for the Sandhurst officers' training school entrance exams. Passed my first try. Then off to Wiltshire to be grilled by the Army Officer Selection Board at Westbury. I got in. Because it was on His Majesty's service, the fees were subsidised. I don't know how my father and mother

did it, although he'd been promoted to fore-
man by then. They managed. They were
proud of me." He stopped abruptly.
"They're gone now."

The drizzle had been increasing steadily,
and in the quiet house the sound of the rain
beat like a frenzied roll on a side drum.

"Entry into the Royal Military Academy
isn't easy," the marquis said quietly. "I
remember my own selection board."

Perhaps that grain of understanding from
Lord MacNeill had emboldened Mullan to
continue.

"There's more," he said. "When I was at
Dulwich I used to go to the drawing room
comedies at the Whitehall Theatre. I'd lost
my Ulster accent and found I was very good
at impersonating the upper crust in school
dramatics."

O'Reilly refrained from comment but was
beginning to understand.

Mullan's smile was dreamy, wistful. "My
dreams came true when I was commissioned." The smile fled. "The Rifles weren't
a swank regiment like your Irish Guards,
my lord, or some of the cavalry, but I'd no
personal funds other than my officer's sal-
ary. My folks had just been able to help with
my fees at Sandhurst. And by then I had
completely hidden my working-class, Irish

roots. One had to keep up appearances at formal mess dinners, race meetings, things like that. You know all about that, my lord."

"Unfortunately I do, but I could afford it."

"I couldn't, but I was stupid. Yes, I stole the money. I'm a thief." He fished out a hanky and blew his nose. "I'm sorry," he said.

O'Reilly wasn't sure if he was apologizing for the tears clogging his nose or the fact that he'd stolen money to pay for his fictional persona.

"So what did you do?" John MacNeill asked. "Life isn't easy for a cashiered officer."

"What you said, sir. I tried to enlist in the Black Watch under a false name as a working-class Ulsterman with a Scottish father, but they found out. Their medical officer who did my entry medical, a Scot who had been with the Rifles, had asked for a transfer to the Gallant Forty-twa."

"What terribly bad luck," said John Mac-Neill. "So what did you do then?"

Typical of the man, O'Reilly thought, to have sympathy for the scoundrel.

"I auditioned at the Whitehall Theatre, got a small part. I was with them when Basil Dean and Leslie Henson founded E.N.S.A.

in 1939." He sniffed. "I still wanted to serve my country. Do you remember the Kipling story?"

John MacNeill nodded.

"I was in that E.N.S.A. sketch as the sergeant because I can," he dropped into broad Belfast, "make a bloody cat laugh when I take off a Belfast docker, so I can," his accent became more nasal, "and people say, 'hold the feckin' lights' at my Dublin Northsider."

O'Reilly had difficulty stifling a grin. "Take off," Belfast for "to imitate," and the man was spot on with both Irish accents and nearly perfect with his usual Oxbridge too.

"After the war I went back to the Whitehall Theatre. I was too young for a colonel so I played a major when I wasn't at the theatre. Gave me an entrée into a much better class of society." O'Reilly had heard enough. He looked at John MacNeill. "I think I've had enough, sir."

The marquis raised a hand, a gentle admonishment. "Nearly enough. An actor can't make a great deal of money or have much of a pension. Where did you get the money to buy this house?"

"That's the really sad part. When I met Margaret Pearson in 1958 I started off try-

471

ing to impress her. We met quite by chance. I'd gone to Lords' to see the MCC play cricket," he hesitated, "against Sandhurst. Silly, I know, but I took the chance. She was sitting beside me and we got chatting. She was most knowledgeable about the game. At close of play at six I took her for an early dinner and, unusually for me with my memory, I quite forgot who won the match, I'd become so entranced with her. She was five years older than me, a wealthy widow with two children —"

O'Reilly wondered if she had been the only one to whom Mullan had paid court. Probably not.

"We fell in love. I'd wanted to marry for money, I'll admit it, but we were in love."

And despite the fact that Mullan was a self-confessed liar and impostor, O'Reilly believed the man.

"We married and I moved into her house in Mayfair. I left the Whitehall Theatre. Margaret was so proud of my having been an officer, I had to keep on pretending."

O'Reilly understood.

Mullan took a very deep breath, swallowed, and said, "Then five years ago —" He hesitated, shook his head, inhaled. "Oh, God, it was all so stupid. She was driving home alone after visiting an old friend I didn't like much and so I had stayed at home. A drunk driver hit her car head on. They said she died instantly. Didn't suffer." Deep breath. "But I did. Still do."

"Och, Jasus," O'Reilly said, unable to control himself.

"I rattled around in London, trying to decide what to do. I had money now. Much of the estate went to the children but Margaret had provided for me quite generously. But Margaret was gone and suddenly it all seemed so pointless. I decided to come home, to Ulster. Buy somewhere in the country, but not too far from Belfast, that still left me enough to get by in reasonable comfort from the interest on the remainder. I looked at several properties, and apart from the nearness to the sporting club, this seemed ideal. And seeing it had worked before, to gain acceptance and be reasonably high up in a local social scene, I gave myself a rank, but this time lieutenant-colonel. Another façade, but" — he was like a chastened small boy trying to find something virtuous he had done — "I have been working on my memoirs. My E.N.S.A. memoirs." He managed a tiny smile. "I know our nickname was Every Night Something Awful because there were some pretty second-rate acts, but a lot of the awful was

473

hilarious and I met quite a few famous people. I have an agent and he says he's sure he can sell it."

"But surely," the marquis said, "if you do, people will realise you were not in the war. Not a lieutenant-colonel."

A slyness crept into the man's smile. "Who was George Orwell?"

The marquis frowned. "The chap who wrote *1984*?"

O'Reilly said, "His real name was Eric Arthur Blair."

"Exactly. If all works out, the author will be one Al Cotton, a combination of Al Bowlly and Billy Cotton, who were E.N.S.A. members. I knew them both."

O'Reilly said, "You really do live in a make-believe world, don't you?"

The smile fled and Mullan nodded and hung his head. He looked from the marquis to O'Reilly. "But I try not to hurt people. I loved Margaret and I was a good husband. Sometimes, yes, I make a mess of things. Doctor O'Reilly, I know that, and you know I behaved badly with Miss Moloney. You were there. I lied to her about India. I've never been, but I've become adept at learning plausible background details. After a while you begin to believe your own stories. And telling people about detached service fended off a lot of awkward questions. Added a touch of glamour." He paused to gulp down some air. "I've — I've been so lonely." The last word was broken and prolonged.

It took all of O'Reilly's resolve to say nothing, rather than try to comfort the man. He looked over to John MacNeill.

"Very well. We understand now. Doctor O'Reilly, if you concur, might I suggest that, as we are the only ones other than Mullan who know this, we say nothing to anyone?"

Mullan's eyes widened.

"If certain conditions are fulfilled and promises kept. Break one and we'll expose you and file a complaint with Constable Mulligan. I want a full, sincere apology to Alice Moloney and Doctor Fitzpatrick, and a solemn promise never to annoy her again."

Mullan nodded rapidly.

"You will withdraw your complaint to the borough council about the sporting club being noisy and never complain again."

"I will, sir."

"And you'll tell everybody that as the war's been over for quite a while you are relinquishing your military title, Mister Mullan."

"I will, sir." Mullan managed a weak smile. "To tell the truth, I was getting tired of the constant pretending." He stood. "My lord, Doctor O'Reilly, I offer you both my most sincere apologies. I will mend my ways. I may leave Ballybucklebo. I don't know. I've had a great shock, been terrified, ashamed, and relieved. You were right, Doctor O'Reilly, I do feel better now, but I'm all a-tremble. I'd really like to be alone."

John MacNeill rose and so did O'Reilly, who said, "We'll be going, but we'll be keeping an eye on you. We'll let ourselves out." As O'Reilly closed the door to the living room he half turned.

Mister Oliver Mullan was sitting, trembling, and his tears freely flowed. You poor bastard, O'Reilly thought. You poor soul.

He joined the marquis beside the pitch. The game was over and the sun was peeping through the parting clouds. The rain had stopped.

"Jasus, John. It was tough on Mullan. I had set out wanting to gut him, but —"

John MacNeill smiled. "Very Hippocratic of you, my friend. I too, felt great discomfort, but on the brighter side, he is going to change his ways. I don't think he's harmed anyone but himself impersonating an officer, so no complaint to the police. We've achieved the goals we wanted. As soon as I get home, I am president after all, I'm going to give the ten days' notice required and convene that extraordinary general meeting. I can't foresee any difficulties and we should be able to get functions started in very short order after it."

O'Reilly grinned. "Mister Mullan's downfall will be the sporting club's victory. There's a certain rightness in that. Indeed there is."

28

HE SAVED OTHERS; HIMSELF
HE CANNOT SAVE

December 3, 1963

Barry signed off on the chart he'd been writing, dated his notes December 3, 1963, and put his feet up on the desk in the staff room. He glanced into the hall, wondering if he dared close his eyes for a few minutes. While the pace on 5 and 6 hadn't been as gruelling as the work on casualty, at least there you'd known when you were off call. Here you could be summoned at any time, and he had been, twice, last night in the small hours.

During the last month he'd helped John Geddes deal with three in-hospital cases needing defibrillation in the coronary care unit on ward 6. The cardiac ambulance had arrived three weeks ago and had already proven its worth. John had told Barry how he'd taken his team to the home of a woman who had suffered a myocardial infarction. Treatment of her condition had been started there and then. Fortunately she had not fibrillated, but had she, the defibrillator had been on the spot and ready to go. She'd been admitted, and discharged eight days later.

He heard a phone ringing, and in a moment the door flew open, and Sister Kearney stuck her head in. "Barry, looks like you're finally going to get your time in the cardiac ambulance. John is over in Royal Maternity looking after a woman with mitral valve disease who's in labour. The GP, Doctor Halliday, has had a call about a man with severe chest pain. The doctor called our hotline and is already on his way. I've called the ambulance depot and the driver's on his way to pick up your team. You'll have to go. Now."

"Right." He dropped the chart and tore after her to meet a staff nurse and a senior medical student in the hall. "Come on."

With Barry leading, they charged out through the plastic doors, down the stairs, along a corridor, outdoors past the tennis courts, across a car park, and there waiting for them was the Daimler the colour of Devonshire clotted cream, its back doors wide open. This was as close as it could get to 5 and 6. Barry, followed by his team, piled aboard. The medical student slammed the doors and headed for one of two fold-down seats on the bulkhead between driver and cabin. In moments, Barry was seated facing into the cabin, at the head of a centrally placed stretcher on wheels. He smiled at the nurse in her seat on the opposite side of the trolley.

"Go," Barry yelled to the driver through a connecting sliding door.

The driver switched on his siren and took off. Barry held on and felt a small smile on his lips as the excitement inside him built. Perhaps the acceleration wasn't quite as powerful as the rocket sleds NASA used to simulate blastoff, but it rocked him as he clung to the hinged seat. "God," he said over the racket, "it's all go."

They should be there in about two minutes, taking a left up Grosvenor Road, a right turn down the Falls, and a left onto Conway Street.

Barry took inventory. There was the ECG machine and the portable defibrillator. The nurse was flanked on one side by a storage cabinet and a case containing resuscitation gear and on the other by a case containing drugs. All was in order.

"Nurse Logan, when we get there you bring the drug case, Jim, the resuscitation gear, and I'll bring the ECG. The driver

480

knows to put the defibrillator on the trolley and wheel it in."

"We're here," the driver yelled as he braked.

Barry and his team bailed out and ran into the house.

"In here," a man's voice called.

Barry led the way into a front parlour.

A man of about fifty with grey eyes and a short moustache was kneeling, taking the pulse of a pale and sweating middle-aged man lying on the floor. His pupils were constricted and he was fully conscious, which Barry knew meant he wasn't fibrillating. At once Barry felt the rush of his adrenaline start to slow down.

"That was quick. I'm Doctor Halliday, by the way. I'll brief you. Brendan Kerr here is fifty-eight. His wife, she's in the kitchen, phoned me ten minutes ago to tell me Brendan had complained of a crushing pain in his chest, radiating down his left arm, and had collapsed on the floor. My surgery is just around the corner so I phoned the hotline as we'd been taught by Doctor Geddes on the Sunday-morning course, and headed here."

As Doctor Halliday spoke, Barry was plugging the ECG machine into a house electricity socket and his team members

481

were opening their cases.

"I got here five minutes ago. His pulse was regular but a hundred and ten beats per minute, he was pale, sweating, and his blood pressure was only one hundred over seventy. I gave him fifteen milligrams of morphine intramuscularly" — that would account for the constricted pupils — "and twenty-five milligrams of Largactil orally as an anti-emetic."

"Absolutely right," Barry said, a little embarrassed that he, a houseman, should be praising an experienced GP. He bent to his work. "Sorry, but this is going to sting, Mister Kerr." He inserted the first of four ECG needle electrodes, one for each limb, and with each the patient sucked in his breath.

"Excuse me, sir." The driver stuck his bus-driver-capped head round the door. "The trolley and defib are in the hall."

"Thank you," Barry said. "Leave them there for the minute. Jim, can you put up the intravenous dextrose, please?" And as the student, assisted by the nurse, bent to his task, Barry switched on the ECG machine. It whirred, and from a slot in its side, a narrow strip of pink graph paper inched its way along. Barry was no world authority on reading these strips, but this one showed

482

the classic distortions of the tracing that indicated an anterior wall infarction, a blockage of one of the coronary arteries that supplied oxygenated blood to the heart muscle. "Your diagnosis was spot on, Doctor Halliday. Thank you. Excuse me for a minute."

Barry went into the hall. "We'll not need the defibrillator. Please return it and come back with the trolley so we can get Mister Kerr into the ambulance."

"Right, sir."

In very short order, Doctor Halliday had explained matters to Mrs. Kerr and had helped her into one of the two seats at the front of the body of the ambulance. Barry disconnected the ECG leads from the machine but left the needles in situ so the patient could be reconnected once aboard and continuously monitored. Barry carried the machine into the ambulance.

Meanwhile, the driver and the student had loaded Mister Kerr onto the trolley, and with the nurse holding the intravenous bottle above, moved into the ambulance. The nurse and student returned to the house to collect the two cases, and by the time they had replaced them, closed the door, and taken their seats, Barry had reconnected Mister Kerr to the ECG machine and plugged the defibrillator into two twelve-volt batteries. The siren blared and off they set for the return trip. Barry was running the ECG strip through his hands when Mister Kerr made a strangling noise and his eyes rolled up.

Mrs. Kerr muttered, "Jesus wept," and started to cry, and the spiky patterns on the graph paper were replaced by a continuous series of low wiggles. "He's fibrillating," Barry said, switching on the defibrillator. He'd waste no time giving CPR. He grabbed the two defibrillator electrodes and held them for the nurse to smear them with KY jelly. He placed one on the upper right-hand side of Mister Kerr's left chest and one over the lower left. "Everybody clear." Quick visual check. Right. He triggered the machine. The patient twitched and, half turning, Barry was able to see that the tracing had reverted to its earlier series of periodic jagged spikes. He heard the patient haul in a deep breath, and his eyes were open.

Barry was jubilant. One shock, just one, and he'd brought the patient back. No, he corrected himself, he and his team had. "Well done, everybody," he said. He was panting, sweating, and wondered what his own heart rate was. This defibrillating business certainly pumped out the adrenaline.

"What happened?" Mister Kerr said in a small, weak voice. "I feel awful."

The ambulance had drawn up outside the ambulance room.

"We're at the hospital, Mister Kerr," Barry said, "and we're going to get you admitted, then I'll explain." While his medical team waited for the driver to come back with another orderly, Barry removed the needle electrodes, turned off the ECG, and tore off the paper strip for further study by the senior cardiologists.

Once inside the ambulance room, the driver and his mate, accompanied by a nurse and Mrs. Kerr, wheeled Mister Kerr into a cubicle and drew the curtains. The nurse would begin the admission procedure.

Barry said, "Thanks for all your help. Pretty dramatic, wasn't it?"

"Absolutely," said the student. "I'm still all jittery." He smiled. "I think I need some grub. Hope there's some dinner left in the East Wing."

"Well, I'm late getting off duty," said the staff nurse. "It's not quite as exciting after you've done a few."

Barry went behind the curtains.

Mister Kerr had been transferred to the hospital trolley and the student nurse was taking his blood pressure.

"You did a great job, driver. Thank you."

The driver laughed. "We call it the flying squad, sir, but the locals are already calling it the 'firing squad.' "

Barry, still collecting himself after the dramatic race to Conway Street, found himself laughing, probably to release the tension, and had to control himself before helping a tearful Mrs. Kerr into a chair at the head end of her husband's trolley.

"Sorry to seem to be ignoring you all this time," Barry said, "but we had to act at once back in the ambulance, and now we have to get your husband admitted."

"That's all right, Doctor," Mrs. Kerr said. "Doctor Halliday explained that my Brendan, God love him, had had a heart attack."

"Yes, he has."

A second nurse came in. "Hello, Doctor Laverty? What have we here?"

"In brief, anterior wall infarction. Ventricular fibrillation successfully treated."

"I see," she said. "I'll send Doctor Sloan in the minute he's finished with another patient. It won't be long." She left.

Barry glanced at his watch and felt as if his own heart had received an electric shock. Damn it to hell. Six thirty. He was going to be late again. A week ago he'd promised, come hell or high water, to take

Virginia to see Barbra Streisand and Omar Sharif in *Funny Girl* tonight. He was to have picked her up at six thirty at Musson House.

Mrs. Kerr brought him back to the present. "I seen a programme on TV about bringing people back from the dead by giving them electric shocks. I think that's what you done, sir. You saved my Brendan's life, so you did." She stroked her husband's forehead.

"Well I —"

"Don't you be shy, sir. I thank you from the bottom of my heart."

Barry smiled and, now wanting to get away to Musson as quickly as possible, said, "Thank you, Mrs. Kerr. It's my job."

Harry Sloan entered. "Doctor Laverty. You've brought me a coronary?"

Now in a rush, Barry said, "Mister Kerr, fifty-six, had an anterior wall infarction about an hour ago, here's the tracing." He gave the ECG strip to Harry. "He was given fifteen milligrams of morphine and twenty-five milligrams of Largactil and was defibrillated in the ambulance coming back here."

"Right," said Harry. "I'll take over. Do the admission. You go and get your tea."

"Thanks, Harry." Barry spoke to Mister Kerr. "This is my colleague, Doctor Sloan. He'll admit you to — ?"

487

"There are no beds in the coronary care unit, so we'll monitor you here in casualty and arrange a transfer to the coronary care unit as soon as possible," Harry said.

Even if that happened in the next few hours, Norma, who was going to cover him from six on the ward, could cope, so as of now Barry really had no more responsibility. "I hope you're feeling much better soon, Mister Kerr," he said, and left at the run for his room.

At least The Huts, three minutes from casualty, were on the way to Musson House, but he'd sweated doing the defibrillation and needed to change his shirt. He barged into his room, stripped off the shirt, sponged under his armpits, dabbed on a bit of deodorant, and flung on a clean one. No point wasting time trying to phone. There were only two lines for the student nurses and they were almost invariably busy.

As he gave his face a lick and a promise, knotted his tie, and put on a sports jacket, he thought about how he had tried to make things up with her since they'd dined at the Causerie in early November. He'd managed to see her nearly every week. They'd been to see *Lawrence of Arabia,* and last Friday had been the Queen's University Boat Club formal in the Sir William Whitla Hall on campus.

He raced out the door, running to the adjacent car park. The strains of the Hank Williams song "Half as Much" pursued him as he left The Huts.

If you loved me half as much as I love
 you
You wouldn't worry me half as much as
 you do.

He fired up Brunhilde, sped over to Musson, parked, and got out. No Virginia. He took a deep breath and began to climb the steps to where Joe the night porter stood. "Good evening, Doctor Laverty. Can I help you?"

"I was meant to pick up Nurse Clarke at six thirty."

"I know, sir. She waited here for ten minutes and went back in. I could let her know you're here."

"Thanks, Joe." Barry paced back and forth until Virginia appeared. Joe, it seemed, must have sensed trouble and had not accompanied her. She was wearing a grey pantsuit with bell bottoms. It was December but she had no coat and Barry found that disconcerting. Damn it all, he was only fifteen minutes late.

He started toward her. "Virginia, I —"

She moved back. "You what, Barry? Had to save another life?" She folded her arms in front of her chest.

"Virginia. I explained to you a month ago that I had to cover for John Geddes if he wasn't available to go out with the cardiac ambulance. The call came at five to six. I had no choice. None at all, nor any way to let you know. I'm sorry."

She shook her head. "Barry. Barry. I really did think I'd fallen in love with you, but we've been going out for four months —"

"I am in love with you, Virginia." Barry's mouth was dry, his palms sweating. "Don't throw it away. Please." He could feel his heart racing for the second time tonight, an ache building in his chest. "Please."

She unfolded her arms. Let them hang loosely by her sides. "Four months, Barry, and you've let me down again." Her voice was flat.

"I know. I'm sorry."

"At our age, a couple like us can decide to have fun together for a while then go their separate ways, or consider making a lifelong commitment." She took a deep breath. "You told me at the Causerie you were pretty certain you were going to try general practice."

490

"Yes."

"Where you could get to know all your patients the way you got to know Mister Peters?"

"Yes."

"Where your wife and family, if you had one, would be expected never to know when you might be called. Always have to take a backseat to your patients."

Barry didn't know how to reply. He hung his head.

"Barry, I'm going to miss you, for a while. I'm sorry because I know I'm hurting you now, but I have to think of me. My life. My future. I just don't see it being with a man like you."

Barry took a deep breath. Looked at her green eyes and saw nothing but resolution.

"Barry, I'm sorry, but it's over. Goodbye." She turned and he simply stood watching as Virginia Clarke walked into Musson House and out of his life.

29
TELLING THE SADDEST TALE

May 24, 1969

Barry, parked outside the Galvins' house, glanced down at the letter that sat on the passenger seat, then up to the door. He wasn't sure why he'd brought the letter. It was a standard notice from specialists to a GP about a discharged patient, but reading it ten minutes ago had prompted a slight change in his plans for the afternoon. He had kissed his wife, briefly explained where he was going, secure in the knowledge that she could accompany Fingal and Kitty to the sporting club, and headed to the car, still clutching the letter.

The door opened and Guffer came out to the front step. Barry climbed out of the car as Guffer Galvin walked slowly toward him. "Och, Doctor Laverty. It is you. What are you doing here on a Saturday?"

"I just got a letter from Marie Curie telling me Anne was discharged yesterday. How is she?"

"Come in." Guffer retraced his steps and stood aside as Barry walked up the path and through the front door. "I have her in her bed." He led Barry into the familiar living room where three ceramic mallard, garishly painted and decreasing in size, flew up at an angle on the white-washed chimney breast.

"Have a seat, Doctor, and I'll tell you what I know." Barry sat on the sofa and Guffer on a chair opposite.

Guffer sighed. "That there radiation has been very rough on her. Quite a bit of throwing up. You can see for yourself how she looks when I take you up til her. The doctors there were great and they've not told her what they told me. I think that's kinder. They told me to understand that while the puking was due to them trying til stop the — you know. It was progressing. It was in her other lung and liver." He stared down at the carpet for so long that Barry had to say gently, "What else did they tell you, Guffer?" Barry, who had always considered telling patients the facts to be an item of faith, decided at once to put his own opinion aside. If Guffer thought it kinder to his wife to hide the truth, so be it.

493

"Dear God, it's a hard row to hoe." Guffer swallowed. "They said nobody can predict accurately for an individual, but their experience with patients who've got what my Annie has, have had surgery, and had all the radiation that's safe til give but aren't getting better, the outlook's very poor. Maybe a matter of weeks. They said it was my choice. They'd look after her or she could come home." He looked at Barry. Guffer's eyes were full of supplication. "Weeks? She's better in her own bed. I've made a couple of long-distance phone calls, told Seamus til come home at once. He's on his way, and Pat, our older boy, he's coming up from Dublin on Monday when Seamus gets here."

"Good," Barry said. He stood, moved to Guffer, and put a reassuring hand on his shoulder. "You'll have to be brave for her. It's going to tell on you. I'll do what I can. Arrange for Colleen Brennan, the district nurse, to visit every day. One of us will call regularly too."

"Thank you, Doctor. Thanks a lot." He sighed and dropped his hands to his thighs, rocking himself up to standing, then headed for the door. "Will you come upstairs, please, sir?"

Barry followed the man up a narrow

staircase where a frayed tartan stair carpet was held in place by dull brass carpet rods. The last time Barry had been here they had been polished. Guffer stood aside to let Barry into a tiny room where chintz curtains were drawn back so he could see across to rooftops, some with broken slates. Spindly TV aerials sprouted from the sides of chimneys.

He parked himself on Anne's bedside.

Guffer slipped into the room and stood at the foot of the bed.

She lay propped up on pillows and wore a pink bed jacket over a blue flannel nightie. Her head was covered by a woolly hat. Irradiation frequently caused total hair loss. Her National Health Service wire-rimmed granny glasses covered pale blue eyes that seemed to be struggling to focus on him.

"It's Doctor Laverty, Annie," Guffer said.

Her voice was reedy. "Hello, Doctor."

"Hello, Anne." Enquiring after her health would be superfluous. This was not the Anne Galvin Barry used to know. Her cheeks were sunken, her cheekbones prominent through jaundiced skin as thin as tissue paper. Her right arm lying above the bedclothes was yellow-tinged too, the result of liver damage, and painfully thin, the fingers moving aimlessly. Her breathing was laboured. "Just dropped by to say welcome home. Sorry I've not brought Kenny this time, but I will soon." Apart from offering the Galvins moral support and, if needed, prescribing antiemetic or pain-killing medication, there was little more any physician could do, and he knew from the letter from Marie Curie what her physical findings were, of weight loss, liver enlargement, and consolidation of the lower left lung base.

"That's nice."

Barry could see that the effort to talk was tiring her. He went through the motions of taking her pulse, more so she could feel the human contact of his hand. "You'll be glad to be home."

"Aye." She managed to take Barry's hand in hers. "Doctor. I want you —" She had to pause and catch her breath. "To do something."

"If I can."

"Give you my uilleann pipes til Angus Mehaffey of the Highlanders — I've not the strength til work the bellows. They're his til keep — Guffer's busy looking after me."

"I will, of course."

She looked into his eyes. "Do you mind a big American — Burl Ives?"

Barry nodded.

She looked at Guffer. "He had a song.

496

'Wayfaring Stranger.' Mind the last two lines?"

Guffer sang,

I'm just a'goin' over Jordan
I'm just a'goin' over home.

"Aye. No one's told me, but I know." She gazed upward for a moment. "I'll be going over Jordan very soon."

Barry held his peace.

"When I'm gone — I want Angus til play 'The Flowers of the Forest' on my old pipes after the service."

Barry was close to tears.

Guffer said, "Excuse me, Doctor."

Barry moved aside to let the man lean over the bed and hold his wife.

Barry, who could see Guffer's broad shoulders shaking, said, "I'll leave you alone now. I'll wait for you, Guffer, in the living room."

"I'll be down in a wee minute til get you the pipes, sir."

As he went downstairs he thought of her request. "The Flowers of the Forest." It was an ancient Scottish tune performed only in public at funerals or memorial services. Perhaps keeping the truth from Anne Galvin had been kindly meant, but she already knew her time was short, and was facing the inevitable with pride and dignity. Barry Laverty straightened his shoulders. He'd not cry for Anne Galvin. He'd control himself and show the same stoicism as his patient.

Five minutes later, having put Anne's precious uilleann pipes in the backseat, Barry climbed into his Hillman and headed for the extraordinary meeting of the Bally-bucklebo Bonnaughts' Sporting Club called by John MacNeill ten days ago.

Barry turned right onto the Belfast to Bangor Road. Anne and Guffer would have enjoyed the events that Bertie Bishop and his committee envisioned for the club, but he knew Anne Galvin would not live to see the first one held there. And when she died, Doctor Barry Laverty would miss her, comfort her family, but recognise that all of it was a sad but ordinary part of being a physician who cared for his patients but now had the ability to cope.

Fingal O'Reilly held a chair so Sue could be seated, then did the same for Kitty before sitting himself at a table close to the platform at one end of the big room.

They were early and the only other people to have arrived were Alan Hewitt and Lenny

Brown, who were completing a game of darts.

"How's about youse, Doctor and ladies?" Lenny Brown said from where he had been keeping score on a blackboard near a circular darts board.

"Afternoon, lads," O'Reilly said. "Mind if we watch?"

"We're near done," Alan said. "Both of us is close. I'm down til twenty-four and Lenny til twenty-three." He squinted at the dartboard. "I'm going for a three and seventeen, and then I'll double out on the two and win."

"And if you don't double out" — Lenny smiled — "you'll 'bust' and I'll get my turn before you get another go to make twenty-four. Don't count your chickens before they hatch."

Alan threw his first dart. It flew straight but instead of sticking in the 3 wedge, lodged in the immediately adjacent 19. He muttered, "Bugger. Sorry, ladies."

Lenny grinned, scratched out *24* and wrote *5* beneath it. "Remember them chickens now, Hewitt."

"Run away off, Lenny Brown. You're dead meat, so you are. I can do it."

O'Reilly grinned. Those were the friendly insults of two old friends. One Catholic, one Protestant. He did the sums. "Alan can still win if he makes one, and double two."

Alan's second dart hit the 1. "I hear cracks starting in them eggshells, Lenny. Wee beaks pecking til get out."

Sue and Kitty both chuckled.

O'Reilly noticed folks starting to arrive. Last dart. Double out or bust.

O'Reilly held his breath and so did Alan in the moments before he released. There was a solid thump as the point hit and stuck into the red line between the wires of the double two at the half past four position on the board's face.

O'Reilly applauded as a smiling Alan Hewitt said, "You were saying about chickens, Mister Brown?"

Alan's last dart had flown true and given him the win.

"Aye. Well done, ould hand." Lenny walked over, and they shook hands. "Well done. If there was no meeting to attend and the bar was open, I'd buy you a pint."

"Aye," said Alan with a laugh, "and if we had any bacon we could have bacon and eggs — if we had any eggs. Next time in the Duck."

"Fair enough." The two friends took a table close by.

O'Reilly turned to Sue. "Interesting game,

darts. I forget which English king in medieval times decreed that all able-bodied men should play darts after mass on Sunday to hone their archery skills, but it's one thing us Irish were happy to pinch from the English. Darts is part of pub life."

"Looks complicated to me," Sue said. "I really didn't understand what was going on."

"Come on then and I'll show you how to play before the place fills up." He waved at Donal and Julie Donnelly.

"You're on, Fingal."

They walked to the blackboard where the score had been kept. O'Reilly wiped it clean and wrote "301" once beneath a letter *S* and again under *F.* "That's you and me, Sue," he said. "During the game, each of us in turn throws three darts. A turn is called a 'leg.' The object is to be the first player to reduce that number three hundred and one to exactly zero."

"Exactly zero? And how's that done?" Sue asked.

O'Reilly moved over. "Come and look at the board." He pulled out three darts, each with a pointed steel tip, tapered barrel, narrow shaft, and flight of three feathers. He used the point of one to demonstrate. "Can you see how the circular green and red board is divided by radial wires into twenty numbered pie-shaped wedges? And each has a designated number?"

"Yes." Sue frowned. "And if a dart lands in a wedge it gets that score?"

"Exactly. I'll show you in a minute."

"What about those two circles in the centre of the board?"

"The bulls. The outer green one's worth twenty-five points and the red inner circle's worth fifty. There are a few finer points, but let me show you."

He walked to a line on the floor opposite the board. "The line's called the oche. It's seven feet, nine and a quarter inches from the target. Stand behind it."

Sue did.

O'Reilly was aware of the arrival of more people. As was customary, so as not to disturb the competitors' concentration, folks made as little noise as possible. He handed her a dart.

"It's quite heavy," she said.

"Hold it and stand like this." O'Reilly half turned, with his right shoulder pointing to the board. He leaned forward and raised his right arm, bent at the elbow. The dart's barrel was gripped between thumb and fingers.

Sue copied O'Reilly.

"Now," he said. "To begin the game you

have to double in."

"Double in?"

"See how the circumference is bounded by two narrow wires? A hit in there is worth twice the pie's score, so a hit there in the twenty is worth forty, a 'double top.' Watch." He sighted, drew back his arm until his right hand was level with his right ear, paused, then snapped his arm forward and released the dart. It flew straight — and hit the rectangular cork wall protector an inch away from the board's edge.

"Bugger," he muttered. As he went to retrieve the dart, O'Reilly heard Alan Hewitt say to Lenny, "And nothing subtracted from three hundred one is?"

"Still three hundred one." Both men laughed.

More people quietly filled chairs.

O'Reilly said sternly, "It could happen to a bishop." But he was smiling.

"If bishops played darts," Kitty said. "Which they probably don't."

"Less of your lip, Mrs. O'Reilly."

Kitty replied by blowing him a discreet kiss, which he was quite sure was not standard darts procedure. He winked at his wife as he helped Sue adjust the position of her feet, corrected the angle of her elbow. "Now, sight along the dart, hold your breath, and snap your arm forward."

Thump.

"I'll be damned," O'Reilly said. "Double top. You're in."

Sue's feat was greeted by applause.

O'Reilly gave her another dart.

Sue's next throw scored nineteen. She grasped the third and final dart firmly, took her time sighting, flicked her arm forward and there, proud as Punch, the metal tip buried itself in the inner bull. "Fifty," she said.

She got another round of applause.

O'Reilly said, "Plus forty is one oh nine, from three hundred and one is one hundred and ninety-two. Well done, Sue."

"Begob," Alan said. "Mrs. Laverty, play like that and you could give last year's News of the World Darts champion Bill Duddy a run for his money."

"I think it's a classic case of beginner's luck, gentlemen," said Sue. "But thank you."

O'Reilly said, "That'll have to be it for now, Sue. Look. The place is full to over-flowing, but I must say" — O'Reilly grinned — "you've a good eye. Inner bull? You really nailed it."

"Aye," said Bertie Bishop, who had arrived, accompanied by Flo, "and let's hope we nail this vote."

30
OF SOME DISTRESSFUL STROKE

February 17, 1964
Barry sat in the clinical room of ward 21, looking out the window and yawning, waiting for his shift to end. Twenty-one, along with ward 22, the neurology unit, were in Quinn House, at the westerly end of the hospital complex, facing east. It was shortly after sunset and his view was fading of the Royal Victoria to his left, Royal Maternity to his right, and The Huts in the distance between them. He smiled. He was fading like the light and never mind dinner. Bed beckoned.

His three months on 5 and 6 had ended three and a half weeks ago, on the last day of January 1964. It had been an interesting time medically, and keeping busy had helped distract him from his sadness at losing Virginia Clarke. But he knew cardiology wasn't for him. Sure, the admission, treatment, and discharge routine had been more

505

satisfying than the "get 'em in and out" of casualty, but it was still so — Barry sought for the word — so mechanical. This was highly technical stuff and there was little time to understand his patients as human beings. He stretched and yawned again, thinking of the hours he'd spent here last night. Unlike the other wards, 21 was on permanent take-in for cases requiring immediate brain surgery. That could happen at any time, so a houseman must always be available. To allow junior doctors some leisure and rest, two were assigned to this rotation, and at present he shared the workload with Norma. He had every other weekend off, a fat lot of good now Virginia had gone, damn it.

The door opened and Norma came in. "Hello, Barry. What are you up to?"

"Having a rest."

"Heard you were busy last night. Anand told me."

Barry nodded. It was Anand Garg, the registrar here, along with John Geddes and Doctor Dennis Coppel, the anaesthetic registrar, who had been responsible for starting CPR on a man who had collapsed outside the hospital, got him to a side ward, and kept him alive until Doctor Pantridge had arrived with the defibrillator and treated the ventricular fibrillation. The case John Geddes had detailed to Barry as the start of the portable defibrillator programme.

"We admitted an unconscious Mister Wilson Warnock at midnight," said Barry. "He'd been hit with a bottle on his right temple and was unconscious. Drink and politics don't mix. According to Wilson's brother, who'd come to the hospital, they'd been in an illegal drinking club on the Falls Road, a general ruction broke out, Mister Warnock tried to intervene and got hit for his pacifist pains. Anand diagnosed a subdural haematoma, and sure enough when we opened the skull there was a pool of blood between the dura matter and the brain, the protective membrane. Anand ligated the torn middle meningeal artery and reckons the patient will make a complete recovery."

"That's good." Norma collapsed into the chair opposite Barry and sighed. "But I could never do surgery, never mind brain surgery." She chuckled. "It takes a certain amount of nerve. I can't see me sticking a scalpel into someone."

"Mister Warnock is a lucky man to have a skilled surgeon like Anand last night, but I agree with you about surgery. Particularly this kind. I've always found the nervous

507

system puzzling."

Norma shook her head. "All of those cranial nerves, sensors for pain and temperature, and orientation in space. Nerves sending motor messages to make the muscles move. It's bloody complicated."

"Can't imagine trying to sort it all on the operating table. I'm pretty good at tying flies, but otherwise I'm a bit ham-fisted."

Norma smiled. "Our boss, Mister Greer, has fingers like sausages, but, boy, is he skillful. I don't know how he does it."

"One of Jack Mills's heroes. Rugby-mad, is Charlie Greer. A graduate of Trinity College Dublin. In the '30s he played in the second row for Ireland at rugby football."

"Very rough game. Good way to get a subdural haematoma if you ask me. Did you ever play, Barry?"

"At school. We had to, but I was a better scholar than an athlete. Jack played at Queens." Barry yawned and covered his mouth with his hand. "Excuse me."

Norma glanced at her watch. "Quarter past five. Go on. Don't wait 'til six. I'll look after the shop. You'd a bad night."

"Thanks, Norma. Thanks a lot." Barry rose and headed for the door. "I hope you have a quiet one." He left ward 21 and was passing the entrance to ward 22 when he saw Jan Peters heading toward the unit. Her winter coat was buttoned unevenly and stray pieces of her usually neatly coiffed hair straggled out from under a blue tam. She must have left home in a hurry.

"Jan, what's up?"

"Oh, Barry. I was at Mum and Dad's getting ready to take them to the Cottars Kitchen for tea when Dad took sick again. He started slurring his speech. Said he had a blinding headache and passed out."

Barry didn't like the sound of that. He was aching to sleep, but knowing his friend was in trouble acted as powerful a stimulant as a Benzedrine pill.

"I had enough sense to call nine-nine-nine, but when the ambulance came, there was only room in it for him and Mum. I've just got here. I don't know what's happening. I'm scared, Barry."

"I'm so sorry. Would you like me to come with you?"

"Please. I'd like that. So will Dad."

Together they entered 22. Jan went to speak to Sister Lynch at the main desk.

Barry waited in the corridor. Not again. The poor man — and his family. Barry had derived great satisfaction from dropping in on Rusky Peters on ward 10 after his amputation in November, getting to know the man better. Rusky had been discharged in mid-November, to be followed up by physiotherapy and the department of prosthetics. Throughout it all he had been having regular bleedings. Jan, when they happened to meet, had given Barry bulletins about her dad's progress. From what she had said, Barry had felt confident that Rusky was holding his own.

She returned, frowning, her breathing shallow. "It's not looking good, Barry."

"He may pull out of it. Your dad is a strong man, and he has a lot to live for." Barry put a hand on Jan's shoulder and she reached up to touch it before letting her hand drop. She sighed.

"Thank you, Barry. I suppose that's true. Sister Lynch says Doctor Millar is with my father now. He's still in a —" She swallowed. "In a coma. We'll get a better idea when Doctor Millar's finished." She pointed to a door. "Mum's in the quiet room. We'd better go to her."

Barry followed Jan into a small, gently lit, windowless room with several chairs and a central table adorned with a vase of flowers. Three tasteful seascapes hung on the daffodil yellow walls.

Mrs. Dora Peters looked up from where she sat. "Oh, Jan," she said. "I'm dead

510

scared, so I am." There were tear tracks down her cheeks. "They wouldn't let me stay with Dad."

Jan knelt in front of her mother and they hugged.

Barry stood silently. Patients with polycythaemia were prone to blockage of major arteries. If that artery happened to be one supplying the brain with oxygenated blood, the result would be serious brain damage. It was medically referred to as a cerebrovascular accident, better known as a stroke. Almost certainly all that could be hoped for now was that the residual permanent damage might be minor.

Jan stood, motioned Barry to take a chair, and sat beside her mother.

"I met Barry in the hall. Asked him to come with me for a bit of support."

"Hello, Barry," Dora Peters said, looking up, then sniffed. "Please excuse me. I'm a bit of a mess."

"Dora, I understand. I know you're worried sick. If I was an expert, I'd try to explain to you what's going on, but you know I'm only a houseman."

"I understand."

"I can tell you that Doctor Harold Millar is a foremost neurologist. Rusky's in very good hands."

"Dad really is, Mum. I work here with Doctor Millar every day. I know."

"Thank you, both," Dora said. "And, Barry, you've been a great comfort to us ever since Rusky took ill."

Barry inclined his head.

The door opened and a middle-aged, silver-haired man with a high forehead over dark-rimmed spectacles entered. "Mrs. Peters, I'm Doctor Millar — please, don't get up." He nodded acknowledgments to Jan and Barry.

Dora Peters sank back into her chair.

Jan held her mother's hand. Both looked up at the consultant.

Doctor Millar stood in front of them, his hands in front of him at chest level, right hand clasped over left. His gaze never left Dora Peters's eyes. "I'm sorry, but —" he said.

Barry held his breath. No. He knew what was coming next.

"I'm truly sorry, but your husband had a massive stroke. I'm afraid he did not recover."

Barry pursed his lips. Screwed his eyes shut for a moment. Inhaled deeply. No. Not my friend Rusky.

Dora stammered, "Massive? Did not recover?" Her eyes widened. She shook her

512

head. "I don't — I don't — Please — I don't understand."

Jan glanced at Barry, squeezed her mother's hand, and said in a soft, level voice, "Mum, Doctor Millar is saying that Dad has passed away."

The consultant nodded, put his right hand on Dora's shoulder. "Please accept my deepest condolences."

Dora Peters shook her head. Her eyes looked unfocussed. Her voice was soft. "No. Not my Rusky. No. He's a tough man. Them bleedings was working. No. Not Rusky. You'll see." Her little smile was self-comforting.

Barry had had to break this kind of news several times when he was working on 5 and 6. Many recipients tried to deny the facts. He had come to believe it was a deep-rooted defence that allowed them to understand more gradually, absorb the shock over time.

Jan kissed her mother's cheek, sat back, and looked her right in the eye. "Mum, I know it's hard to believe. Doctor Millar knows his job and he's not making it up."

"Och, Jan. No."

Barry wondered how Jan, a trained nurse, would handle this. Certainly he didn't want to interfere, and he could feel his own grief welling up.

Jan took both of her mother's hands in her own. She kept her voice level as she said, "Mum. I know it's hard to believe. I don't want to believe it either, but Dad's gone. He really is."

Dora Peters's eyes came back into focus. "Are you certain sure?"

Doctor Millar intervened. "I'm afraid I am. Absolutely certain."

Dora gave one sob, but Barry could sense she was holding herself rigidly. Either refusing to show her pain or still not able to grasp the situation. She said, "Thank you, Doctor Millar. Thank you for telling us the truth."

Doctor Millar said, "If there's anything we can do? Perhaps send in one of our chaplains?"

She shook her head. "No. It's all right, thank you." She swallowed. Exhaled. Her eyes glistened.

"If you'd like to come and say good-bye?"

Dora's voice cracked. "I don't want to say good-bye to my Rusky." She patted her left chest. "He's still alive — in here." She looked at Jan. "I want til remember him like he was, not all cold."

Young doctors and nurses were taught that there was benefit in seeing the departed. Denial was often the next of kin's first reaction. Facing the incontrovertible facts was the first step in the long process of healing.

Jan stood and put a hand under her mother's elbow. Helped her to stand. "Come on, Mum. Dad would want you to."

"Do you think so?"

"I do."

"Barry?"

"Yes, I do, Dora."

"I really must? We can't just go home?"

"I'm sorry, Mum."

Together they followed the consultant.

Barry, out of respect for their privacy, sat down to wait and see if he could offer any comfort when they returned. And being alone, let flow the tears he had been holding back.

31
ONE MAN SHALL HAVE ONE VOTE

May 24, 1969
"Nail the vote?" O'Reilly said to Bertie Bishop. "I'm certain we will."

Bertie smiled. "I hope so. I've til bring in the subcommittee's report, so I'd best join the rest of the platform party." He pointed to where the marquis, as president, and Fergus Finnegan, as secretary, sat behind a wooden table on a raised platform facing the hall. The marquis had a gavel and Fergus the minute book.

Flo said, "And I'm going over there til sit with the rest of the committee, Father Hugh and the Reverend Robinson." She waved at them and they waved back.

Myrna Ferguson approached, mouthed, "May I join you?" over the now loud hubbub, and pointed at a chair.

O'Reilly stood. "Of course." As he held her chair, then sat himself, he glanced 'round. Standing room only.

The clock above the platform said two o'clock, and the marquis bent his head so his mouth was close to Bertie Bishop's ear, said something, and nodded in agreement with Bertie's reply. He sat and rapped his gavel. Conversation lessened. Another rap. The volume decreased. A third rap and he rose. "Ladies and gentlemen. Ladies and gentlemen, may I have silence, please?"

The only sound to break it was the tapping of Barry's heels as he crossed the floor and sat beside Sue.

The marquis smiled at Barry and said, "Thank you, ladies and gentlemen. Thank you for coming to this extraordinary meeting of the Ballybucklebo Bonnaughts Sporting Club to discuss and vote on a proposition to open the club to nonmembers for functions on Saturday nights. First I am going to ask Councillor Bishop to read a report from his committee, then I will ask for a motion in support and a seconder. We'll open the floor for discussion and then take a vote. In order to approve the committee's recommendations, we will require a majority of the members present to be in favour." He paused for breath, then said, "Councillor, if you please."

Fergus scribbled in his minute book.

Bertie Bishop rose and tucked his thumbs

under the lapels of his dark double-breasted suit. "My lord, ladies, and gentlemen, arising from a conversation in April, a small group of Father Hugh, Reverend Robinson, my wife, Flo, and me was struck to consider what the marquis just said, having functions here on a Saturday night. We had three reasons in mind, not just wanting a venue where men and women could get together and have a drink or two. One, in light of the recent outbreak of sectarianism, which praise the Lord seems to have settled down for a while but which could rear up again, we wanted til demonstrate how the two communities can and will continue to live in harmony —"

"Hear him. Hear him."

O'Reilly saw Alan smiling at his darts partner and heard the approving murmurs and applause.

One gavel rap. "Order, please."

Silence.

"Two, we wanted more than a drink. We wanted til hold functions like dances and talent contests, and three, we wanted to charge admission so we might put up seed money for a good cause like sending kids from both communities to camp together in the summer. That there's the proposal. I need a motion to approve the opening of

518

the club to nonmembers on Saturday nights for the purpose of strengthening our community ties by holding functions, and raising money for charity. I'd like a proposer."

Up went many hands, but the marquis said, "Please, minute proposed by Father Hugh O'Toole."

"Seconded by?"

More hands.

"Please, minute seconded by Reverend Robinson."

O'Reilly whispered to Kitty. "When it passes that'll look good in the *County Down Spectator.*"

The marquis said, "Fergus, will you please read the duly proposed and seconded motion?"

Fergus did.

"I now declare the motion open for discussion."

Mister Coffin, the undertaker, rose. "Mister Chairman, 'function' can mean a lot of things. Can we please have clarification of exactly what kinds of functions are to be proposed?"

"Mister Bishop?"

"Your committee is thinking of four things: dances to small local bands like the Belmont Swing College or the White Eagles, because they're not very expensive. That

519

there *Come Dancing* on BBC with ballroom stuff's quare and popular with the older crowd. All you'd need would be a DJ. Donal Donnelly's a dab hand at that —"

"Dead on, Donal," someone yelled, and everyone laughed.

One rap. "Order."

O'Reilly whispered to Kitty, "Judging by the mood of the crowd, I think this is going to breeze through."

"And so it should," she said.

Bertie Bishop continued, "Me and Flo's got a brave clatter of Glenn Miller and Tommy Dorsey records."

Kitty said to O'Reilly, "And you have Count Basie, Cab Calloway, Earl Hines. We used to dance to their records when you were a student."

O'Reilly nodded and remembered those days fondly.

A hand was raised.

"Yes, Mister Brown."

Lenny Brown rose. "That's all very well for older folks. I've a wee lad. Would there be anything for the younger crowd?"

Bertie said, "If you want to save money, a DJ could play rock-and-roll records. New stuff like The Beatles, The Rolling Stones —"

Lenny wanted to know, "And would there

be stuff by bands like The Who, Led Zeppelin, Creedence Clearwater Revival. Dy'ever hear CCR's new one, 'Proud Mary'?" Before the marquis could stop him, Lenny had sung with an affected American accent,

Big wheel keep on toinin'
Proud Mary keep on boinin'
Rollin', rollin', rollin' on the rivah.

Whistles and catcalls. Applause.

The marquis played a serious gavel concerto until everyone had settled down, then said, "I have and will continue to allow questioners to interrupt a speaker, but please can we have a little more order?" The seriousness of his words was only slightly diminished by his wide grin.

Jasus, O'Reilly thought, where else would a man want to live?

"I'm sure music for the younger set could be arranged," the marquis said.

Mister Robinson asked, "Would there not be some kind of fee to pay to the record companies?"

Bertie dropped a slow wink and said, "What the eye doesn't see, the heart doesn't grieve over."

"I didn't hear that," said the marquis.

"Besides," said Bertie, "this will still be considered a private club rather than a public venue."

"Ah, thank you, Councillor. An important distinction. Yes, Dermot Kennedy?"

"If we're going to have dances for the younger ones, and I know my Jeannie would go, could we serve drink or would the guests have to be over eighteen?"

The marquis asked, "Constable Mulligan?"

Malcolm Mulligan, wearing his bottle-green RUC uniform and very much on duty, said, "In a private facility, if food is also served, those under eighteen may be present, but it is still an indictable offence to serve or for them to consume alcoholic beverages."

"Thank you, Constable. Please carry on, Mister Bishop."

"Thank you, sir. I said there was four things, but the last couple are two sides of the one coin. The Ballybucklebo Highlanders. Them fellahs don't just play pipes and drums. They've a uilleann piper, a fiddler, two pennywhistle guys, a banjo player who also has a mandolin, a squeeze-box lad who doubles up on the spoons. That's enough to hold a traditional *céilidh.*"

"*Céilidh?*" Father O'Toole called. "Then

I'm your man, so. I love that music."

As do many of your flock, O'Reilly thought. Diplomatic, Bertie. Diplomatic. Although it might appear on first sight that traditional Irish music was more favoured by Catholics, it was actually a division based more on class. The upper and middle tended to be Protestant and liked ballroom dancing and hops. Many more Catholics were working class, and their tastes tended to traditional Irish music handed down from generation to generation.

"And," said Bertie Bishop, "we've not only talented musicians, we've singers and dancers, and reciters. We've a notion to run talent contests too."

"I draw the line at being a judge," the marquis said.

Me too, O'Reilly thought, remembering the judging of a pie contest.

When the laughter had died down, there was silence for a while.

The marquis said, "If there are no further questions?"

A hand went up.

O'Reilly recognised Hubert Doran as he stood stiffly, his other hand rigid at his side.

"I thought this here was a sporting club. Them as wants dances is quite at liberty til go til Caproni's in Ballyholme. I'd rather have a quiet drink here on a Saturday. I don't approve of this talk of dances and talent contests and *céilidhs* at all. Not one bit."

A voice O'Reilly did not recognise yelled over a communal groan, "Jasus, Hubert, if you ever get til Heaven, you'll be bellyaching that your halo's too tight."

The groan turned to derisive laughter. Hugh Doran continued to stand, his feet planted widely, as if ready to take on the whole crowd.

"Thank you, Mr. Doran," said the marquis. "Your comments will be duly noted in the minutes. Now, if you have no further comments, I believe someone else has something to say. Reverend Robinson?"

Hubert Doran dropped back into his chair with a grunt as the Presbyterian minister, in black jacket and white starched dog collar, rose, waited for silence, and said, "It's a small point but I, and I'm sure a large number of people, will want to be reassured that these festivities will not spill over into the Sabbath."

"Last orders ten thirty. Twenty minutes' drinking-up time. Everyone out by eleven o'clock. That's a promise," Bertie Bishop said.

"Bless you."

The marquis waited, and waited, and waited.

O'Reilly rose. "My lord. I call the question."

"Very well, Doctor. Mister Secretary, please read the motion once more."

Fergus did.

"Those in favour?"

O'Reilly's raised hand was lost in a forest of others.

"Those against?"

A single hand went up and O'Reilly recognised the owner. Hubert Doran. He leaned over to whisper to Kitty, "That little gobshite could sow dissension in a deserted house."

"Luckily, we have a full house today," Kitty said with a smile.

"Those abstaining?"

Not a hand.

One gavel bang. "I declare the motion carried. Now, unless there is any other business?" The marquis scanned the room. "No? I declare this meeting adjourned. Thank you all very much."

He rose, left the platform and, accompanied by Bertie Bishop, joined O'Reilly and company. "That was all very satisfactory, I thought."

"I agree," Myrna said. "It's been a while

since I watched you chair a meeting, John. Nicely done."

Kitty said, "I agree. I thought you handled that perfectly, John." She turned to Bertie. "Your report was terrific. Clear, brief, and right to the point."

O'Reilly laughed. "It ought to have been. How many years have you been in local politics, Bertie?"

"A brave wheen," Bertie Bishop said, "but thanks for that. All I did was reflect the great work done by my committee."

John MacNeill said, "I think that even though things have been politically quiet for a while, the whole business of cross-community bridge-building is vital. I for one, and I think I can speak for Myrna, are very happy to be a part of it."

"I'll drink to that," O'Reilly said, "and as the bar won't open here until five, I propose a quick nip down to Crawfordsburn and the inn's Parlour Bar."

"I've a better idea," John MacNeill said. "Bertie, why don't you get your lovely wife and Father Hugh and Mister Robinson, see if they'd like to join us and let's all go back to Ballybucklebo House. I'm sure Thompson will be able to find something in the cellar to toast tonight's achievement in private."

"By God," said O'Reilly. "I'll certainly drink to that."

32
I Have of Comfort and Despair

February 17, 1963

Barry had said good-bye to Dora and Jan on ward 22, leaving Dora to weep softly in the quiet room and Jan to work with the staff on the formalities of a death certificate, registering the death, and making the funeral arrangements. He had promised to attend the funeral.

Ignoring the usual comings and goings, Barry walked slowly along the main corridor toward the stairway to The Huts. He still needed sleep but knew his concern for Rusky's family — and being deeply saddened by the loss of the one patient he had really got to know — was going to make dropping off difficult. He took a deep breath, puffing out his cheeks as he exhaled. He might as well get something to eat even if he wasn't particularly hungry.

He turned left into the junior doctors' and students' quarters and into the common room to find Jack Mills alone, sitting in an armchair with his feet up on another, smoking a cigarette. "Hello, mate. Off early?"

"Mmm." Barry flopped into a chair. He didn't feel much like chatting.

"Me too," Jack said. "Things are quiet on 5 and 6 and Harry's covering me this evening. You remember that wee blonde staff nurse from Carrickfergus who works there?"

Barry nodded. She was a good-looking lass.

"I'm picking her up at seven and —"

"That's nice." Barry's voice was flat.

Jack frowned at Barry. "You all right?"

Barry shook his head.

"What's up?"

Barry heard the concern in his friend's voice. "I just lost a patient."

"I'd have thought after six and a half months . . ." Jack paused and gazed at his friend. "Don't mean to sound callous, but it is part of our job and I'd've thought you'd have got used to that by now. Was this one special?"

"Yes. Yes, he was." Barry looked Jack right in the eye. "Very. It —"

Two other housemen came in, loudly discussing how a surgical team in Leeds General Hospital had carried out the first kidney transplant from a cadaver last Friday.

Jack looked over at the two men, stubbed out his cigarette, and stood. "Come on. I know you need to talk about it. I'm taking you to the Oak for a bite to eat. You can tell me all about it there once you've got a pint in front of you."

They sat at a Formica-topped table in the window alcove of the upstairs room of O'Kane's Bar, the nearest pub to the Royal and much used by students and young doctors.

"What would you like to eat?" Jack asked.

"I'm really not very hungry."

"You have to eat something."

"All right. Whatever you're having."

Jack half turned. "Brendan."

"Yes, Doctor Mills," the barman said.

"Two pints and two steak and mushroom pies and chips."

"Right." He called the order through a hatch and put two pints on the pour.

"So, tell," Jack said.

Barry took a deep breath. "It was Rusky Peters —"

"The fellow you admitted our very first day in casualty? You've told me a little about him."

Barry nodded. "After I'd made my diagnosis of polycythaemia, I explained it to him."

"That's a bit unusual."

"I know. He told me he felt safe with me. Asked me to visit him after he'd been admitted. You know Nurse Jan Peters?"

"Aye. A right decent lass."

"She's his daughter. I said I would."

" 'Scuse me." Brendan set two pints of Guinness on the table.

"Thanks, Brendan," Jack said, and lifted his pint. "Cheers." He drank.

"Cheers." Barry sipped the creamy stout. It tasted bitter tonight.

"Go on," Jack said.

Barry stared at the table. "To cut a very long story short, my diagnosis was confirmed. Rusky had a phlebotomy but lost two toes. I got to visiting him and we'd play draughts. Two months later, he lost a leg below the knee. I visited him then too, because by now he and his family weren't patients. They were friends." Barry looked Jack in the eye. "I was coming off duty today and met Jan going onto 22. I was there when Doctor Millar broke the news to Jan and her mum. Rusky had had a massive stroke." Barry's eyes misted. "He's on his way to the mortuary." He grabbed his pint and took a gulp. "And here I sit, trying to sort out how I feel. But one thing's for sure.

I'm bloody miserable."

"Excuse me, Doctors." Brendan set two plates on the table. "And will there be anything else?"

"No, thanks, Brendan," Jack said, sprinkling vinegar on his chips.

Barry took the opportunity to turn away and dab his eyes with a hanky that he stuffed back in his pocket.

"That is tough, mate. I'm sorry for your troubles. I truly am." He touched the back of Barry's hand.

Barry ate a chip. "I've had people I know die before, but none of them hit me like this." He frowned. "My grandfather died when I was nine. My parents sent me off with an uncle to go fishing for a few days. Until the funeral was over. I understand now they were trying to shelter me. I didn't understand what was going on back then."

Jack was tucking into his pie and frowning. "It's not the same, but you know I grew up on a dairy farm. When I was eight I had this pet cow named Bessie. I loved that cow. She'd follow me around the place like a dog. Well, she died, and my dad told me she'd gone to a retirement farm. He was trying to protect me. It really hurt when an older boy at school told me the truth."

Barry nodded. "Kids can be cruel."

"Come on, Barry. Eat a bit of your pie."

Barry did, but it was tasteless. "The summer I was sixteen, one of my best friends from Bangor was drowned in Belfast Lough."

"How did you take it?"

"It's strange. After the immediate shock and a vague feeling of loss, I accepted the fact that life had to go on without Ron."

"I reckoned I was immortal when I was sixteen. I think we all have to be a bit older than that before we really understand how final death is."

"You're right. And I do know now, and it's odd because when I heard Rusky was dead there was no sense of shock. I suppose our medical training forewarned me of the real possibility after Rusky's toes had been amputated in August and his leg in November."

Jack nodded. "We do have an advantage as doctors. We can make realistic appraisals of possible outcomes. I know it's trite, but forewarned is forearmed. At least it is for me. And there's another thing. Anyone who thinks doctors save lives hasn't got it quite right. Medical intervention, if it works, merely delays the inevitable. Death comes to all of us. I think you understand that, Barry."

Barry nodded. "I do. It's true. In Rusky's case, I was, at least intellectually, fully prepared."

Jack pushed away his empty plate. "Intellectually prepared, but not emotionally?"

"You know how we're told that as doctors we need to get a thick skin? I think I am getting a bit of one. Death is part of life." Which was something of which Barry had become very conscious when he had thought he was facing his own imminent demise when he'd had mono. "I can accept that. Rusky would have felt no pain after he became unconscious. His suffering's over. My doctor half tells me that."

Jack touched Barry's hand again. "I think, my friend, you're going to survive this."

"Mebbe, Jack, but inside I'm aching for my lost friend. Rusky Peters was a brave man, a man who had accepted the hand life had dealt him and faced the future with courage." He took a pull on his Guinness. "I told you we'd played draughts. He was a true craftsman. You should see the beautiful marquetry draughts board he made me. He gave it to me in November."

"And you'll treasure it, won't you."

"By God I will, as a constant memento of a good man."

"Despite what our profs keep telling us,

you got close to the man. Let him into your life."

Barry nodded. "And because I didn't keep him at arms' length, I got a great deal of satisfaction knowing I was helping him." Barry took a deep breath. "And just like people have warned me, I'm going to have to pay the price. I have to face my own sense of loss." Even though he was in public, Barry fished out a hanky and for a while let the tears flow, dried them, blew his nose, pocketed his hanky.

Jack was clearly putting every ounce of sincerity in his words. "You're a good man, too, Barry Laverty. And you're a good physician. You're going to have an empty place inside you for Rusky Peters for quite some time. But you're strong."

"Thank you, Jack, and both as a physician and friend of the family I must be strong for them."

"You will be."

"I wondered when Harry Sloan said he found it difficult to handle death if he was a man of deeper feelings. Do you think all those losses so soon after the beginning of his houseman's year overwhelmed him?"

"Harry's a sound man and he has the ability to be honest with himself. I admire that, and I see it in you too, Barry. For now, you'll have to grieve and mourn, but you'll cope."

"Thanks, and do you know what? I'll still want to get to know my patients."

"I wouldn't have thought otherwise."

Barry felt the tension leave his muscles. He was a lucky man to have a friend like Jack Mills.

"But you won't be able to if you starve to death."

Barry looked down at his barely touched meal and half-finished pint.

"I told you about the wee blonde from Carrickfergus. I'll have to get my skates on." He rose. "You sit on and mull over what we've talked about. I'm going to pay and get Brendan to reheat your dinner. Now promise me . . ."

"What?"

"You'll eat it up."

"I will, Doctor." Barry managed a smile. "Bless you, Jack. Thanks for listening."

And for once the never-serious-for-long Jack Mills did not make some flippant quip in an assumed accent but instead made a small, solemn bow, laid a hand briefly on Barry's shoulder, and was gone.

Brendan appeared. "Warm it over for you, Doc?"

"Please."

"Excuse me, sir."

"Yes, Brendan?"

"You've been coming in for years. Now you can tell me til mind my own business, but you look a bit down. You all right, like?"

"I am a bit low, and you're not being nosy. I appreciate your concern. I'm going to be fine, but thanks for asking."

"Even if you are, sir, your pint's as flat as a pancake. I'll bring you a new one. On me."

"Decent of you. Thank you."

Brendan collected the plates and glasses. "Back in a wee minute with your pint, sir." He left.

Barry was thinking over what he and Jack had discussed when a young man came in and started to help a woman off with her coat. She turned and her green eyes opened wide.

Barry jerked back in his seat. Apart from glimpses at a distance in the hallways of the Royal, their paths had not directly crossed since December. Virginia Clarke was as lovely as ever, but today he had only room in his heart for the Peters family. He looked away, but in a moment had to glance at her again.

She was standing bending over, obviously explaining something to the young man now seated at the table. He had sleek black hair, blue eyes, and a look of surprise on his open face as he looked at Barry. He was Alan Baskett, a newly qualified surgeon.

Barry watched as she approached his table.

"Barry. How are you?"

He rose. "I'm fine." His current problems were not something he wanted to discuss.

"May I sit down for a moment?"

"Please." He held what had been Jack's chair and wondered what this was all about.

She sat and he followed.

"How have you been?" she asked.

For a moment Barry debated whether to pretend he was perfectly fine, implying that he was over her already, as if she'd never mattered to him, and let her stew over it. "How am I?" He breathed in. "I still miss you." And he did, but he was not going to embarrass himself by saying he was still in love with her.

"I'm sorry, Barry. I really am. I know how much I hurt you, but I truly believe we weren't right for each other and it was better to get it out in the open rather than pretend."

He was tempted to say, "I wasn't pretending," but what was done was done. No need to be vindictive. "I believe you're right," he said, and forced a smile.

"Thank you. You were always a gentleman. Still are."

He couldn't mouth "thank you" again. He shrugged.

"There's something I want to tell you before you hear it on the rumour mill, unless you've already heard."

"Heard what?"

"I think you know Alan Baskett."

"I do. He was a registrar on 13 and 14 when I was a surgical dresser there last year. Decent chap. Funny as hell."

"He is." Her voice softened. "He's a superb surgical technician too. I've been scrubbing for him since early January."

Barry had heard that admiration of professional skill could be the start of an attraction between doctors and nurses. "I see." He knew that his voice was flat.

"We've been keeping company for six weeks."

God, that was quick. It stung Barry to think she could get over him so quickly. He glanced over at Alan Baskett, but he was hidden behind his menu.

"Barry, I know this is hurtful for you, but it's important to me that you understand."

"I'll try."

"Excuse me, sir. Your pint."

"Thanks, Brendan."

Virginia glanced up at Brendan, then back to Barry. "Alan enjoys his time off and doesn't get too close to his patients."

A common trait among surgeons, Barry knew. "Which I am afraid is one of my faults," and, boy, was this a time to be reminded of it. "Virginia, I'm trying to understand, but could you get to the point?"

"Very well. Last week he asked me to marry him. I said yes and —"

Virginia paused and Barry felt a crushing weight on his chest.

"I want to explain something else."

What more could there be?

"Do you remember our first date on Cave Hill?"

"Yes." Did he? He'd never forget the softness of her kisses.

"And I told you I was serious about nursing, wanted to be a midwife, and I wasn't in it like a lot of the girls to snag a young doctor."

"I do." He swallowed down the words that wanted to be said: But you have, and bloody quickly too.

"It's not like that. Alan is quite happy for me to have a career." Her voice caught in her throat. "I just didn't want you to be angry, that's all."

"I'm not angry." I'm heartbroken — again.

"Thank you."

Barry sat silent for several moments before he was able to collect himself enough to force a weak smile and offer the Ulster well-wishing. Not congratulations, but, "I wish you both every happiness. I really do."

Virginia rose. "Thank you, Barry. You are a generous man. Good luck." She crossed the floor and sat with her face to her fiancé and her back to Barry, who now was as low in spirits as he had ever been. Free pint and reheated meal be damned. He stood, turned, and walked away.

33
ARMS OF COOL-ENFOLDING DEATH

June 4, 1969

"Come in, Doctor Laverty, Doctor Emer," Guffer Galvin called from where he held his front door open. "Thank you for coming so quick."

Barry, clutching his bag, ran after Emer, dodging through an early June afternoon's sudden downpour and into the terrace house.

Guffer closed the door and leaned back heavily against it. "We're sure our Annie's gone."

Barry stopped brushing the water from his jacket. "We're so very sorry, Guffer."

"Thank you, sir." He sighed. "We all was expecting it, and, praise be, she didn't suffer. Youse doctors and the district nurse seen til it she was comfortable. It was dead nice when you brought Kenny til see her last week. She was daft about the big dog. Talked about him for a whole fifteen minutes after you'd gone."

"I'm glad it helped," Barry said.

"She seemed til be fading this morning, so Mister Robinson our minister come and seen her again. They had a wee prayer together." Guffer opened the door to the living room. Pat, tall, broad-shouldered, and the younger Seamus, slight, blue-eyed, both stood. Pat said, "Thank youse for coming, Doctors."

Seamus, eyes glistening, merely nodded. He'd arrived from Palm Desert, California, eight days ago.

"Me and our boys was with her at the end there now. I was holding her hand and her skin was freezing and she'd got paler in spite of her jaundice. She smiled and whispered, 'I love youse all,' closed her eyes, and never opened them again. Her breathing got very shallow, then she give a big sigh. She'd" — Guffer's voice cracked — "stopped breathing." He inhaled deeply. "I should've known what til do, but I just stood there both legs the same length. It was Pat said, 'Da, you'll have til get the doctor.' "

"I asked what for?" Seamus said. "Doctors don't do resurrections. I was powerful upset, so I was. Still am." He sniffed. "I wasn't thinking straight."

Pat said, "I've been through this with a

543

friend's granny in Dublin last year, so I know there's paperwork and stuff like that the doctor has til do."

"You're right, Pat," Barry said. "We'll take care of it. Why don't you all sit down and Doctor Emer and I'll go and see Anne, and maybe, Guffer, you could put the kettle on?" A cup of tea was, and always had been, the great comforter.

"I'll see to it, Doctor."

"Come on," Barry said to Emer. "We know our way."

Together they climbed the narrow stairs. Barry noticed that someone had polished the brass carpet rods. The chintz curtains over the bedroom window were drawn shut and the upper sheet had been pulled over Anne's head.

"I'll examine her. I know you know how to confirm death," Barry said. He set his bag beside him and pulled back the sheet. She lay motionless in her nightie, hands crossed over her breast. "The skin of her face is paler than the last time I saw her." Someone had taken her glasses away, but she was still wearing her woolly hat. "Her eyes are open and her pupils dilated." Barry took out his penlight, shining it directly into each eye in turn. "No response." He took a small mirror from his bag and held it before her lips. The glass did not steam up. He bent and put his ear near to her lips. No sound of breathing, nor could he feel the passage of air. "She's not breathing and . . ." Barry moved her head slightly to one side and it moved easily. Rigor mortis only set in two to four hours after the heart stopped, about the same time as the appearance of cadaveric spots. "Her skin's cold."

His right index finger pressed over her carotid artery but detected no pulsations. Statistically, the terminal event causing death was ventricular fibrillation causing cardiac arrest in 93 percent of cases, and in Anne's, not even Doctors Pantridge or Geddes could have, and in Barry's opinion, should have, attempted defibrillation. She had drifted into unconsciousness before the end and it had been a painless way to her inevitable passing. "No carotid pulse, so no heartbeat." He stood up. "Good-bye, Anne Galvin," he said. "I'm glad it was an easy death." He used his thumb and index fingers to close her eyelids, and pulled the sheet back up.

Emer was standing, quietly crying. "It's very sad," she said. "She was a lovely woman and bolstered by her faith." She inhaled. "Sometimes I think you Protestants miss out by not being given extreme unction. When I worked in the *Mater Infirmorum,* I saw several people die. I could tell how much comfort they took from the last rites."

Barry, remembering how he had felt when Rusky Peters had died five years ago, kept his voice gentle when he asked, "Did you cry for those patients?"

She shook her head. "No. I didn't know any of them like I knew Anne. I didn't watch any of them falling in love with a big dog. I'd cry if a friend died too."

Barry moved to her and hugged her. He felt her head on his shoulder, warm tears on his neck, and her sobs. He gently led her to a chair and helped her sit. "Here." He gave her his hanky.

She dried her tears. "Thanks, Barry." She returned the handkerchief. "Thanks a lot."

"I know why you're crying. I don't cry now — men aren't supposed to — but when I was a houseman I made friends with a man — a patient. I saw him on my very first day and watched him get worse between that admission and another one three months later. He faced up to things, tried to keep his spirits up. The third time he was admitted, he died before I could see him. And it hurt me. A lot. I'd lost a friend. A friend who'd given me a draughts board he'd crafted himself. I have it yet, and I have a wee bit of me that still remembers and misses him."

She nodded and managed a small smile, but her head drooped.

"People kept telling me, 'Don't get close to patients. Thicken your skin.' But I didn't. I know most of my patients here. And looking after them is the most satisfying thing I've ever done, even though sometimes I have to mourn their passing, grieve for them. Look at me, Emer."

She looked up. Her eye makeup was smeared.

"I told you before I think you're going to make a wonderful GP."

"If I can find a place."

"When, not if. When you find a place. I'm only a few years ahead of you. I learned the hard way to get to know my patients, and do you know something?"

"What?"

"So does that great unsung hero of a man, Doctor Fingal Flahertie O'Reilly. Learn from him as well as me. Know your patients and you'll never tire of your work."

"Thanks, Barry."

"Now," he said, "the bathroom's across the hall. You go and fix your face and I'll talk to the family." He put the mirror back in his bag and left.

Barry let himself into the living room. All three men were seated, drinking tea. "Please accept my deepest sympathy. Anne's gone," he said. "And from what you told me, Guffer, and what I've just seen, she went gently. No suffering."

Pat said, "That's good to know. Thank you, Doctor."

Seamus nodded.

"Thanks." Guffer made a hiccupping kind of noise and said, "Would you take a cup of tea in your hand, sir?"

"Please."

Guffer stood, poured, and handed Barry the cup and saucer. "I'm sorry we've no biccys." He swallowed. "Annie always took care of things like that." He remained standing. "Now sit you down, sir."

Barry put his bag on the floor and sat in what had been Guffer's chair. "Doctor Emer'll be down in a minute. She just wanted to powder her nose." There was no need to let the Galvins know she was upset. He took a mouthful of tea, set his cup and saucer on a convenient small table, and withdrew a book of death certificates from his bag. "It'll only take a minute to fill this in."

Seamus said, "Back in America, they're

desperate keen on them autopsies. Ma'll not have til be cut open will she, sir?"

Barry managed a reassuring smile. "No. She won't. Here it's only for unexplained" — he was going to say "deaths" but changed to — "passings. I'm quite able to certify the cause, so don't worry yourself, Seamus." Barry finished writing and signed the form. "This has to be taken to the Registrar of Births and Deaths over in Newtownards, but I can save you a trip."

"Oh?" Pat said.

Barry sipped a mouthful of tea. "Yes. I assume Mister Coffin will be making the arrangements?"

"Aye," Guffer said. "I know it sounds heartless, but I went round a couple of days ago and had a wee word."

"It wasn't heartless, Da," Seamus said. "Didn't Ma ask you to, and didn't she and Mister Robinson pick out the hymns and readings from the scriptures?"

Barry shook his head. Anne Galvin had been a remarkable woman. "I'll drop in on Mister Coffin. His folks can take care of all the paperwork, including going to Newtownards."

"Thank you, Doctor," Guffer said as Emer, face now repaired, came in.

"Cup of tea, Doctor?" Pat asked, rising,

"and please have my chair."

Emer sat. "Thank you on both counts. Just milk, please."

Pat handed her a cup.

"Do you know, Doctor," Guffer looked from Pat to Seamus, "it was a great comfort til Annie and me having our boys here at this sad time. At the heels of the hunt, there's nothing more important than family." He smiled at his two grown sons.

"You're right, Guffer," Barry said. "Nothing in the whole world."

"My Annie was the religious one. I went along til please her," Guffer said, "but would everybody please bow their heads and close their eyes for a wee minute and send their thoughts til her."

Barry did.

After some time, Guffer said, "Thank youse all very much."

All three Galvin men had hankies out and were dabbing their eyes. Finally Guffer said, "Do you mind when you come til see Annie, sir, after they sent her home from Marie Curie and she asked about that Burl Ives's song, 'Wayfaring Stranger'?"

"Yes. Yes, I do."

"She wants that sung at her funeral, and youse all know that Alan Hewitt has a great tenor voice. I talked til him a couple of days back. He says he'd be pleased to."

"That's wonderful," Emer said.

"Aye," said Guffer. "There's a couple of lines in the first verse that I think sum things for our Annie." He recited, ". . . there's no sickness, toil nor danger in that fair land to which I go." His inhalation was shaky. "And it's true. I know she's in her heaven now. Rest in peace, love. Rest in peace."

34
LET'S GO ON WITH THE SHOW

July 11, 1964

"Here you are, folks." Jack Mills handed his friends each a typed and stapled sheaf of papers. "As the writers, directors, and lead performers, we get the programme hot from the presses. Tada!" Barry, Jack, Harry Sloan, and Norma Fitch had come earlier than the rest of the cast. The four had dealt with some last-minute details before the doors opened and the curtain went up on this year's annual Houseman's Concert. For now they were taking a breather before changing into costume.

Jack stood in front of his three friends seated in the first row of seats in the Bostock House auditorium, named for the matron appointed in 1901, Mary Frances Bostock. The building provided subsidised housing for single staff nurses, and its auditorium was the ideal venue for the annual concert, taking place this year on Saturday, July 11.

Barry stared at the date on the front page of the programme and realized their house-man's year was almost over.

He set his dinner suit on the chair beside him, opened the programme at page 1, and read aloud, " 'The Royal Victoria Hospital Houseman's Concert 1964. Copyright. All rites, including last, reserved. For any resemblance to characters living, or to all intents and purposes dead, we accept no responsibility, it's entirely their own fault.' " He smiled and scanned the next few pages. Every one of the fourteen sketches and comic songs either took the mickey out of the senior consultants and administrators or was filled with risqué humour or off-colour limericks. "Hey, who put this one in? 'She wasn't what men would call pretty/And other girls offered her pity/So nobody guessed/Her syphilis test/Involved half the men in the city.' "

"Me," Norma said. Her grin was feral. She moved a hold-all onto a chair beside her.

The men laughed.

"Good for you," Harry said.

Every houseman had a role. For tonight, God bless them, the senior house officers, doctors like John Geddes, were carrying out the juniors' duties. The four friends had been the prime movers of the concert. Jack

553

had a monologue and Barry a lengthy narrative poem, "The Snake," he'd written. The senior staff to be guyed went under distorted but recognisable names. In one sketch, Jack Mills would portray Doctor Cranky Cartridge, an unsubtle caricature of Doctor Franky Pantridge. In another, Barry would be playing Sir Bosom Gazer, a reference to a senior man with a penchant for well-endowed young women.

After the list of acts were more one-liners. He read, " 'Have you heard about the psychiatrist who slept under the bed because he was becoming a little potty?' " Barry groaned. "God, that's an awful pun. 'Potty' meaning out of his mind, or chamber pot."

Jack, in the accents of a well-known Cockney comedian, said, "I don't wish to know that. Kindly leave the stage. Ba-boom-boom." He dropped on one knee with his right arm extended.

"You're so sharp," said Harry with a smile, "you'll cut yourself, Mills." He riffled through the pages. "I don't know when the tradition started, but I think it's a terrific way for us all to let off steam. It was great *craic* putting the show together, and it lets us get in some home truths too, under the protective umbrella of a fool's pardon."

" 'Our grateful thanks to the consultants

for allowing us to take their illustrious names in vain,' " read Norma. "That should cover it, don't you think?" she said with a bark of laughter.

"That may cover the medical staff, but personally I feel an apology is in order from the dining room. Still, I got my licks in, so to speak." Harry stood, looking solemn, and cleared his throat.

" 'The houseman's meals are all the same/ and don't we know the man to blame?/He sees no point in wasting food/When burned-up crap is just as good.' "

"Aye, dishes like savoury mincemeat á la dunghill or potato soup with less spuds than the great famine. But it's nearly all over, the grub and the year, and I've never worked so hard in my life. I've learned a lot, and I've gained a lot of confidence —"

Barry, with no steady girlfriend since Virginia Clarke, said with a smile, "And you've worked your way through almost every student nurse, you old lecher."

Jack grinned, blew on the tips of his right fingers and thumb, and rubbed them up and down on his left lapel in the Belfast gesture of self-congratulations. "You're only young once, my son."

"Aye," said Harry, "and I feel more than a year older, but I'll say one thing. It was great to sample all of the services, get a taste for what might interest you."

"And is it still pathology for you, Harry?" Norma asked.

"It is. Professor Biggart has a job for me in his department, starting next month."

"And you'll not miss seeing patients?" Barry said. The death of Rusky Peters back in February had hit him hard, but partly thanks to Jack's sage advice on the night and his continuing support, and partly from some inner reserve, Barry had coped. And more than ever he wanted to get to know the patients he was treating.

Harry shook his head. "I meant what I said back in the fall. I'm impressed by the work clinicians do, but I'm going to help them from the lab. Particularly the surgical specialities."

"That's where I'm going," Jack Mills said. "Mister Sinclair Irwin of 13 and 14's going to take me as his senior house officer in August."

"Sinky's been a great boss to work for on my last rotation," Barry said, "but I'm just not cut out to be a surgeon."

"We knew you couldn't hack it," Jack said.

"Not cut out? Can't hack it?" Norma groaned. "I think you two are still working on tonight's script. We were talking about our futures. I've definitely decided on paediatrics. The new professor, I. J. Carré, has a house officer position for me at Sick Kids, and Barry?"

He didn't hesitate. "Eventually I want to try general practice, but there's no starting date of August the first like there is in hospital posts, so I'm going home to Bangor, having a break, and then I'm going to start looking for an assistantship in County Down. I'll have the luxury of all the time in the world to decide, and unlike you lot, no more exams to face."

Jack put his fingers to his forehead.

"Hey, old friend. Attack of the nerves?" said Barry.

"No, not at all. There's something I wanted to tell you that might be able to help with a job."

"Oh?" Barry was interested.

"No, it's gone. But it'll come back to me and I'll let you know."

Norma said, "None of us are thinking of emigration?"

Jack went into his upper-class English accent he'd be using later in a sketch. "Are you suggesting one should head for the colonies? What a positively ghaaaastly thought."

When he'd stopped laughing, Barry said,

"Nothing would persuade me to leave Ulster. Not one thing."

And Harry, with seriousness in his voice, said, "I think we all feel like that."

Heads nodded in agreement.

Norma fiddled with a ballerina's tutu in her hold-all. She'd need it later. "It's going to feel strange next month. We've all been together for the last seven years. Then on August the first, we'll all be going our separate ways. I'm going to miss you lads."

Jack, never one for displays of emotion, looked distinctly uncomfortable. "But hey, bye, we'll have our memories," he said brightly. "You know, like that first day in casualty. You missed that, Harry, but the housemen from the class before arranged for us to be swamped with customers on our very first day."

"The waiting hall was packed," Barry said, "and in rapid succession, as one patient was called, each patient moved up one seat, sort of a serpentine movement. Some irreverent medical student of bygone years named the unfortunates who came to casualty 'the snakes.' That's what gave me the idea for my poem."

"Go on then," said Jack, "give us a verse or two."

"This piece is in the rhythm of Oscar

558

Wilde's 'The Ballad of Reading Gaol.' "

"Oscar Wilde," Jack said. "I've remembered. I'll tell you later, Barry. Please go ahead."

"Right."

Deep in the gloom of the Ambulance
    Room
White-coated figures make
A silent plea that you not me will make
    the dread mistake,
That has led the brave to an early grave
When they tried to treat a snake.

"There's twelve more verses —"

"Twelve more verses," said Jack. "Oh, the anguish."

"I guess I've added a few since you heard it last."

"Remind me not to be around when they start pelting you with rotten tomatoes."

"Pay Jack no mind," said Norma. "Give us another stanza, Barry."

"Okay. In the penultimate verse, our hero's fate is described."

With courage sapped, his nerve had
    snapped
His mind had given way.
With lips that shake, "A snake, a snake,"

    was all that he could say
  That's the only word we've ever heard
  Him gibber since that day.

"And here I thought you liked patients, Laverty," Jack Mills said.

"I do. But sometimes I think a bit of gallows humour helps us cope with some of the less pleasant ones."

"Quite right, Barry," Harry said. "I find gallows humour helps with the less alive ones as well."

Barry heard a sound behind and turned to see the other housemen coming in. "Come on. Time to go backstage." He picked up his dinner suit and followed Jack and the others up onto the stage and into the wings, where Norma, clutching her hold-all, headed off for the women's dressing room and the lads went into the men's.

"Norma's right about seven years together," Harry said. "I know you two went to Campbell. I went to Belfast Royal Academy. The lot in my sixth form had been together for five years when we left school in '57. We got together a group. We called it the Fifty-seven Club and we meet once a year. Formal dress. What would you think about us Royal Victoria housemen calling ourselves the Sixty-four Club and meeting, formal dress, first Friday in December, say, at the Dunadry Hotel near Templepatrick on the way to the airport?"

Jack was taking off his jacket. "Brilliant idea. Barry and I'll help you organise it."

"Absolutely," Barry said, hanging his costume in a locker. "We've shared a lot."

"And who knows what's ahead," Jack said. "Barry, I've remembered what I wanted to tell you."

"Go on."

"I was reading *The British Medical Journal* the other day. Looking at the ads. There's a GP, a Doctor Fingal Flahertie O'Reilly, in a place called Ballybucklebo, between Cultra and Holywood. The good doctor's looking for an assistant. Might be worth a look. I'll give you the journal when we get back to The Huts so you can get his address and phone number."

"Thanks, Jack."

The room was filling up now with the other male housemen.

Ten minutes, Barry thought, and the curtain would go up on the Houseman's Concert 1964 — and in twenty-seven days they'd lower the final curtain on seven years of training. Seven years of making friends for a lifetime through shared crises and triumphs. He glanced at Jack, and Norma, and Harry. Seven years to prepare them for their next chosen steps in medicine. Barry smiled. He wondered what kind of a man this Doctor O'Reilly might be and what sort of a place Ballybucklebo was. Barry shrugged. He reckoned he might as well find out soon.

35
A PARTY OF FRIENDS AND RELATIONS

July 5, 1969

O'Reilly watched as, hand in hand, Jack Mills and Helen Hewitt left the bar hatch where they had been talking with her father, Alan Hewitt, and approached the table in the main hall of the Ballybucklebo Bonnaughts Sporting Club, where O'Reilly sat with Kitty, Lord John MacNeill, and his sister Myrna.

"Excuse me my lord, Lady Ferguson," Helen Hewitt said, making a small curtsey. "I know I wrote the night in June that I learned I'd passed, but I wanted to thank you both in person for the MacNeill Scholarship."

"You already have given me the best possible thanks, Doctor Hewitt. Not only did you pass, you took first-class honours and the gold medal in medicine. There's only one man prouder than me here tonight, and that's your father."

"Actually, sir, you might have to fight me for that honour," said Jack with a broad smile.

Myrna laughed. "Well, no other woman here tonight could be prouder of you than me." Myrna's face suddenly became serious and she took one of Helen's hands. "And your mother, Doctor Hewitt. She would have been so proud."

"Thank you. Thank you both," said Helen. "I am very grateful. And I never would have known about the scholarship if it hadn't been for Doctor O'Reilly. Thank you, sir."

"My pleasure. It seems only a few weeks ago when the marquis awarded you that scholarship, and by all that's holy, you've done the MacNeills, indeed the whole village, proud."

"Fingal and I are delighted for you," said Kitty. "I still remember you curled up in our lounge reading *Popular Science* and now, here you are, a doctor."

"Please excuse us. The place is starting to fill up. I think we should claim our table, Helen," said Jack.

The marquis said, "Quite right. We'll get a chance to buy you a drink later."

O'Reilly watched as Jack seated Helen at an adjacent table, then threaded his way through the nearly full tables to the bar hatch.

The nearby stage was hidden by closed curtains. Several tables away, Kinky and Archie were sitting with Maggie and Sonny Houston and Julie Donnelly, who had put her handbag on the empty chair beside her. Ronald Fitzpatrick and Alice Moloney, as they had at Donal Donnelly's housewarming party, were sitting with Emer and Nonie and a young man O'Reilly did not recognise. Connor Nelson was on call tonight. The organising committee of Bertie Bishop and Flo, Dapper Frew and Lenny Brown sat together with Connie and Colin Brown. The fifth member, Alan Hewitt, was serving behind the bar because Donal Donnelly had other duties tonight.

The loud buzz of conversation was punctuated with laughter and the clinking of glasses, and the tobacco fug was building. Someone had already opened the door to let in some fresh air. He looked around but did not see Oliver Mullan anywhere. Indeed O'Reilly hadn't seen hide nor hair of the man since that Tuesday in May. He felt for the fellow, sitting alone in his house, hearing the festivities over here. O'Reilly shrugged. It couldn't be helped. "Here we are, only the first Saturday in July, and already the organising committee had put on a dance, a disco, a *céilidh,* and a hop, and the place is packed again tonight."

"And," said John MacNeill, "the honorary treasurer tells me that after expenses, the money's mounting up. We'll be able to send some children to that multidenominational summer camp in Cushendall next year if the cash continues accumulating the way it has been."

"That's terrific," Kitty said. "So good for the kiddies. I've come to love that part of County Antrim. It's so peaceful."

"And great social successes the events are too," John MacNeill said. "I think we put on a wonderful show for BBC Ulster, Ulster ITV, and RTE on the first night. Father Hugh and Reverend Robinson were ecumenism personified, and Alan Hewitt and Gerry Shanks, a republican and a loyalist, shaking hands? What a powerful symbol that was. Bertie Bishop's idea of showing the rest of the world how one little Ulster community can forget its differences and get along was brilliant. I had a letter from a friend in Philadelphia. The story was picked up by the major American networks. He was most impressed."

Kitty said with a mischievous smile, "That unity may not hold true tonight."

"Good gracious, Kitty," Myrna said. "Of course it will. Why ever would you say it wouldn't?"

"Because," Kitty said, "folks can fall out over things other than politics and religion. Talent contests can be great fun, but . . ." She let the idea hang.

"Which is why neither Fingal nor I volunteered to judge," John MacNeill said. "Kitty's right. You need someone with the wisdom of Solomon."

"And a skin as thick as a rhino's." O'Reilly sat back in his chair and laughed. "By God, some of our citizens can be pretty competitive."

"And speaking of God, you can't do much better than Father O'Toole and Reverend Robinson," Myrna said, nodding to their front-and-centre table. "They'll keep the peace."

"True," O'Reilly said. "And I think tonight's going to be a lot of fun."

"Bound to be," Kitty said, "with Donal Donnelly as our master of ceremonies."

"Speak of the devil." O'Reilly watched as the curtains jerked open to reveal an empty stage, a microphone on a tall stand, and behind it the carroty-thatched Donal Donnelly clutching the top of the stand in both hands.

A series of hisses, squeaks, and a low booming came from two tall speakers, one at each side of the stage. "My lord, ladies, and the rest of youse lot, can you hear me at the back?" Donald roared out.

Gerry Shanks yelled, "They can hear you in Donaghadee, Donal, and that's nine miles away. Turn it down a bit."

Donal fiddled with a control panel.

"Right," Donal said. "Is that better?"

"Dead on," Gerry called. All other conversations had stopped.

"Good. Now, youse all know me, I'm Donal Donnelly, so I am, and I'm your MC the night and I want til tell youse all how matters will proceed up here on the stage so you know what to expect from the, well, from the proceedings." Donal paused for breath.

"Go on then," a stranger called out. "Get on with it. We want some music."

Donal shook his head, rolled his eyes to the heavens, and said with scorn in every syllable, "There's one in every crowd. If the bollix was at a wake he'd only be happy if he was the centre of attention — and that would mean being the corpse."

The room erupted then the noise faded.

"As I was saying, welcome to the first Ballybucklebo Bonnaughts' talent contest.

We have a number of acts, and each one will perform, and be judged, by Father O'Toole and Reverend Robinson. Will youse gentlemen stand, please?"

Father Hugh in his cassock and Reverend Robinson in his black jacket and dog collar stood and faced the crowd and were politely applauded.

As the clergymen sat, Donal said, "Now, in order that neighbours can chat with neighbours and the odd jar can be bought, when I've finished talking I'm going til sit down over there for a while beside my beautiful wife, Julie, and youse can mingle. In about ten minutes I'll bring the first act up. Not sure yet who it's going to be, but all will be revealed in good time. Then, when they've done their party piece, and youse all have shown your approval, like, by clapping and cheering and doing whatever else you want to do to show you liked the act, as long as it's civil, mind, that'll give the judges your opinions. Then, we'll have another wee break, another turn, and so on. When everybody's done singing and dancing and playing their instruments, we'll find out the winner from our judges, who will have as tough a job as your man Hercules had when he mucked out them stables back in Greece. Now is all that clear?"

"As mud, Donal, as usual," Gerry Shanks called, "but we love you."

Laughter and applause.

Donal grinned his bucktoothed grin and hopped down from the stage. The curtains closed.

The sounds of practice scales on a set of uilleann pipes and the high notes of a pennywhistle rang out over the buzz of the crowd. A short queue had formed in front of Alan Hewitt's bar hatch.

O'Reilly became aware of two people standing beside him. He turned to see Lenny and Colin Brown. "Hello, Browns," O'Reilly said. "How are you?"

Lenny said, "I hope we're not intruding, my lord, but could Colin and me have a wee word with Doctor O'Reilly?"

"You are not intruding at all. Please do, Mister Brown."

"Thank you, sir."

"Doctor O'Reilly. Do you mind when you and me had a kind of falling-out four years ago when I wanted Colin til work in the shipyards and you and Doctor Laverty and Mister Bishop ganged up on me and got me til let him sit the Eleven Plus exam and go to grammar school?"

"I do, Lenny."

"Colin has something til say. Go on, son."

A blushing Colin, with both hands clasped behind his back, took a deep breath, straightened his shoulders, and looked O'Reilly in the eye. "Doctor O'Reilly, I want to say thank you very very much. You know I want to be a vet. You're part of the reason I'm going to get that chance."

"Well, I —"

"I sat my first of the national school exams in June." He offered O'Reilly a sheet of paper. "This here come, I mean came, in the post this morning. Mum and Dad are very pleased. I'd like you and Doctor Laverty, and Mister Bishop, to read it too."

O'Reilly took the sheet and scanned it. "Holy Mother of — Sorry." He turned and cleared his throat to address the whole table. "Everyone, listen to this. Young Colin Brown here has passed eight subjects in the national school exams, and every one of them with distinction. My most sincere congratulations, Colin."

"Eight? All eight. Good Lord," Myrna said, clapping her hands. "As a university type I can tell you what that means. The pass mark in the national school exams is forty percent. They are tough, tough tests. A distinction is awarded when marks are over eighty percent. Achieving that in eight subjects is practically unheard of. Very well done, young man."

John MacNeill offered his hand. "I think you'll go far, Colin Brown. Congratulations."

"Thank you, my lord." Colin completed the handshake.

Kitty, always the most demonstrative, stood up and kissed Colin's cheek. "Well done, young man. Well done."

"Thank you, Mrs. O'Reilly."

"His mum and me, we're dead chuffed, so we are," Lenny said. "Imagine. Our wee Colin going to university in two years with money from Mister Bishop after he passes the next set of national exams."

"And I'm certain you will, Colin," John MacNeill said.

"Now I said we didn't want til intrude, so we'll be going to see Mister Bishop next, but thanks again, Doc."

"And I'll tell Doctor Laverty when he gets here. He'll be delighted," O'Reilly said to their departing backs.

"Isn't that wonderful?" Kitty said, sitting back down, but before anyone could answer, Donal's voice came over the loudspeakers as the curtains opened. "My lord, ladies, reverend gentlemen, and youse lot. Let me present our first act, the Jolly Beggarmen." With a flourish of his arm, he indicated a group of five men. Accordion, uilleann pipes, mandolin, penny whistle, and bodhran. "Let's hear it for them."

O'Reilly recognised all five as members of the Ballybucklebo Highlanders. The piper was Angus Mehaffey. O'Reilly had heard from Barry that Angus would be playing the very pipes Anne Galvin had given him.

Applause and whistles.

O'Reilly, whose musical tastes covered the spectrum, sat enjoying the group's set of jigs, reels, a hornpipe, and a vocal rendition of "Whiskey in the Jar." He sang along,

As I was goin' over the far-famed Kerry
   Mountain
I met with Captain Farrell
And his money he was countin'
I first produced my pistol . . .

He joined in the great round of applause when the set ended, and glanced at his empty glass. "The trouble," he said, "with the singing is that it gives you a thirst. Anyone else?"

"Please, Fingal," Myrna said. "A small dry sherry." She handed him her empty glass. O'Reilly, glasses in hand, headed for the bar hatch, exchanging pleasantries on his way. Picking up snatches of conversations.

"D'yuh see that there Rolling Stone Brian Jones drowned in a swimming pool on Wednesday?"

"Right enough? Desperate. Poor lad."

"Likely he was stoned. No pun intended."

"Hello, Doctor. Grand evening," Kinky said when he stopped at their table.

"Good evening to this table," he said.

"Maggie and I do have an idea, so," Kinky said. "Next time, if the committee would give us a small budget, Maggie and Cissie — she's baby-sitting Julie and Donal's brood so they can be here tonight — Maggie and Cissie and I would cater, and you could charge for the food and make a profit for the kiddies' charity."

"We could, you know." Maggie's hatband sported one red and one yellow carnation. "I'll bet my plum cake would sell like hotcakes. There wasn't a bit left after Donal's housewarming. And I've a new recipe for cherry cake."

"I'll bet it would. I'll mention your suggestion to Mister Bishop. Now I've to be off to get drinks. Enjoy yourselves." O'Reilly headed on but had to stop at the doctors' table, where Emer was grinning from ear to ear and beaming at Nonie and her young man.

"Have your Premium Bonds given you a

big win, Emer?"

She bounced on her chair. "Nonie, introduce Michael."

"Doctor O'Reilly, please meet Doctor Michael O'Driscoll."

The two men shook hands.

"Michael, could you give Doctor O'Reilly your seat for a minute?" Emer said. "We've something amazing to tell him. I want him sitting down when he hears."

Michael stood.

Frowning, O'Reilly sat and put his empty glasses on the tabletop. What the hell was going on?

"Tell him, Nonie. Tell him."

"Fingal, you remember when we all had lunch in April the day you and Emer saw the boy with mumps, and I said I might have something to offer with respect to Emer's job prospects?"

"I do, and as I recollect you said your lips were sealed. Are they about to be unsealed?"

Nonie nodded. "The something, or rather somebody, was Michael." She looked into his eyes. There was love there.

O'Reilly thought he was beginning to understand.

"Michael is an immunologist. He's accepted a consultant job with the Bay of Plenty Health Board in Wellington."

"It's in New Zealand," Emer said, and laughed.

Nonie held up her left hand to display a diamond-and-sapphire engagement ring. "He's asked me to go with him and there's a GP job available too. It took longer than we had anticipated making the arrangements, but we wanted to keep it all to ourselves until everything was certain. We finalised our plans last night."

"Well, I'll be damned." The implication was obvious to O'Reilly. "Well done, both of you. Nonie, it's been a pleasure having you here, and I hope things turn out wonderfully for you both Down Under and that you'll write and keep in touch."

"Thank you," Nonie and Michael said in unison.

Nonie continued, "We will, and I'm sorry about the short notice, but they'd like us in post by August the first."

"I'll tell Barry when he gets here. He'll be pleased for you and for Emer, and as soon as I can arrange things with Professor Gibson, Emer, you can consider yourself as an assistant with a view to partnership with Barry and me, with no break in the continuity of the practice."

Emer leapt to her feet and bent to give O'Reilly a smacking kiss. "Thank you, Fingal. Thank you. Thank you. I can't . . ."

But her words were drowned out by Donal's amplified voice. "And now for your pleasure. Alan Hewitt will give us some songs from Old Ireland, and I'll take back my usual job as barman."

O'Reilly looked at the empty glasses he'd deposited on the table and back to where his party sat. Damn. It would be considered coarse to get up and walk to the bar just as Alan started singing.

"Please, sir, stay where you are." Michael O'Driscoll motioned for the senior man to remain seated.

Alan, with no preamble, began to sing "My Lagan Love."

Where Lagan streams sing lullaby
There blows a lily fair
The twilight gleam is in her eye . . .

He sang four numbers, finishing with a rousing rendition of the "Rocky Road to Dublin" with everyone, O'Reilly included, belting out the choruses.

One, two, three, four, five, hunt the hare
    and turn her down the rocky road
and all the way to Dublin,
Whack fal-al-dee-rah

577

When the applause died down and the hubbub of conversation restarted, O'Reilly rose. "I've drinks to get, but good luck to you both Michael and Nonie, and welcome aboard, Emer."

"Fingal," Ronald Fitzpatrick said, "before you go, could you wait one more minute?"

"Of course."

"You will recall how a certain Colonel Mullan was, well, rude to Alice back in May?"

"You needn't worry about him, Ronald. His house is up for sale."

"I know, but what happened got me thinking." He gazed fondly at Alice Moloney, who returned his loving look. "Well I, that is, you see —" His Adam's apple bobbed and he blushed beetroot red.

Alice said with a smile, "What my dear tongue-tied Ronald is trying to tell you is that he asked me to be his wife three weeks ago. We didn't tell anyone but," she smiled, "we tied the knot in Belfast and went to Dublin to have a little honeymoon. We only got home two days ago. And we wanted you, Fingal, to be one of the first to know. This seemed like the ideal spot to tell you."

O'Reilly's roar, which would have made a bull elephant's trumpeting sound like a mouse's squeak, cut off every other voice in the hall. All eyes turned on the doctor. "Bloody marvellous. Well done, Ronald and Alice. May your troubles be as few and as far apart as my late grandmother's teeth." His gaze covered the room. "I've just had some excellent news, in fact two excellent pieces of news, and I'm a very happy man, so quit your rubbernecking and go back to talking to each other." He seized Ronald's hand and pumped it. "You old dog. Bless you both."

Conversations began again, everyone, no doubt, commenting on the eccentricities of their senior medical advisor. O'Reilly shrugged. It wouldn't be the first time nor the last.

"Thank you, Fingal."

O'Reilly lifted the empty glasses. "If I had a drink, I'd drink to the health of both couples and my new assistant. But now if you'll excuse me, I must get back to my own party and tell them your news, so if you'll give me your orders, it's drinks on me for the table. Alan or Donal will bring them over."

As O'Reilly walked away from the serving hatch, carrying his pint and Myrna's sherry, he reckoned he must be the most contented person in all of Ballybucklebo, until he saw Barry coming in holding Sue's hand. They were laughing like two kids who'd just robbed an orchard and not been caught. Perhaps he might have some competition for that position? He'd find out what was so amusing after Barry had got their drinks, joined Jack and Helen, and dealt with the usual pleasantries.

Donal's voice rang out, "My lord, ladies, and — och sure you know all the rest. I now have for your defeacation — no, that's not right, for your edification — the Dympna Kelly's school of dance. Six of the prettiest girls in Ballybucklebo and the townland will dance in hard shoes to two hornpipes and a treble jig to the music of the Jolly Beggarmen, who youse saw earlier. A hand, please."

O'Reilly walked on as the applause rose and fell and the music and staccato rattle of the dancers' hard shoes stifled any chance of conversation. Och well, he'd get a yarn with Barry and Sue and their friends later. See what their news was. For now, Fingal O'Reilly was full to overflowing. Emer would have a job here; Ronald and Alice? He smiled and shook his head. Colin Brown was academically on his way, and Bertie's idea for strengthening the community was becoming a roaring success. He thought back to Father Hugh's blessing at the housewarming: "May you hold them in the palm of your hand." It seemed that prayer had been answered, and included not only the Donnellys but all of Ballybucklebo and the townland. Long may it last.

36
JUST TO CELEBRATE THE EVENT

July 5, 1969

Barry led Sue to the bar hatch, and by the time he'd said hello to Alan Hewitt and got himself a pint and her a vodka and orange, the first hornpipe, "Off to California," was over. They headed for where he could see Jack waving, moving past occupied tables and mouthing "Good evening" to folks they knew. Many were Barry's patients, others were parents of children Sue had taught or was teaching.

He kept glancing at the dancers. Six girls with identical plaits wore matching plain white blouses, dance skirts, white knee socks. Their black leather footwear in the style of Oxford shoes had reinforced heel and toe taps. They hopped and skipped, arms held rigidly to their sides, their taps clattering rhythmically, their movements perfectly synchronised.

He recognised the four-four time of the

hornpipe "The Boys of Bluehill," the melody carried by the accordion and embellished by the pipes and pennywhistle while the mandolin and bodhran kept the beat. The Irish had been dancing to hornpipes since the seventeenth century. Despite his high spirits, Barry frowned. The long memory that kept some traditions going to this day was both the blessing and the curse of the Irish. Still, he told himself, his smile returning, all was harmony in here, and the bigger world outside had been quiet for a good two months.

Jack rose, held Sue's chair, seated her, and sat as Barry took the seat beside her. Conversation would be impossible until the dance set was over, so glasses were lifted and smiles exchanged.

The hornpipe ended, but the crashing applause inhibited speech until the music of the treble jig "Blackthorn Stick" rang out. Barry sipped his pint, hugged his news to himself, and waited for the music to stop.

When it did and the fresh applause had died, Donal Donnelly took the microphone. "Wasn't that sticking out a mile? Well done, dancers. Dympna, you and their mammies and daddies must be very proud of them. And Beggarmen? Dead on. Now, we'll take another wee break until our next act and

I'll give Alan Hewitt a rest from bar duty."

Conversation began at once.

Barry said, "Thanks for keeping us seats."

"Glad you made it," Jack said, "because I've something important to tell you. Something I think you're going to like."

"Go on."

"You remember the day back in April when we were sailing, Barry, and we saw the basking shark?"

"I'll never forget it."

"And I told you how Helen was having second thoughts about mebbe going to Canada? Worried about leaving her dad. That taking her new skills out of Ulster so soon would hardly be repaying the marquis's kindness?"

Barry had been hoping ever since Jack had mentioned how Helen was considering doing her houseman's year here that they would stay. And it was that remark that had got him reminiscing about his own houseman's year. "And?" He wanted his friend to say they were staying at least for another year.

Jack looked fondly at Helen. "I told you soon after we got the results of her finals that Helen had taken a first and the gold medal in medicine."

"You did, and Sue and I were delighted."

"Thrilled," Sue said.

"Well, it gets better. Sue — Barry and Helen and I know how juniors have to ask consultants if they'll accept them in a training post. There's a lot of competition. This time Professor Bull got in touch with Helen and asked her to be his houseman. She'll start next month there for her first three-month stint."

Barry whistled. Not only was he pleased for Helen's success, his best friend would be staying in Ulster for at least a year.

"And," Helen said, "he's offered me the chance to come back next hospital year to begin and ultimately complete my training as a specialist nephrologist. Sue, that's the discipline that focuses on the kidneys. So, we'll be staying for another four years at least," Helen said.

"What? The pair of you are staying?" Barry reached across the table and shook Jack's hand. "Terrific, isn't it, Sue?"

"Wonderful."

"This," said Barry, "calls for drinks all round." He glanced at Sue, who smiled and nodded. "I'll buy, and I'd suggest, Sue, you ask Fingal to push our two tables together. We've some news too, but it'll keep." He saw Sue smile and nod her agreement. "Jack, come and give me a hand to carry."

Barry finished the last of his pint and took note of what they were drinking at the other table. They set off for the bar hatch but were waved at by Alan Hewitt, who was standing alone near the bar holding a two-thirds-finished pint. "Jack, Doctor Laverty. Have you a wee minute?"

"Of course, Alan," Jack said, "and I must say you were in fine voice tonight."

"Thank you."

"Helen's over with Sue, and the Mac-Neills, and O'Reillys. We'll be over to see you again later."

Alan shook his head. "It's yourself, Jack, I want a word with. I didn't get a chance when you bought your drinks. The queue behind you was too long, and I don't mind Doctor Laverty hearing. I know you two's like brothers."

Barry wondered what was coming.

Alan said, "I've not seen much of you or Helen for most of this year. I know she's been awful busy studying and living at the hospital. It's been grand having her home since she finished her exams in June. Now, you've been walking out with my wee girl for nigh on three years, so I've a question."

Barry saw Jack stiffen.

"I seen the way you look at her and she at you." He stepped closer to Jack. "Tell me

586

the truth. Are you in love with Helen?"

Jack took a deep breath. "Yes, Alan, I am. Very much. And she with me."

Barry braced himself for an explosion. Jack and Helen had decided to keep their engagement secret from both their families, Jack's Protestant and Helen's Catholic, until she was qualified.

Alan Hewitt nodded, kept a solemn face, but said, "Then why the hell don't you ask her to marry you?"

"What?" Jack took a step back. His eyes widened. He inhaled. "You don't mind?"

Alan shook his head. "I do. I'd not be human if I didn't, but Helen's all I've got and I'll not do anything to spoil her happiness. Just because you and yours and me and mine worship the self-same God in different ways is no reason til hate each other. I mean that, so I do. The Saviour preached, 'Love thy neighbour,' and he made it mean everyone, not just your own kind."

Barry had a vivid memory of saying to Jack on the basking shark day, "I don't know Alan Hewitt all that well, but by reputation he's a fair-minded man. And he loves his daughter." It was true.

Alan Hewitt extended his right hand, which Jack took and shook. "Thank you, Alan. Thank you with all of my heart."

Barry was sure there was a moistness in Alan Hewitt's eyes when he said, "Just you be good to my wee girl. Hear me now."

"I will, Alan. I promise."

"You're staying in Ballybucklebo the night with Doctor and Mrs. Laverty, but I'll see you the morrow when you come to dinner at one with me and Helen."

"That's right."

"After what we've just talked about, bring you Helen til see me here when Donal's behind the bar so I can give you both my blessing right away."

"I will, Alan."

And Jack's right, Barry thought, not to mention their engagement to her father until Helen was present. He said, "Mister Alan Hewitt, you're a sound man. I'm proud to know you."

"I'm just doing what's right, but thank you, Doctor. Now, I reckon you're here to buy drinks, so I'll finish my pint while you do and then I'll spell Donal. And I'll see you and Helen later, Jack."

Barry and a jubilant Jack, each carrying a loaded tray, made their way back to the now enlarged table.

O'Reilly stood. "Here, let me give you a hand, Barry. And welcome home." O'Reilly put a sherry in front of Myrna, slid a gin

588

and tonic over to Kitty, placed a neat whiskey in front of the marquis and a pint in his own place opposite them.

Barry gave Helen, who was sitting next to Myrna, a half pint of Smithwick's and another vodka and orange for Sue, who sat beside Kitty. He and Jack took seats opposite and each held a fresh pint.

Before anyone could say "Cheers," or *"Sláinte,"* Barry, who could contain himself no longer, said, "Sue has something important to tell you."

All eyes were on her when Sue, beaming from ear to ear, said, "On or about the thirty-first of January 1970, the Laverty family will increase to three. Barry and I are expecting."

Kitty squealed and hugged Sue. Myrna said, "Congratulations, Sue. What wonderful news."

Jack leaned over and, because he was not supposed to have been in the know, said sotto voce to Barry. "Any treatment?"

"No. Graham Harley was right. It just took time. We saw him yesterday and Sue's test was positive."

"Jasus Murphy," O'Reilly said, "that beats Bannagher. Folks, please raise your glasses and drink with me to Helen Hewitt's success and to Barry and Sue — may all your troubles be little ones."

"I'll forgive you that dreadful pun, Doctor O'Reilly, and on behalf of Sue and I, thank you all for your good wishes. I must confess I'm a bit concerned about being a new father."

"It's easy," John MacNeill said, "as long as you don't confuse the end to wipe with the end to feed."

Everyone laughed, and before conversation could resume, Barry noticed Donal and Fergus Finnegan standing beside O'Reilly. Donal said, "Excuse me, my lord and lady, but Fergus here has something to say to Doctor O'Reilly. Go on, Fergus. He won't bite you."

"Doctor O'Reilly, do you remember back in April there was a bit of a session here and someone asked you, sir, for til give us a sea shanty?"

"I do. And I said, 'Not tonight, if you don't mind.'"

"And I said, 'But mebbe some other night, Doctor, sir?' Donal and me thinks tonight would be the time."

"I heartily agree," John MacNeill said. "You've a fine baritone, Fingal."

Kitty said, "Go on, old bear. Up on your hind legs."

Barry looked at O'Reilly's grinning face

590

as he took a long pull on his Guinness. His senior partner did not need any more encouragement.

O'Reilly rose.

Donal said, "Give me a wee minute til introduce you, sir, then come on up." He and Fergus walked away, Fergus to an adjacent table, Donal to the microphone. "My lord, lady, and the rest of youse, and now for your def — No. Now for your edification, we are to be treated to a sea shanty by one of Ballybucklebo's most illustrious citizens. Let's hear it for Doctor Fingal Flahertie O'Reilly."

Barry was deafened by thunderous applause. He heard whistles, calls of "Go on Doctor, you-boy-yuh." He looked at O'Reilly, who, judging by his grin, was not one bit embarrassed by being asked to sing in public, and when he stood and stretched out one arm and bowed to the room it was clear he was revelling in their affection. O'Reilly stood in front of the mike and waited for the room to settle. "All right. I'm going to sing 'Haul Away, Joe,' a tack-and-sheet shanty. The shanty-man, that's me, stood behind the men on the ropes and sang a line. When he sang, 'To me,' " — to Barry's ear the words were clipped and sounded like "tuhme" — "it was the crew's cue to begin to haul the lines in unison in the direction of the shanty-man. You all know how the line 'Way haul away, we'll haul away Joe' is repeated over and over. I want you all to let her rip and raise the rafters and sing it along with me every time. In real life on a sailing ship, the ropes were pulled each time you roared 'haul,' and you'd get a rest from pulling while I sang the next line."

Barry watched as O'Reilly clasped his hands, opened his mouth, and filled the hall with the first line in a voice that made Barry think of rich mahogany wood.

When I was a little boy, so, me mammy
    told me,
Tuhme,

O'Reilly and the entire room roared,

Way haul away, we'll haul away, Joe
If I never kissed the girls, me lips would
    all grow mouldy.
Tuhme,
Way haul away we'll haul away, Joe.

Barry smiled, took Sue's hand, leaned to her, and said, "I'm so proud of you, darling."

"Thank you," Sue mouthed, then, smiling, dropped her head to his shoulder for a moment.

Not wanting to interrupt the song, Barry contented himself by holding and squeezing her hand.

> King Louis was the king of France until
>   the Revolution.
> Tuhme,
> Way haul away we'll haul away, Joe
> Until he got his head chopped off. It
>   spoiled his constitution.
> Tuhme,
> Way haul away we'll haul away, Joe

Barry looked over at Jack and held a thumb up. His friends were going to stay in Ulster and they had Helen's father's approval. In six short months, he and Sue, God willing, would be parents. And while things were quiet now in the province, Barry, like all moderates who were the vast majority, hoped things would stay that way but had his concerns. At least here in this hall, Bertie Bishop, with the help of O'Reilly, the marquis, and a hardworking committee, had succeeded in running these events and bringing the communities together.

As if to underline that thought, O'Reilly

yelled, "Everybody sing the last verse in unison."

And the walls shook to

And it's way haul away we'll haul for
    better weather.
Tuhme,
Way haul away we'll haul away, Joe
Way haul away, we'll all haul together
Tuhme,
Way haul away, we'll haul away, Joe.

The audience applauded O'Reilly, who in turn applauded them, then said into the mike, "And that's all you're getting from me for now," hopped down off the stage, retook his seat, and took a deep pull of his pint.

"Well done, Fingal," John MacNeill said.

Kitty blew him a kiss.

Barry asked, "Did you pick that particular one for a reason, Fingal?"

O'Reilly shook his head. "Not really. It's just a great one that gets everybody singing together."

"We'll all haul together." Barry Laverty repeated the words. "It's certainly what's been happening here in Ballybucklebo." He looked at Sue. "I said before Donal came and dragged Fingal away that I was concerned about being a father, but while Fingal was singing I thought I have no need to be. We won't be alone. We'll have the support of three families."

Sue smiled. "Unless you've got a secret family hidden away somewhere, my folks and your folks are only two."

Barry smiled and shook his head. "They're blood family. I count them as one."

O'Reilly nodded. "True."

"The other two are our friends who've been part of Fingal's practice. You all know who they are."

"Of course we do," Kitty said, and waved at Kinky and Archie.

"And you've us," Jack said. "Me and Helen."

"Thanks, Jack." Barry opened his arms wide to encompass the whole room. "And then there's all of Ballybucklebo: Donal and Julie, Bertie and Flo, Sonny and Maggie, the Browns, the Shanks, Constable Mulligan, and you, sir," Barry inclined his head to John MacNeill, "and Myrna — everyone."

Barry took Sue's hand and looked her straight in the eye. "I thought I had concerns, but honestly can you think of a better place than Ballybucklebo to start our family? I'm damned if I can."

AFTERWORD

Hello there. It's me again, Mrs. Maureen "Kinky" Auchinleck, so. You'd've thought that after all the recipes I put in 2017's *Irish Country Cookbook,* with help from Dorothy Tinman, Doctor O'Reilly himself would have given me peace, but I knew there'd be no rest for the wicked when after the cookbook was published he asked me for more recipes to go with *An Irish Country Cottage* for 2018. Now your man Patrick Taylor has done it again and written a fourteenth Irish Country story, and as usual I've been asked for some more recipes. Here they are, and I hope you'll try and enjoy my savouries: tomato soup, beef and dumplings, and its variation, beef cobbler. For those of you with a sweet tooth, I have also added ginger biscuits (or, if you prefer, cookies) and at the request of a reader, cherry cake. And that cake is a departure from my usual. It's not my own. I got it, believe it or not, from

Maggie Houston, née MacCorkle. Eat up however little much is in it.
Until the next time,
MAUREEN AUCHINLECK,
lately Kincaid, née O'Hanlon

TOMATO SOUP

Serves 4 to 6

1 tablespoon olive oil
2 medium onions, peeled and chopped
2 carrots, peeled and chopped
2 medium potatoes, peeled and chopped
2 lbs. / 910 g. ripe tomatoes, skin taken off,
   or equivalent weight in canned tomatoes
1 clove garlic, crushed
1 teaspoon sugar
34 oz./1 L. vegetable or chicken stock
   (good-quality stock cubes are grand for
   this)
Salt and freshly ground black pepper to
   taste
Cream and chopped fresh basil or parsley
   to garnish

When I am in a hurry, I like to use the canned tomatoes instead, which I think have a better flavour anyway. Heat the oil in a saucepan, add the onions, carrot, and potato. Cover with a lid and cook gently for about 10 minutes until softened. Add the chopped tomatoes and cook for a further 5 minutes. Then add the garlic, sugar, and stock, and simmer for about 15 minutes. With an immersion blender or in a food processor, puree until smooth, season with salt and pepper to taste, and serve with a swirl of cream and chopped basil or parsley.

Kinky's Note: If using fresh tomatoes, immerse them in boiling water for a minute, then plunge them into ice-cold water and draw a line round the tomato with a sharp knife. This will make it easy to peel off the skin.

BEEF AND DUMPLINGS

4 to 5 lbs./2 1/2 kg. brisket (bone in)
2 medium onions, chopped
3 or 4 carrots, peeled and chopped
25 fluid oz./740 mL. beef stock
8 fluid oz./ 235 mL. red wine
2 tablespoons tomato puree
4 bay leaves
2 tablespoons fresh thyme leaves
1 tablespoon black peppercorns
Salt and freshly ground black pepper
1 bunch parsley, chopped

Preheat the oven to 225°F / 100°C. Put everything except the parsley into a Dutch oven or a large lidded casserole dish. Cover the pot with foil and then the lid. You want this to be a really tight fit so that it will not evaporate too much.

Cook for about 8 hours or overnight. Alternatively, you could use a slow cooker.

Let the beef cool in the cooking liquor, and when cool remove the meat, leave to one side, and slice into portions. Remove the bay leaves. Before you skim the surface fat from the liquor it helps to chill it in the refrigerator first.

Skim off the fat and liquidise the stock, adjust the seasonings, and bring up to a simmer on the stovetop. If the stock seems a little watery, just turn up the heat and reduce the quantity. Return the beef to the cooking pot, together with the chopped parsley.

Now make the dumplings.

SUET DUMPLINGS

7 oz./200 g. suet
14 oz./400 g. self-raising flour
2 tablespoons chopped parsley
2 teaspoons salt
A little water

Rub or cut the suet into the flour, parsley, and salt and make into a dough with the water. Form the dough into egg-shaped pieces and add to the meat and the stock. Cover and simmer for about 15 minutes, by which time the dumplings will have doubled in size. Serve in individual dishes with some chopped parsley sprinkled over.

Kinky's Note: For really light dumplings, do not open the lid when cooking and keep it just at a simmer.

Variation:
Beef Cobbler: Instead of suet dumplings you could try this scone topping for a nice change.

COBBLER SCONE TOPPING

3 1/2 oz./100 g. wholemeal flour
3 1/2 oz /100 g. plain flour
2 teaspoons baking powder
1/2 teaspoon bicarbonate of soda (baking soda)
A pinch of salt
1 tablespoon finely chopped rosemary
5 1/2 oz./156 g. cheddar cheese, grated
1 egg, beaten
4 to 5 tablespoons buttermilk
Chopped fresh parsley

Mix all the dry ingredients in a bowl, but reserve some of the grated cheese. Stir in the milk gradually to make a soft dough. You may not need all the milk or you may need a little more.

Work quickly on a floured surface and roll out to about 1 inch thick at least. Now cut out round scones, glaze with beaten egg, and cover the surface of the beef stew in the casserole with the scones. Top the scones with the reserved grated cheese, pressing it down a little so that it sticks to the scone.

Bake on top of the beef casserole in a hot oven (220°C / 425°F) uncovered for 25 minutes or until the scone topping has risen and is golden brown.

Sprinkle some chopped parsley on top before serving.

GINGER BISCUITS

3 oz./85 g. plain flour
1/2 teaspoon bicarbonate of soda (baking soda)
1 teaspoon ground ginger
2 1/2 oz./60 g. sugar
3 oz./85 g. rolled oats
Ginger root, about 2 inches, peeled and chopped or grated finely
4 oz./113 g. butter
1 tablespoon syrup — golden or maple
1 tablespoon milk

Preheat the oven to 150°C /300°F.

Line 2 large baking tins with baking parchment. Put all the dry ingredients and the ginger into a large bowl and mix together. Melt butter, syrup, and milk in a saucepan and mix into the dry ingredients. Pop it into the fridge for about 5 minutes, until it has firmed up and cooled.

Now put heaped teaspoons on the baking sheets, very well-spaced apart as they spread while cooking. Flatten the top of each biscuit with the back of a spoon and bake until lightly browned.

This can take between 10 minutes and 20 minutes depending on your oven. Now you need to let them cool on the trays, otherwise they would disintegrate. When they are cool enough to move, transfer to a cooling rack and store, when cold, in an air-tight box.

CHERRY CAKE
Serves 6

7 oz./200 g. glacé cherries
8 oz./225 g. flour
2 level teaspoons baking powder
6 oz./175 g. softened butter
6 oz./175 g. sugar
1 lemon, grated zest only
2 teaspoons vanilla essence
3 large eggs

To Decorate
6 oz./175 g. confectioners' sugar
Juice of 1 lemon
6 extra glacé cherries, quartered

604

Grease and flour a round 9-inch cake tin. Preheat the oven to 350°F/180°C.

Cut the cherries into quarters and toss in flour.

Beat the remaining ingredients well and fold in the floured cherries.

Put into the prepared baking tin and bake for 35 to 40 minutes until well risen and golden. Press gently with a finger on top, and if the cake springs back, it is cooked. Alternatively, you could insert a skewer into the centre of the cake and if it comes out clean it is properly cooked.

Leave to cool in the tin for 10 minutes and then cool on a wire rack.

Icing the cake

Mix the confectioners' sugar with the lemon juice and drizzle randomly over the cake. Place the cherries in the icing to decorate.

Kinky's Note: Tossing the cherries in flour stops them sinking to the bottom of the cake.

GLOSSARY

I have in all the previous Irish Country novels provided a glossary to help the reader who is unfamiliar with the vagaries of the Queen's English as it may be spoken by the majority of people in Ulster. This is a regional dialect akin to English as spoken in Yorkshire or on Tyneside. It is not Ulster-Scots, which is claimed to be a distinct language in its own right. I confess I am not a speaker.

Today in Ulster (but not in 1969, when this book is set) official signs are written in English, Irish, and Ulster-Scots. The washroom sign would read Toilets, *Leithris* (Irish), and *Cludgies* (Ulster-Scots). I hope what follows here will enhance your enjoyment of the work, although, I am afraid, it will not improve your command of Ulster-Scots.

999: Emergency telephone number like 911 in North America.

anyroad: Anyway.

away off (and feel your head/bumps/and chase yourself): Don't be stupid.

beat Bannagher: Wildly exceed expectations.

beeling: Suppurating.

biscuit: Cookie.

bejizzis/by jasus: By Jesus. In Ireland, despite the commandment proscribing taking the name of the Lord in vain, mild blasphemy frequently involves doing just that. See also **Jasus,** Jasus Murphy, Jesus Mary and Joseph.

bleeper: Pager.

bodhran: Irish. Pronounced "bowron." Circular hand-held drum.

boke: Vomit.

bollix/bollox: Testicles (impolite), or foulup.

bonnaught: Irish mercenary of the fourteenth century.

borrowed: Loaned.

both legs the same length: Standing around uselessly.

bout ye?: How are you. See also **How's about ye?**

boys-a-dear or boys-a-boys: Expression of amazement.

brass neck: Arrogance.

brave: Large number.

bravely: Very, large, or good/well.

brung: Brought.

bum: Borrow with little intention of repaying.

burroo: The unemployment bureau which paid benefits.

bye: Boy. Often tacked on to the end of sentences by people from Counties Cork and Antrim.

by jeekers: By Jesus.

cadger: One who is constantly **"bumming."**

can't feel nothing: Double negative. Can't feel anything.

céilidh: Irish. Pronounced "kaylee." Party with traditional Irish dancing and music.

chips: French fries.

chuffed: Very pleased.

chuntered: Kept going on about.

clatter: Indeterminate number. See also **wheen**. The size of the number can be enhanced by adding **brave** or **powerful** as a precedent to either. As an exercise, try to imagine the numerical difference between a **brave clatter** and a **powerful wheen** of **spuds**.

coarse: Rude and abrasive.

come on on (on) in: Is not a typographical error. This item of Ulster-speak drives spellcheck mad.

cow's lick: Fringe of hair diagonally across forehead.

craic: Pronounced "crack." Practically untranslatable, it can mean great conversation and fun (the *craic* was ninety) or "What has happened since I saw you last?" (What's the *craic*?). Often seen outside pubs in the Republic of Ireland: *"Craic agus ceol,"* meaning "fun and music."

cracker: Very good. Of a girl, very good-looking.

cross my heart: Completed by "and hope to die." Implied, if what I am telling you is not the truth.

cup of tea/scald in your hand: An informal cup of tea, as opposed to tea that was synonymous with the main evening meal (dinner).

dab hand: Expert.

dead/dead on: Very/absolutely right or perfectly.

dickie-bird: Cockney rhyming slang. Word.

dinner suit: Tuxedo.

divil: Devil.

docker: Longshoreman.

do-re-mi: Tonic sol-fa scale, but meaning "dough" as in money.

dosh: Money.

duncher: Flat cloth cap.

dunt: Blow or strike.

ECG: Electrocardiogram; in North America, EKG.

eejit/buck eejit: Idiot/complete idiot.

ferocious: Extreme.

fire away: Go ahead.

flying: Drunk.

Fomorian: One of the early races said to have inhabited Ireland.

fornenst: Nearby.

forward: Impertinent.

gander: Look-see or male goose.

git: Corruption of begotten. Frequently with **hoor's.** (whore's.) Derogatory term for an unpleasant person. Not a term of endearment.

giving off: Scolding.

glipe (great): Idiot (imbecile).

goat (ould): Stupid person, but used as a term of affection.

grand altogether/so: Very good.

ham-fisted: Clumsy.

have or take a pew: Be seated. A pew was a bench in a church.

having me on: Trying to baffle me.

heart bled: Had great empathy for.

heart of corn: Very good-natured.

heels of the hunt (at the): When all is said and done.

hide nor hair: Not a trace.

high doh (up to): Very agitated.

higheejin: Very important person, often only in the subject's own mind.

hold-all: Soft bag like a sports bag.

hooley: Boisterous party.

how's about ye?: How are you.

I'm your man: I agree and will follow where you lead.

jag: Prick or jab.

jar/jug: Alcoholic drink.

let the hare sit: Let sleeping dogs lie.

like the hammers of hell: Moving very rapidly or powerfully.

liltie: Irish whirling dervish.

Jeekers (by): Jesus, by Jesus.

kipper: A herring which has been split, gutted, rubbed with salt, and cured with smoke, preferably from oak shavings. **kippered:** Physically destroyed.

learns me: Teaches me. In Ulster, meanings are often reversed, as in "Borrow me a cup of sugar."

lug(ged): Ear, kind of marine worm. (Carried awkwardly.)

marley: Child's marble.

marry up: Marry into a higher social class.

MC: Master of ceremonies.

medicine: The speciality of internal medicine.

midder: Midwifery, now called obstetrics.

mind: Remember.

more power to your wheel: Words of encouragement akin to "The very best of luck."

muck out: Remove all droppings and soiled straw from a byre or stables.

no harm til you, but: "I do not mean to cause you any offence," usually followed by, "you are absolutely wrong," or an insult.

no rest for the wicked: Self-deprecatory humorous remark of someone who is feeling slightly put upon.

not as green as you're cabbage-looking: You may look a bit dim but inside you're sharp as a tack.

not at oneself: Feeling under the weather.

och: Exclamation to register whatever emotion you wish. "Och, isn't she lovely?" "Och, he's dead?" "Och, damn it." Pronounced like clearing your throat.

operating theatre: OR.

orange and green: The colours of Loyalists and Republicans. Used to symbolize the age-old schism in Irish politics.

ould/oul: Old.

ould hand: My friend.

oxter/oxtercog: Armpit/help walk by draping an individual's arm over one's shoulder.

paddy hat: Soft-crowned, narrow-brimmed Donegal tweed hat.

Paddy's market: Disorganised crowd.

party piece: Performance to be given at social events.

pavement: Sidewalk.

peely-wally: From lowland Scots. Unwell.

pethidine: Demerol.

pipes: Three kinds of bagpipes are played in Ireland. The Great Highland pipes, three drones; the Brian Boru pipes, three drones and four to thirteen keys on the chanter; and the uilleann (elbow) inflated by bellows held under the elbow.

piss artist: Heavy drinker.

plaits: Braids.

plum cake: Fruitcake.

potato crisps: Potato chips.

Premium Bonds: A UK government-sponsored lottery begun in 1956. No interest was paid but every bond had a chance to win a prize once a month. The bonds could be redeemed for face value at any time.

quare: Ulster and Dublin pronunciation of "queer," meaning "very" or "strange."

Radió Éireann: Irish State radio network. Pronounced, "Raddeeo Airann."

Radió Telefís Éireann (RTE): Irish State Television network. Pronounced, "Raddeeo Telluhfeesh Airann."

ranks of junior medical staff and North American equivalents: Houseman/intern. Senior house officer/junior resident. Registrar/more senior resident. Senior registrar (usually attained after passing the speciality examinations)/chief resident.

rickets, near taking the: Nothing to do with the vitamin D deficiency disease, but an expression of having had a great surprise or shock.

rightly (do): Very well. (Be adequate if not perfect for the task.)

Róisín: Irish. Pronounced "Rowsheen." Little rose, or rosebud.

ruction: Brawl.

shenanigans: Carryings-on.

shite/shit: "Shite" is the noun ("He's a right shite") "shit" the verb ("I near shit a brick.")

sicken your happiness: Disappoint you greatly.

skitters: Diarrhoea.

sláinte: Irish. Pronounced "slawntuh." Cheers. Mud in your eye. Skoal. A toast.

snaps: Photographs.

soft hand under a duck: Gentle or very good at.

solicitor: Attorney.

so sharp you'll cut yourself: Too clever by half.

so/so it is, etc: Tacked to the end of a sentence for emphasis in Counties Cork/Ulster.

sound (man): Terrific (trustworthy, reliable, admirable man).

speak of the devil: Is completed by "and he's sure to turn up" when someone whose name has been recently mentioned appears on the scene.

sticking out/a mile: Good/excellent.

stocious: Drunk.

sweets/sweeties: Candies.

taking a hand out of: Teasing.

tat-ta-ta-ra: Boisterous party.

tea: The main evening meal.

that there/them there: That/them with emphasis.

the night/day: Tonight/today.

the sick: Benefit paid by the state to people who are off work because of illness.

the wee man: The devil.

thole: Put up with. A reader, Miss D. Williams, wrote to me to say it was etymologically from the Old English *tholian,* to suffer. She remarked that her first encounter with the word was in a fourteenth-century prayer.

thon/thonder: That or there. "Thon eejit

shouldn't be standing over thonder."

thran: Bloody-minded.

tights: Pantyhose.

tongue hanging out: Dying for a drink.

took the mickey: Teased.

townland: A mediaeval administrative region comprising a village and the surrounding countryside.

tube: Medical-student slang for a useless person. Klutz.

walking out with: Going steady.

wee: Small, but in Ulster can be used to modify almost anything without reference to size. A barmaid, an old friend, greeted me by saying, "Come in, Pat. Have a wee seat and I'll get you a wee menu, and would you like a wee drink while you're waiting?"

wean: Pronounced "wane." Small child.

well mended: Healed properly.

wheen: An indeterminate number. "How many miles is it to the nearest star?" "Dunno, but it must be a brave wheen." See **clatter**.

wheest/houl' your wheest: Be quiet or shut up.

worser (nor): Worse (than).

wrench: Severe twist, or kind of spanner used for twisting.

617

you-boy-yuh: Words of encouragement.
youse: Plural of "you."

ABOUT THE AUTHOR

Patrick Taylor, M.D. was born and raised in Bangor County Down in Northern Ireland. Dr. Taylor is a distinguished medical researcher, offshore sailor, model-boat builder, and father of two grown children. He lives on Saltspring Island, British Columbia. He is the author of the bestselling Irish Country series, including *An Irish Country Cottage, An Irish Country Practice, An Irish Country Doctor* and many more.

The employees of Thorndike Press hope you have enjoyed this Large Print book. All our Thorndike, Wheeler, and Kennebec Large Print titles are designed for easy reading, and all our books are made to last. Other Thorndike Press Large Print books are available at your library, through selected bookstores, or directly from us.

For information about titles, please call:
(800) 223-1244

or visit our website at:
gale.com/thorndike

To share your comments, please write:
Publisher
Thorndike Press
10 Water St., Suite 310
Waterville, ME 04901